Dear Aunt Ch—

I left out the part about the settlers coming up the Cumberland River. You can pencil in what you remember.

Love. Joel

Cherokee
Chronicles

Cherokee Chronicles

1540–1840

Joel S. Koenig, M.D.

Cherokee Chronicles 1540–1840
by Joel S. Koenig, M.D.

ISBN 0-9741373-0-8

First Edition, June 2003
1 2 3 4 5 6 7 8 9 10

To the memory of my grandmother, Leona DeMoss Stephens

Acknowledgments

I would like to apologize that I am neither a writer nor an historian, and I am not even a Cherokee! In fact I'm a pediatrician. My family has lived in Tennessee since before it achieved statehood, and so I have had a lifelong interest in the history of the state. Most history books are written about white men for white men, so I began to explore Tennessee's Native American heritage. I was disappointed that the Cherokee history books available at the time were somewhat incomplete or inaccurate and difficult to read. I felt challenged to do better. I didn't have the time, money, or skill to review original documents, but when I found the collections of synopses of William L. Anderson, James A. Lewis, and Paul Kutsche, I decided to go for it!

I have organized Cherokee history into a chronicle, from the first contact with Europeans to their reunification under constitutional government after removal. Some details of the early history are sparse, but the last eighty years are easily organized into yearly summaries. I have tried to organize each yearly essay so as to put the tribal history into the context of European or American history. Most of the information comes from sources outside of the tribe; the history of the internal politics of the Cherokee is obscure. I have concentrated on political history and have discussed Cherokee culture only as it has been relevant to their history.

Some of the documents seem to contradict each other, and I have had to make decisions as to what sounds logical. This is especially true for the period between 1735 and 1750. Again I apologize for any inaccuracies. Since I do not have academic credentials as an historian I decided that it was pointless to keep meticulous footnotes. I acknowledge that all of my work is dependent on the writings of others, listed in the bibliography. I have made efforts not to quote sources directly.

I would also like to apologize if any of my words are offensive or culturally insensitive. No lapses of that sort are intentional and might arise only out of ignorance.

I would like to extend special thanks to Sam Kidd for her help with the illustrations and to Chris Armour and Jan Stinson for editorial advice. I am indebted to my wife, Diane, and three children (Caroline, Ben, and Sam) who have tolerated the difficulty of living with an eccentric Dad!

I hope that this book will be useful to students of Cherokee history. I would have written about the history of the Cherokee beyond 1840, but I didn't have enough time. If I had the talent and time I would also have created an atlas of Cherokee history, a biography of Cherokee notables, and a compendium of Cherokee documents such as treaties, constitutions, and so forth. I hope that somebody else will be inspired to write a better version of this book and tackle the other projects.

Introduction

Cherokee Chronicles traces the history of the largest native tribe of southeastern North America from its first contact with Europeans to the resurrection of its constitutional government after a removal holocaust. Since the Cherokee did not have a written language until the 1820s, much of this history is dependent on the recordings of Europeans and European-Americans who may or may not have been biased against the tribe. Despite these limitations, it is clear that this remarkable people not only survived the harshest of betrayals and abuse, but actually assimilated the highest ideals of the Europeans into their own evolving culture.

Cherokee origins are obscured by the veil of time, and much of their internal history was not preserved. As the tribe engaged more fully with the European immigrants, their story became more intertwined with those of the newcomers, and thus better recorded.

First contact between the Cherokee and the Europeans occurred in 1540 during the expedition of Hernando de Soto. The Spaniard set the tone for relations between whites and Indians by betraying his generous hosts and slaughtering the innocent. After a hundred years of minimal contact, a formal trade relationship was ratified in 1684 between the Cherokee and the British colonists in Charleston, Carolina. Over the next generation the economic engagement became so thorough that many of the aboriginal customs of the Cherokee would forever be abandoned. They came to rely on guns to hunt game for furs and to capture foreign warriors as slaves for trade. They could no longer compete with surrounding tribes without the imported technology.

The Cherokee formed alliances with the colonists in the 1710s against the Tuscaroras and the Yamasees, thus gaining most favored trading status with the British. The Cherokee ceded a small tract of land to South Carolina in 1621—the first of some thirty-six cessions that would eventually lead to their removal. The land might be useful to the agrarian Carolinians, but it was over-hunted and depleted of game and was thus worthless to the Cherokee anyway.

In 1730 the rogue diplomat Alexander Cuming convinced seven Cherokee chiefs to travel with him to London, England. After an audience with King George II, the parties inked the Treaty of Dover, committing the two nations to a military and commercial alliance. As the rivalry between Britain and France heated up over the domination of North America, the Cherokee desperately tried to avoid becoming pawns and continued to welcome French influence even while officially allied with Britain. The internal power structure of the tribe was changing to adapt to the new reality. The new emphasis on hunting for profit enhanced the power of the young, brash hunters and warriors at the expense of the more moderate elders. The devastating small pox epidemic of 1738 further eroded authority of the old ways as the priests' incantations against the virus proved impotent.

During the next half-century the Cherokee were caught in the crossfire between the British and the French as the European powers struggled for hegemony. Just as the British were winning their protracted war, Governor Lyttleton dragged the Cherokee into a needless conflict that proved devastating for the tribe. The aftermath of this first war between the Cherokee and a white army was painful and humiliating. Western settlers established a pattern of encroaching onto Cherokee lands despite King George III's Proclamation of 1763. The colonial governments could not control the actions of these independent frontiersmen, and feared that their own regimes could be destabilized if they asserted too much pressure to keep them off Indian lands.

A second Cherokee War broke out as the Americans declared their independence. This time the Cherokee were in the crossfire between the British and the Americans. The results were the same as before, but this time the recovery was purposely drawn out for years. The Americans kept the Cherokee in misery and abject poverty to set an example to other tribes that might dare to oppose the new republic.

On the eve of the American Revolution several Cherokee elders had agreed to the sale of vast hunting lands in what is now Middle Tennessee and Kentucky. The Treaty of Sycamore Shoals divided the tribe into a faction that was willing to accommodate the Americans and a faction that was ready to defy them. The elder leader Attakullakulla bears most of the responsibility for this cession, but it was his son, Dragging Canoe, who led the rebellious Chickamaugans in opposition to it. The terrorist-like actions of the young Chickamaugans were used by the Americans as justification for arbitrary raids against the entire Cherokee people.

With the premature death of Dragging Canoe the Chickamauga movement disintegrated. American victories had left the Cherokee homeland essentially an enclave within the boundaries of the United States. President George Washington introduced a "civilization" program in which he envisioned assimilation of the Indians over a fifty- year period. They would be taught the principles of agriculture, animal husbandry, and manufacturing while being introduced to education in English. Christian missionaries would bring the "savages" into the fold.

The civilization program divided the Cherokee once again into two factions. A traditional group of mostly full-blooded illiterate Cherokee opposed the program and gave consideration to voluntary emigration to western territories to avoid further contact with the vulgar influences of the white men. An elite group of mostly half-blooded educated and Christian capitalists arose to power. Many of them amassed fortunes operating estates with mills and ferries, manned with slave labor.

A period of poor leadership brought the tribe to a crisis over the illegal sale of lands by unscrupulous chiefs for personal gain. The assassination of Chief Doublehead for his role in an illegal cession treaty led to tribal reforms in which a representative government was formed. No longer would a consensus of all chiefs be required for legislation, and no longer would individuals be able to sign treaties without the consent of the Council.

The legal reforms were sidetracked by a religious revival aroused by the Shawnee orator Tecumseh and the coincidental occurrence of a tremendous earthquake in 1811. Once again war intervened as the Cherokee were united in their alliance with the United States against the Upper Creeks during the Creek War phase of the War of 1812. The humiliating betrayal of the Cherokee allies by General Andrew Jackson after the war set off a removal crisis, and indeed many traditional Cherokees moved to Arkansas during this period. A penultimate cession treaty in 1819 resolved the removal crisis and gave further impetus to tribal reform.

In the 1820s the Cherokee refined their new constitutional government, establishing a bicameral legislature and an independent judiciary. The executive leadership of the republic was elected openly by the legislature for defined terms. The half-blooded George Gist (Sequoyah) introduced a syllabary for the Tsa-La-Gi language in 1821—thus making it possible for the Cherokee to keep records in their own language. Within a short period of time most Cherokees were literate in their own tongue, and in 1828 the *Cherokee Phoenix* began publication. It was the first time a Native American people had its own newspaper. The Cherokee had achieved the pinnacle of civilization.

At the peak of progress, the Cherokee people were subjected to another disastrous series of betrayals. The State of Georgia began pressing claims to Cherokee lands located within its borders (the bulk of the Nation). The discovery of gold within the disputed territory hastened the pace of illegal settlement, and the administration of President Andrew Jackson did nothing to prevent it. The Cherokee appealed to the Supreme Court of the United States, but despite a victory in *Worcester v. Georgia*, Jackson continued to allow Georgia to take over Cherokee land.

As the illegal white settlers began to outnumber the Cherokee inhabitants, it became apparent to some that removal was the only option left for the tribe. A small group of educated elite, led by Elias Boudinot, Major Ridge and John Ridge, signed the infamous Treaty of New Echota in 1835. This treaty ceded the entire territory of the Cherokee Nation for land west of the Mississippi River. Principal Chief John Ross presented evidence to the United States Senate that ninety-five percent of the tribe opposed the illegal treaty, but nevertheless it became law. The Cherokee who opposed the treaty could not believe that it would be implemented and made no efforts to prepare for removal. When the deadline arrived for the removal the United States Army rounded them into concentration camps to prepare for deportation.

The tragedy of the removal along the Trail of Tears has become a focal point for modern Cherokee history. *Cherokee Chronicles* does not end with this holocaust but rather ends with a new beginning. Chief John Ross and many other capable leaders formed a new united tribal government with a new written constitution. The Chief addressed the first meeting of the new Council in Tahlequah, Indian Territory, speaking of the importance of education for the future of the Cherokee.

Contents

Chapter One

1540–1700

From First Contact to the Establishment of Permanent European Colonies

Cherokee Origins

History of the Cherokee before Contact with Europeans

At the time of first contact with Europeans, the Cherokee were the most populous native tribe in southern North America, with perhaps as many thirty-two thousand people. They settled in villages along rivers and streams in the southernmost valleys of the Appalachian Mountains, giving them access to both the Savannah River and the Tennessee, Ohio, and Mississippi rivers. The villages were divided into three geographical areas: the Lower, Middle, and Overhill Towns. (See Map 1, page 2.) The Lower Towns were situated mostly along the Keowee River and were the most exposed to the Creeks and the coastal tribes. The Middle Towns were subdivided into the Valley, Middle, and Out Towns. The Middle Towns were established along the upper Little Tennessee River just beyond the high grounds above the Lower Towns. The Valley Towns, which were the most populated, sat along the Hiwassee River further west and were surrounded by excellent hunting grounds. The Out Towns were built along the Stecoe River and were the most isolated. The Overhill Towns lay along the Little Tennessee River over

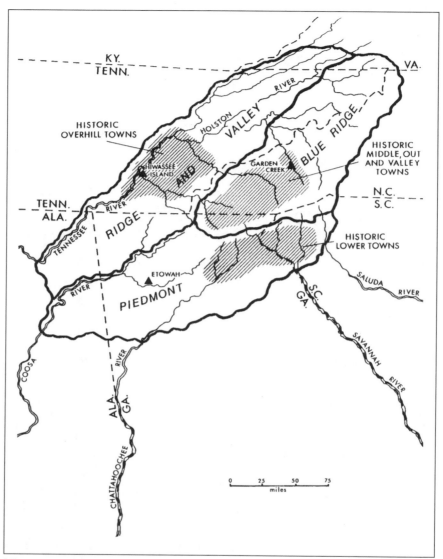

Map 1

the Unaka Mountains and were the most vulnerable to attack from the north and west. Vast unsettled areas, which were used as hunting grounds, surrounded the towns and were often shared peacefully with neighboring tribes. (See Map 2, page 3.) These hunting grounds were of vital importance, not just for procurement of food but as buffer zones between them and the surrounding tribes. The Cherokee did practice agriculture, but it was mostly limited to small plots of corn tended to by the women.

The origins of the Cherokee are not entirely clear, but linguistic evidence suggests they migrated from the Great Lakes region. The language of the Cherokee, Tsa-La-Gi, is an Iroquoian language, while the surrounding southern tribes were mostly speakers of Muskogean tongues. They had few oral traditions of their origins and no written records prior to their eventual encounters with Europeans, but it is likely that the Delaware Indians collaborated with the Iroquois to drive the Cherokee southward, perhaps a few hundred years before the arrival of the Europeans.

The Cherokee then followed the Appalachian Mountains to their southern extremity, undoubtedly displacing the original Musk-

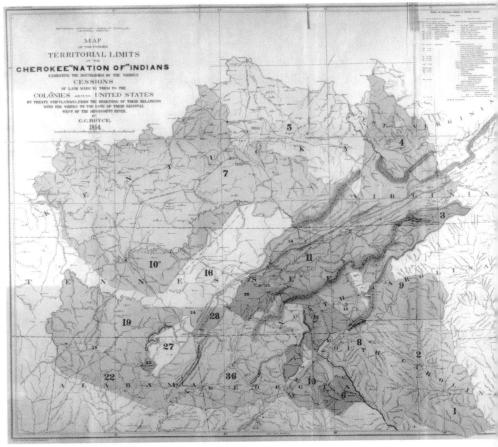

Map 2

ogean inhabitants. The origin of the name "Cherokee" or "Tsa-La-Gi" is obscure, but it may have been a term used by the Muskogeans. They called themselves the Ani-Yun-Wiya, or Principal People. They believed that in the beginning of time, they either sprung from the earth or fell from the clouds. Asga-Ya-Galun-Lati, the Great Spirit, gave them land in the southern Appalachian Mountains for their eternal use.

Clan membership was the dominant form of organization of Cherokee society. There may have been many clans in ancient times, but by the sixteenth century seven clans were recognized by the Cherokee. An individual always belonged to the clan of his mother and was obliged by such membership to marry outside of the clan and to defend other clan members through a system that demanded eye-for-an-eye retribution. Each village may have had members from all seven clans. Since an individual was considered to be a close relative of all members of his clan, each village was bound to the others by kinship. Each town had its own chiefs, a "white chief," or *Uku*, to lead in times of peace, and a "red chief," or *Skiagunsta*, who lead during times of war.

Although each village had its own chiefs, governmental decisions were based on the consensus of the town leaders and mediated by the priests, who gave advice through the interpretation of oracles. Each village was essentially independent from the others, and yet Cherokee villages never fought each other—even when the Overhill and Lower Towns had different opinions about foreign policy.

The Cherokee had traditional enemies on all fronts. Since wars were often precipitated by individual incidents and driven by obligations of clan membership, the scope of warfare tended to be limited. War parties were seldom large, and battles were limited to raids during a single season. Conflicts were usually defensive in character and not driven by a desire to acquire land or to conquer another people for economic gain. Much of the warfare was with local neighbors, such as the Creek, Chickasaw, and Shawnee, but many of the raiders traveled much further to settle scores. The second largest tribe in North America was the Iroquois Confederation (settlements in the Great Lakes region). The Iroquois had a traditional hatred for the Cherokee and the Catawba, who were located to the southeast of the Lower Towns. Amazingly, steady streams of warriors headed north and south to fight limited wars of retribution at the same time that there were local conflicts between neighboring tribes. In the days before the European settlements few lasting alliances

ROSEANN MAIKIS, MD

Minimally Invasive Surgery

Gynecology • Obstetrics

2222 State Street • Suite A • Nashville, TN 37203

tel: (615)321-0513 fax: (615)321-0358

email: roseann.maikis@firelinedsl.com

existed between Indian tribes, perhaps because the limited scope of warfare did not make such entanglements necessary. The arrival of the Europeans would change everything.

1492–1526

Europeans Discover and Explore North America

Episodic Encounters with the Cherokee

Spanish Discover, Explore, and Exploit America

By the late fifteenth century, the social and political organization of the Europeans encouraged entrepreneurial exploratory endeavors and new technological advances made them possible. Although the Portuguese were the first to embark on long sailing expeditions to the Orient in search of spices and wealth, the Spanish were the first to explore what would become known as the New World. The Treaty of Tordesillas paved the way for Spain to dominate the exploration and exploitation of the newly found territories.

In the early sixteenth century the Spanish established trading posts and small fringe colonies on Hispaniola, Puerto Rico, Cuba, and other Caribbean islands that they had discovered. They found that profitable sugar plantations could be established, much as they were on the Canary Islands, closer to home. In 1519 it became clear that a "New World" had been discovered. Hernando Cortes discovered the Aztec Empire in Mexico and proceeded to conquer it. The brutal subjugation of the Aztecs was followed by Pizarro's vicious conquest of the Inca Empire. These victories brought enormous wealth to Spain, transforming the nation into a world power.

The realization of treasure in South and Central America led Spain and others to look northward as well. England sent John Cabot to explore the northern Atlantic coast in search of a northwestern passage to the Orient. The English asserted claims to the lands that he discovered, by virtue of getting there first. France hired Verrazano to explore the Atlantic coast of North America in 1524, and in 1535 Jacques Cartier established a settlement on the St. Lawrence River and a French claim for Canada. The stage was being set for a contest among the Europeans to control the continent—a contest that would rage for centuries and have dire consequences for the Cherokee and other native peoples.

Spaniards were the first Europeans to have indirect (and later direct) contact with the Cherokee. In 1521 Judge Lucas Vasquez de Allyon of Hispaniola sponsored the exploration of the coast north of Florida. On August 18, 1526, Allyon established the ill-fated settlement of San Miguel de Guadalpe at Santa Elena Bay in what is now South Carolina. The location was swampy and proved unhealthy. Allyon was among those who died within a few months of a febrile illness. Mutineers imprisoned his successor and proceeded to mistreat natives and slaves to the point of provoking wars and rebellions. After the mutiny was quelled and the guilty executed, the survivors faced the prospect of starving through the winter. By the end of the year the remaining one hundred fifty (of six hundred) settlers abandoned San Miguel and sailed back to Hispaniola.

1540

De Soto Encounters the Cherokee

Hernando de Soto (c. 1496–1542) was the leader of the first European expedition to encounter the Cherokee. De Soto had served brilliantly as cavalry commander and was instrumental in Pizarro's subjugation of the Incas. De Soto became dissatisfied with Pizarro's command in Peru and returned to Spain as one of the wealthiest of the conquistadors. His real desire, however, was to return to America to continue his search for gold and to acquire political power. In 1537 he was named Governor of Cuba and commissioned to explore the interior of Florida.

In May 1539 de Soto sailed from Havana, Cuba, to the western coast of Florida with nine ships and about seven hundred men. After wintering at an Indian settlement named Apalachee (near modern Tallahassee), de Soto and his men headed northward into the interior, searching for treasure. They would discover several tribes of natives (including the Cherokee) as well as natural wonders such as the Blue Ridge Mountains and the Mississippi River. De Soto took his men on a brutal path of destruction that would lead not to further riches for him, but rather to his own death.

It is uncertain exactly when and where de Soto's expedition first encountered the Cherokee, but it is thought that the Europeans crossed the Savannah River (into what is now South Carolina) on April 30, 1540. In a few days they entered the town of Cofitachequi. There de Soto found the influence of the previous Spanish establishment at San Miguel de Gualdape: There were crosses and other Spanish religious artifacts, and half the population was gone—apparently victims of a plague transmitted by Allyon's settlers.

De Soto's meandering path was driven by rumors of gold. He would befriend the natives along the way in order to obtain information and comforts and then betray them once his needs were met. He would kidnap the leaders of a village and ransom them for supplies, slaves, and women and then repeat the process at the next village. If the natives were unable to lead them to gold or treasure, de Soto often would have their hands axed off. His legacy would be that of hatred between European and native. Although the rest of his sojourn was plagued by skirmishes with outraged natives, his death in 1542 was from an infectious disease that he acquired somewhere on the western bank of the Mississippi.

The extent of de Soto's dealings with the Cherokee is uncertain. Some of the villages that his expedition encountered were certainly Cherokee, but the identity of others is not certain. Most likely Guasili (Guaxule) and Canasoga (Canasagua) were Cherokee towns that they visited. It is reported that the Cherokee leaders greeted the Spaniards with hospitality and gifts, presenting them with berries and barkless dogs (opossums?) for food, although the natives did not eat the animals themselves. Whether or not the Cherokee were subjected to de Soto's cruelty is uncertain. The precedent was set for European dealings with the natives of the region: They were seen as heathen savages with no rights and who would be tolerated only so far as they could be useful.

1559–1565

Spain and France Attempt to Colonize North Florida

In the decades following de Soto's expedition into the Florida interior, Spain continued to show interest in the region but faced stiffer competition from both the French and the English. The conditions for settlers and explorers remained difficult, but the ultimate success of the colonies would depend on circumstances on the European continent.

In 1559 King Philip II of Spain directed that a colony be founded at Punta de Santa Elena in order to provide safe harbor for ships bound from South America back to Spain, to help establish an overland route to Mexico, and to guard against expansion by the French. Two years later Angel de Villefane sailed from Havana toward Santa Elena, but the project was abandoned after a hurricane killed a quarter of his men.

The French attempted to establish settlements along the coast of present-day South Carolina in 1562 and 1564, but both projects failed. The latter post was destroyed after the Frenchmen attacked the new Spanish settlement of St. Augustine. The Spanish went on to build Fort San Mateo and Fort San Felipe at Santa Elena and were left in control of the southern Atlantic coast.

1566–1567

Pardo's Expedition

In 1566 Menendez sent Captain Juan Pardo on an expedition two hundred fifty miles northwest along the Savannah River. A small fort, Fort San Juan, was erected among the Cheraw, very close to the Cherokee Lower Towns. The following year Pardo returned to Fort San Juan and from there he followed Indian roads across the Appalachians and into the Tennessee Valley. The party crossed through the Cherokee territory much as de Soto had, visiting the towns Otariyatiqui (Otari), Quinahaqui, Issa, Aguaquiri (Guaquili), Tocax (Toxaway), and Tanasqui. Apparently the trip through Cherokee territory was peaceful. The

Pardo Expedition returned safely to Santa Elena although it discovered neither an overland route to Mexico nor gold.

1568–1586

The British Drive the Spanish Further South

The success of the Spanish in this territory was short-lived. The small forts that Pardo established were all abandoned or destroyed by natives. Famine and ineffective leadership continually plagued the settlement at Santa Elena. The desperate settlers attacked nearby Indian villages in order to steal food and supplies, provoking retaliatory raids from the Edisto, Guale, and other coastal nations. During this Emascu War, all Spanish settlements except for St. Augustine were destroyed.

During this time the French remained interested in northern Florida. They did not try to resettle in the area, however, until after the Emascu War. In December 1576 the French attempted to re-establish a colony, but within months it failed.

English exploration in North America had been stymied in the 1570s when Martin Frobisher's search for a Northwest Passage met with the Arctic ice and when Sir Humphrey Gilbert died at sea near Newfoundland. Sir Walter Raleigh, Gilbert's half-brother, took up his patent and organized an expedition to explore the coast of North America. In 1584 Philip Amadas and Arthur Barlowe reached the outer banks of what is now North Carolina—an area where the climate was mild and not too close to Spanish Florida. In 1585 Raleigh sent another expedition to the area he now called "Virginia." In 1585 Richard Grenville sailed to Virginia to explore the territory and to establish a military base. The project was hampered from the first by the lack of a deep harbor, forcing the men to search for a better location for a permanent military base. Just over a hundred men were left under the leadership of Captain Ralph Lane to build a fort and to continue scientific studies, while Grenville sailed back for supplies and reinforcements. Both Grenville and Lane had set precedents for cruel abuse of the native peoples, despite overtures of cooperation from them. Without help from the natives, however, the settlers became more and more desperate for relief from home.

Meanwhile in Europe, Spain and England headed into war. The coronation of Queen Elizabeth re-established England as a Protestant power. Elizabeth threw her support to the Protestant rebels in the Netherlands and in 1585 sent six thousand English troops to support them. She also sent Sir Francis Drake on an expedition to destroy as much of Spanish America as possible. In 1586 he rescued the imperiled settlers in Virginia then rampaged against the Spanish settlements in Florida, forcing them to abandon Santa Elena and to consolidate at the damaged St. Augustine. Later Drake would be instrumental in defeating the Spanish Armada's attempted invasion of England. Thus the coastal areas closest to Cherokee lands would be controlled and settled by Englishmen.

French Forts and English Colonies in the Seventeenth Century

In the years following the Spanish retreat from Santa Elena, the English established settlements along the coast of North America, from New England south toward Florida. The colonization efforts were fueled not by a thirst for gold, but rather by a multitude of economic, political, and religious forces. Further Spanish losses in the Caribbean allowed for the establishment of English plantation colonies such as Barbados. Success in raising sugar cane and later tobacco in those areas would be repeated on the continent in Virginia and the Carolinas. In contrast to the Spanish who were driven to find treasure without regard to the welfare of the local inhabitants, the English were more interested in establishing safe strongholds near the sea and establishing friendly trade relations with the natives when possible.

While the English slowly encroached upon Cherokee territory from the coast, the French approached from the west. The French had established a permanent settlement in Canada by the early seventeenth century and then established a series of forts at the Great Lakes, along the Mississippi River, and on the Gulf of Mexico. The French developed trade relations with the native tribes and used every opportunity to influence them against the English. In general the French were less threatening to the Indians because they confined themselves mostly to their forts and posts and did not have large populations that would encroach upon native hunting grounds and villages. The French were also more likely than the English to intermarry with the native peoples.

The Cherokee's vast western hunting grounds served as a buffer between them and the French. Although the French built forts near the periphery of the Cherokee claims and within the Creek Nation at Fort Toulouse, they did not erect posts near the Cherokee villages. The Cherokee people were in general supportive of the French, but their leadership tended to support the English. The Cherokee saw their relationship with the Europeans as being less important than their relations with their traditional friends and enemies, the other native tribes. All of the tribes sandwiched between the English coastal colonies and the French Mississippi Valley establishments would become pawns in the European competition for domination of the continent. The Iroquois and to a lesser degree the Cherokee would become adept at playing one colonizing power against the other, but the ever-increasing European population made native diplomatic efforts more and more futile. Early on the Indians may have united against the white encroachers and destroyed the settlements in their infancies, but traditional animosities and linguistic and cultural differences prevented such collaborative efforts and ensured their doom.

1607

Jamestown Founded

The first permanent English colony to border Cherokee territory was Virginia, established at Jamestown in 1607. The introduction of West Indian tobacco in 1612 and African slaves in 1619 led to the successful development of a plantation economy. Relations with the local tribes soured as the population grew and the settlers felt less dependent on them. The Powhatan Confederation attacked the Virginians in 1622 in retaliation for the murder of a native, and although the colony survived the attack, the Virginia Company was bankrupted. In 1625 King Charles I established Virginia as a royal colony and encouraged its growth "for the propagation of the Christian Religion, the increase in trade, and the enlarging of his Royal empire." An uneasy peace between the colonists and natives held until 1644, when Chief Opechancanough launched another surprise attack in retaliation for offenses committed by the Englishmen. This time, however, the Powhatan Confederation was outmatched. The chief was captured and killed and his empire was destroyed. At the conclusion of the war, the entire James peninsula had been ceded to the colonists.

1654

Virginians Encounter the Cherokee

In the aftermath of the war, Virginia built Fort Henry on the Appomattox River. From there the Virginians launched several exploratory expeditions over the next thirty years. The first known contact between the Cherokee and the English occurred in 1654. Apparently several hundred Cherokee warriors and allies had amassed at the fall of the James River, taking advantage of the vacuum created by the collapse of the Powhatans. The Virginians and their Pamunkey allies marched against the Cherokee and defeated them. It is unknown how long the Cherokee remained there or what their purpose was. It is possible that the tribe had lived there before they settled permanently to the south.

The Virginians continued to be interested in exploring their western territories. There was widespread belief that the Pacific Ocean would be found just west of the mountains until John Lederer's expedition proved otherwise in 1670. Lederer probably did not travel into Cherokee territory, but he evidently did accumulate some reports of their whereabouts from neighboring tribes.

1673

The Needham and Arthur Expedition

There were several other expeditions from Fort Henry in the 1670s, but for the Cherokee the most significant was the Needham and Arthur Expedition of 1673. In the same year that the Frenchmen Marquette and Jolliet reached the western fringe of the Cherokee hunting lands, the Englishmen reached the heart of the Overhill Towns. It was also the first time that Englishmen had ever spent a significant amount of time in the company of the Cherokee. They would find, however, that the Cherokee already maintained hostilities with the Spanish in Florida and that they already had guns.

The veteran trader Abraham Wood organized this expedition under James Needham and Gabriel Arthur with the intention of establishing a trade relationship with the Cherokee. They planned to open an overland route to Chota, the largest town in the Overhill region. They hoped to trade guns, metal implements, cloth, beads, and trinkets in return for Cherokee products such as furs, beeswax, and animal oils, which could then be exported to England.

Needham and Arthur strode into Chota accompanied by Occaneechee Indians as guides and interpreters. The Cherokee chief was friendly and hospitable to his guests and upon their arrival placed them on a scaffold so they could be seen by the amassed clansmen without being endangered by the crowd. After the successful establishment of friendly relations, it was decided that Arthur would stay in Chota to learn the Cherokee language and customs, while Needham would head back to Fort Henry for supplies.

On the way back to Virginia Needham argued with Indian John (the Occaneechee interpreter) with disastrous results: Indian John shot Needham in the head, sliced open his chest, and held the white man's heart in his hands. Indian John cursed the Englishmen and sent word back to the chief in Chota to have Arthur killed as well. When the message arrived in Chota, some of the Indians tied Arthur to a stake and prepared to burn him. The Cherokee chief, who had been out of the village, arrived just in time to spare his life. He shot and killed an Indian who was starting the fire and then cut Arthur loose himself.

Arthur remained as guest among the Cherokee for over a year. He dressed like a Cherokee warrior and accompanied them on raids against the Spanish in Florida. Arthur was wounded and captured while on a raid against the Shawnee towns on the Ohio River. Instead of executing him, the Shawnee inexplicably nursed his wounds and released him. Upon returning to Chota, Arthur was greeted by the Cherokee chief, who then personally escorted him safely back to Virginia.

It would seem that the Needham and Arthur expedition should have encouraged further contact with the Virginians, but a major trade relationship was not established. By 1675 settlers had expanded into the backcountry, antagonizing the Susquehannocks. After raids committed against the settlers were left unanswered by Virginia's Governor Berkeley, the defiant Nathaniel Bacon organized a militia. Bacon allied with the Occaneechee to defeat the Susquehannocks, but then turned on his allies and destroyed them too. The destruction of the Occaneechee left no tribes between Virginia and the Cherokee, but even after Bacon's death in 1676 there was not much organized interest in pursuing further trade with them.

1663–1674

South Carolina Established

From the time of de Soto's Expedition to the exploration of Needham and Arthur, European contacts with the Cherokee had amounted to no more than sporadic brief encounters. That would change with the founding of Carolina and the permanent settlement of white men in the vicinity of the Cherokee lands. The prolonged interaction with the English would have a profound impact on the Cherokee economic system and culture. While the native peoples became more and more dependent on the Europeans for manufactured goods such as guns, an explosion in the white population in Carolina placed increasing pressure on the Indians to provide trade items and cede land. Eventually the excessive hunting of game and the encroachment by white settlers caused such environmental devastation that much of the land they desired was no longer useful to the Indians anyway.

King Charles II granted a proprietorship to a group of investors to establish a colony south of Virginia in 1762. Although the first attempt failed, one of the proprietors, Lord Anthony Ashley Cooper, convinced the other proprietors to invest their own money in another attempt to colonize Carolina, predicting great profits in return. Charleston was established in 1670, and it served as the seat of government. Immediately factional division sprung up among the colonists, which caused instability in the governor's office throughout the Proprietary period. Settlers from Barbados, known as the Goose Creek Men, were an aggressive breed who defied the proprietors whenever needed to protect their own financial interests. They were experienced slave owners who had no regard for the native Americans either.

Wars were fought against the small Kussoe and Stono tribes in 1671 and again in 1674, supposedly in retaliation for raids against the settlements. Captured natives were sold as slaves and exported to the northern colonies and West Indies. The profits from the sale of these captives inspired the development of a much bigger Indian slave trade that pitted tribe against tribe and settler against proprietor.

1674

South Carolina Establishes Trade Relations with the Cherokee

Lord Ashley suspected that the Spanish at St. Augustine were inciting the Indian attacks against Carolina. He recognized the importance of establishing Indian allies, who would serve as buffers between Carolina and Florida, so he sent Doctor Henry Woodward to negotiate with the surrounding tribes in 1674. This mission made contact with the Cherokee and established a trade relationship. The most important outcome, however, was that the Westo were awarded an exclusive arrangement with Carolina, thus becoming the most heavily armed and powerful tribe in the area. In return for guns, cloth, rums, and trinkets, the settlers received deerskins and Indian slaves whom the Westo captured from surrounding tribes.

For the next three years the Indian trade brought profits to individual entrepreneurs, but none to the overseas investors. In 1677 the proprietors declared a seven-year monopoly on the trade with the Westoes. The settlers complained of various abuses committed by the Westoes against them, and by 1680 the alliance had collapsed. The colonists formed a new alliance with the Creek and the Shawnee, and succeeded in destroying the Westo nation. Ironically the Shawnee had been chased southward by the Iroquois, and the Cherokee had allowed them to settle along the Savannah River to serve as a buffer between them and the Catawba. The presence of the Shawnee in the area had invited continual attacks by the Iroquois on them and neighboring tribes. Apparently many of the Shawnee relocated to the Cumberland basin where they served as a buffer between the Cherokee and the Chickasaw. By another agreement, the Yamasee, who were unhappy with their treatment by the Spanish in Florida, were induced to migrate north and settle in the coastal area south of Charleston.

Soon the Cherokee found themselves being victimized by the so-called buffer tribes, with the Lower Towns being close enough to make convenient targets. Although permits were granted to allow exportation of captured Cherokee as slaves, the proprietors did not believe that was appropriate policy. The proprietors were losing money while financing wars against Indians and did not benefit financially from the slave trade. They were also aware that France had established Fort Prud'homme on the bluffs overlooking the Mississippi, near Cherokee hunting grounds. Certainly they recognized the potential power of the Cherokee and did not want this large tribe driven into the hands of the French. Ordinances were passed prohibiting the capture of slaves within four hundred miles of Charleston, but the abuses continued.

1684

The First Treaty between the Cherokee and South Carolina

In 1684 a delegation of eight chiefs from two of the Cherokee Lower Towns arrived in Charleston to negotiate a treaty of protection. Among the delegation were Kalanu (the Raven), Tlanuwa (The Hawk), Nellawgitehi, Gorhaleke, and Caunasaita from Toxaway. Keowee sent Canacaught (The Great Conjurer), Gohoma, and Caunsaita. They were successful in obtaining promises that Carolina would protect them from raids by the Catawba (Esaw), Congaree (Coosaw), and Shawnee (Savannah). This document apparently no longer exists and it is unknown what other provisions were in it. It is believed to be the first treaty between the Cherokee and Europeans. It would prove to be ineffective.

Commercial relations became established between the Carolinians and the Cherokee, and trade routes between Charleston and the Cherokee towns were soon in regular use. In 1690 Cornelius Dougherty established a trading post in one of the Lower Towns; he lived with the Cherokee for the rest of his life. The Congaree, Catawba, and Shawnee, however, continued to kidnap Cherokees to sell as slaves. In 1693 a delegation of twenty Cherokee leaders traveled to Charleston to meet with Governor Thomas Smith to protest the continued sale of slaves in violation of trading regulations. Smith told them that the captured men were already sold as slaves and could not be recovered.

Over the next twenty years the Carolina colony became more deeply divided between those who opposed the proprietors and those who supported them. The Anti-Proprietary Party was dominated by the Goose Creek men whereas the Dissenters (named so because they were not Anglican) were Huguenots, Quakers, and other persecuted groups recruited by the proprietors to settle in Carolina and dilute the power of the Barbadians. The Indian slave trade persisted despite objections from the proprietors, thus compromising their ability to control Indian policies.

1697

Small Pox Destabilizes the Cherokee

An epidemic of small pox broke out in Charleston in 1697 and it had spread to the Cherokee by the next year. The extent of suffering is unknown, but the death toll may have been as high as fifty percent. The Iroquois enlisted the support of the Creek and attacked the Cherokee during this period of weakness. They may have been encouraged by the French, who had established a trading post on the Cumberland River with the Shawnee and who were erecting posts along the Gulf of Mexico at Biloxi and Mobile. Evidently the attack did not go well for the Iroquois in 1698, and in 1700 the Cherokee expelled the Creek from their villages in what is now southeast Tennessee in retaliation for their support of the northern tribe.

In the thirty years after the founding of Charleston, the relationship between the Cherokee and English changed from sporadic contact to an established diplomatic relationship in which trade principles were documented in treaty form. The permanent presence of Englishmen in Carolina encouraged traditional intertribal hostilities and escalated their warfare by providing new means of destruction. The Cherokee, like all of the other tribes in eastern North America, would soon be drawn into new European conflicts in which the natives would fight each other as clients of colonial powers.

Chapter Two

1701–1753

The Cherokee and the European Wars for Empire

Traditionally wars between the Cherokee and their rivals were brief engagements of small parties of warriors who had limited objectives. Often members of a single clan would be out to obtain blood revenge for a murdered relative, and would halt the battle after the appropriate number of enemy deaths had been secured. Captive warriors might be adopted as fellow tribesmen or might be retained as slaves, though not in the European sense. The Cherokee had a subsistence economy so there was nothing to be gained by exploiting them for their labor. The introduction of guns among the native tribes led to the depletion of game and also gave them the capability of waging genocidal war. With inadequate numbers of deer available to pay for guns and for other items the Indians could not produce for themselves, it became expedient for them to hunt each other. The Cherokee entered into this trade a little later than the coastal nations, but they had the advantage of a large population. The warriors gained more and more power in the Cherokee government as the influence of the traditionalists and religious leaders waned. The Cherokee would soon be able to assemble large armies to fight wars for political gain, not just blood revenge.

Just as the Cherokee concept of war was changing, so were the European attitudes toward war in America. From the end of the seventeenth century to the middle of the next, four wars were fought in North America that were extensions of European conflicts representing a struggle for imperial domination of the continent. The native tribes, sandwiched between the English coastal colonies and the French interior settlements, were courted as allies, or simply destroyed if necessary. Spain was a relatively minor player. The persistent influences of the Europeans altered the traditional alliances among the various nations, and their exploitation of long-standing rivalries ensured that no grand alliance of natives could destroy the white colonies.

At the end of King Williams's War, the French were able to ensure the neutrality of the large Iroquois nation. The French realized the importance of linking Louisiana with Canada, limiting the English colonies to the coastal region. In the event of war in Europe, the English would be hard-pressed to divert enough troops to defend the long Atlantic coastline. In order to implement their strategy, the French needed to maintain the ability to navigate the Ohio region. It was not necessary to inhabit the territory if the English could be kept out and if the Indians were kept friendly. The Iroquois Confederation, sandwiched between Canada and New England, had fought against the French in the indecisive King William's War, but it became neutral at the turn of the century. Iroquois neutrality was the keystone of their foreign policy, and was necessary to maintain the internal political stability of the confederacy. The Iroquois used their neutrality to play the French and English against each other, and over the next few decades often succeeded where the Cherokee failed at the same game. The Iroquois maintained hostility with the Catawba and the Cherokee while establishing friendly relations with the pro-French western tribes (some of whom had been displaced by the expansionist Iroquois in the first place). The Iroquois cooperated with Pennsylvania to dominate the Ohio tribes and turn them into vassal states. The Delaware and the Shawnee were forced to allow the Iroquois safe passage in order to attack the southern tribes, while they would resist northern intrusions from the Cherokee.

The Chickasaw, who were allied with the English, stymied French navigation of the Mississippi. The English were also friendly with the Yamasee, but that alliance had more impact on their rivalry with Spain. Whereas many of the southern tribes maintained pro-French foreign policies, the Cherokee were neutral at the beginning of the eighteenth century.

1702–1713

Queen Anne's War and the Tuscarora War

In 1702 the War of the Spanish Succession (Queen Anne's War) broke out in Europe over who was the legitimate heir to the Spanish throne. Specifically, the English and the Holy Roman Empire feared that France and Spain, united under Bourbon monarchs, would destroy the European balance of power and dominate the world of commerce. The war was the first truly "world war" since it was fought on parts of five continents.

Charleston felt particularly vulnerable to attack, considering its proximity to Spanish Florida and potentially hostile Indians. Governor James Moore, a member of the Anti-Proprietary Party, organized a preemptive strike against the Spanish at St. Augustine, without approval of the proprietors. Eight ships carried fifty Carolinians and thirteen hundred Yamasees, but they were unable to breach the defenses of the Castillo de San Marcos. The next year Moore led a party of Carolinians and Creek allies against Spanish missions across northern and western Florida, butchering the Appalachee savagely. A combined French and Spanish naval assault on Charleston was launched in 1706 in retaliation, but was repelled successfully. Moore's military accomplishments enhanced the prestige of the English among the southeastern Indians, at the expense of the Spanish, whose influence continued to decline. The war increased the debt burden of the colony (and exposed the inability of the proprietors to finance the protection of the settlers) while individual soldiers profited by the capture and sale of Indians into slavery. The House of Commons passed a comprehensive Indian trade regulation act in 1707, but it would prove to be as unenforceable as the previous efforts.

The Cherokee became involved in several military excursions over the next few years. The Delaware (a traditional foe) drove them out of the Ohio Valley in 1708. In the same year the Cherokee joined a group of Creeks and Catawba and attacked the pro-French Choctaw near the French post at Mobile. Soon the Cherokee would support the English in a more direct way. In 1711 Swiss settlers in North Carolina had settled beyond the immediate coastal region, in Tuscarora territory, in defiance of official colonial policy. The Tuscarora attacked and killed more than two hundred settlers, nearly wiping the settlement out. While the Virginians subdued the northern Tuscarora, the South Carolinians sent in a punitive force of colonials and Yamasee under Colonel John Barnwell. The fighting led to a stalemate, but Barnwell was forced to retreat in order to secure the release of captured soldiers, whom the Tuscarora were torturing. A short-lived peace treaty was arranged but when violations persisted, South Carolina sent another expedition, this time under Governor Moore. The Cherokee joined Moore and his men against the Tuscarora in 1713 and this time the tribe was nearly destroyed.

Surviving remnants of the Tuscarora fled north and joined the Iroquois as the Sixth Nation. The territory of the Tuscarora was so injured that the land would remain sparsely occupied for years to come.

Queen Anne's War came to an end officially in 1713 with the signing of the Treaty of Utrecht. The Bourbon grandson of King Louis XIV of France was confirmed as King Philip V of Spain, but the French had lost Newfoundland and Nova Scotia to England. Spain retained its American holdings but had to give up its European possessions. The English emerged as a world power and its Protestant monarchy was preserved. Imperial tensions among the French, English, and Spanish in North America would continue to fester. The Spanish had granted the English the *asiento*—the right to deliver African slaves to Spanish American colonies, as well as some other trade concessions. English violations of the *asiento* would be a continuing source of friction for years to come. Meanwhile local wars between colonials and Indians would continue, as would inter-tribal conflicts. For the Cherokee, there would be several military campaigns over the next several years.

1714

Cherokee Expansionism

The Cherokee had tolerated the presence of the Shawnee along the Cumberland River for years, allowing them to serve as a buffer against the Chickasaw, who also claimed the territory. Around 1710 the French established a trading post among the Shawnee (near present-day Nashville) and in 1714 they erected Fort Toulouse among the Creeks (near Montgomery, Alabama). After their successful expeditions against the Tuscarora, the Cherokee decided to attack the Shawnee settlements. The Chickasaw, who were allied with the English, were threatened not only by the French influence along the Cumberland, but also by their growing presence on the upper and lower Mississippi River and Gulf Coast region. The Chickasaw cooperated with their traditional enemy, the Cherokee, and helped to drive the Shawnee from the Cumberland region into the Ohio River valley. The two victorious tribes shared the region as common hunting ground, but disagreement over their boundaries would be a problem for them to settle later. Also in 1714 the Cherokee under Chief Uakwalena (Big Head) defeated the Creeks at Pine Island. Later they established a village there.

The proprietors of South Carolina tried to control the corrupt Indian trade practices, but the abuses only multiplied. Traders led Indians into impossible debts and then kidnapped their women as payment. Thomas Nairne, South Carolina's Indian Trade Commissioner, tried to prosecute the son-in-law of the governor for kidnapping friendly Cherokees and stealing deerskins. Governor Johnson responded by jailing Nairne for committing acts of treason. In 1714 the commissioners found two Cherokee traders, Alexander Long and Eleazer Wiggan, guilty of inciting the Cherokee into attacking the Yuchi village of Chestowe. The two traders, who bore a grudge against the Yuchi over some unpaid debts, convinced the Cherokee (who were themselves heavily indebted to Long and Wiggan) that the governor had sanctioned the raid. The raid was successful in that the captured Yuchi villagers were sold into slavery and the Cherokee debt was forgiven. The official Indian policy of the colony, however, was undermined.

1715–1716

The Yamasee War

The increasing frequency and severity of trade abuses and the growing encroachment by settlers onto Indian lands particularly offended the Yamasee. In April 1715, a large party of Yamasee warriors (with Catawba and Cherokee allies) attacked settlements north of Savannah. The raiders destroyed most of the buildings, killed over a hundred people, and drove the survivors to Charleston. The English suspected that the Spanish at St. Augustine were inciting the Yamasee, and that the French were encouraging the Creeks to abet them. The colonials realized that they were desperately vulnerable to a joint attack by an alliance of southern tribes. The proprietors did not appreciate the grave danger of the situation and offered no significant help. Governor Charles Craven sent an expedition of three hundred armed men under Colonel Maurice Moore up the Savannah River to the Cherokee Lower Towns to negotiate an alliance. A contingent under Colonel George Chicken was sent to Tlanusiyi, one of the Lower Towns. The Cherokee had recently been at war with the Shawnee and were engaged against the Illinois at the time and were not willing to go to battle against the Yamasee, with whom they had no grievances. The Cherokee were angry with the Creeks, however, who had secretly assisted the Shawnee, and agreed to join the attack against them. This alliance with the Cherokee allowed Craven to direct the full brunt of his forces against the Yamasee. By April 1716 the tribe had been nearly annihilated, with the remnants seeking refuge among the Spanish in Florida. The lands of the Yamasee, like those of the Tuscarora, were a wasteland.

1717–1729

Diplomatic Relations with South Carolina

The colony of South Carolina had suffered the loss of a substantial percentage of its white inhabitants, and half of its cultivated land had been abandoned. The colonists realized that they needed to pay for the war and to prevent another one. They also realized that the proprietors would not help them. Excises were established to provide for border patrols, and private trade with Indians was prohibited. Provisions were made for the encouragement of new immigrants and for the orderly settlement of captured Yamasee lands. Furthermore, efforts were begun to invite the King to charter South Carolina as a royal colony and to end the proprietorship.

South Carolina was vulnerable to attack by the Spanish at St. Augustine and by the Creeks, Cherokee, or some combination of native groups. While they were on good terms with the Cherokee, the English asked them to send a delegation to the Illinois, to counter the influence of the French. The diplomatic mission apparently backfired, and hostilities erupted between the two tribes. The French rejected Cherokee overtures for expanded trade relations, and they were falsely accused of murdering two French noblemen. The French were probably responsible for the encouragement of Seneca and Creek raids against the Cherokee in 1717. The Cherokee planned an invasion of the Creek town Coweta the next year, but aborted it upon learning of the presence of European officers among the Creek. The Cherokee and the Creek traditionally fought over conflicting claims to hunting grounds, but the Cherokee realized that it would not be wise to start a war with a European power.

Early in 1718 South Carolina learned that war had broken out between England and Spain. The colonists' first troubles did not come from St. Augustine. English naval efforts in the Caribbean evicted pirates from the southern waters, but that did not prevent them from harassing Charleston. Shipping in and out of Charleston was plundered by the likes of Edward "Blackbeard" Teach and Stede Bonnet until a concerted effort by the fleets of North and South Carolina captured and executed the pirates. The settlers were nearly in a state of panic when rumors surfaced of an eminent Spanish attack. Fortunately, the French attacked and captured the Spanish fort at Pensacola, thus diverting their attention from Charleston.

Meanwhile, relations between the colonists and the proprietors continued to deteriorate. Not only did the proprietors fail to support the settlers' self-defense, they also challenged their independent legislative actions, made necessary by the extreme conditions and the proprietors' own inaction. In 1719, in a bloodless coup, well-organized revolutionaries replaced the proprietary governor, Robert Johnson, with the hero of the Tuscarora and Yamasee wars, James Moore Jr. Although Johnson attempted to continue a parallel government in South Carolina, the colonists were united in their contempt for the proprietors. The counter-revolutionary efforts of Johnson were ended when the King declared South Carolina a royal colony and appointed Francis Nicholson its first governor.

When the provisional government passed Indian trade regulations, Virginia expressed concern that if South Carolina prohibited trade with the Cherokee, then the tribe might be forced into the French fold. After the Cherokee assisted Charleston in establishing peace with the Yamasee in 1720, South Carolina did re-establish trade with them. Although there was some interest in trying to keep the Cherokee and Creek at war with each other, the British government felt that such a policy would give France and Spain opportunities to exert their influence. Nicholson was instructed to remain on friendly terms with the Cherokee and other Indians favoring the English. He would go on to sign treaties with both the Cherokee and Creeks.

Governor Nicholson invited thirty-seven chiefs representing various Cherokee towns to a conference held in Charleston. A treaty was negotiated specifying trade methods and delineating the boundary between the white settlers and the Cherokee. (See Map 3 #1.) Wrosetasatow was commissioned as supreme chief of the Cherokee nation with authority to punish all offenses. He was to represent Cherokee claims to the colonial government. The chiefs also agreed to the appointment

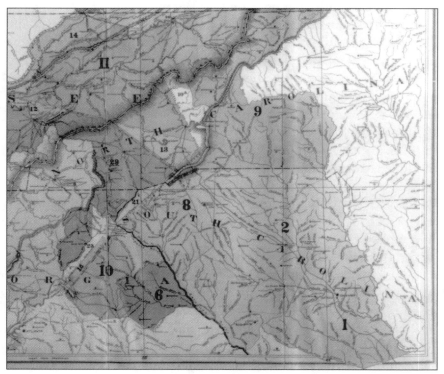

Map 3

of George Chicken as a commissioner to supervise traders residing in Cherokee territory.

The appointment of a supreme chief was a problem for the Cherokee since their governing structure was based on the township level, with no tradition of a central political figure having influence over all of the towns. There was also a tradition of governance by consensus; chiefs did not make decisions without the unanimous consent of representatives of all the clans. There must have been problems with the language of the treaty. The Cherokee did not have a written language at the time so they had to depend on translations by the English themselves. Ironically, the Cherokee language does not allow the expression of land ownership; the concept was alien to their culture. The land that they gave up was a small, game-depleted tract that they scarcely used anyway, but it was valuable to the settlers who would use it for planting. Whatever their intentions, this small tract of land in South Carolina was the first Cherokee land ceded to the Europeans. Over the next one hundred fourteen years there would be more than thirty more land cessions to the English and the Americans, and the titles to all of the original tribal lands would be gone forever.

Fifty years after Charleston was established the combined white and black population of South Carolina had grown to equal that of the Cherokee nation. Once the coastal tribes were virtually eliminated, large tracts of land became available for further settlement and cultivation. Within another twenty years the population tripled and the mainland colonies became more important as trade partners with Britain than the plantation colonies in the Caribbean. The uneasy peace between the French and the English collapsed as these European rivals fought for territorial expansion and domination of the North American Indian trade.

The Cherokee were drawn more deeply into European politics as they underwent drastic cultural changes. The Indian slave trade disappeared as the importation of African slaves and the immigration of white laborers increased and the population of natives waned. As English demand for peltry increased, the Cherokee economy was transformed into a capitalistic system that tended to concentrate more political power in the hands of the hunter/warriors. The demands of the new economy increased Cherokee reliance on the English traders while game depletion caused by excessive hunting and white encroachment into traditional Indian lands increased the pressure for warfare. The first Cherokee overseas diplomatic mission to Windsor in 1730 had profound and lasting (and sometimes divisive) effects on Cherokee politics. Ten years later nearly half the tribe would be dead from small pox, and the power of the sacred traditions would be forever challenged.

After the first cession treaty was signed in 1721, South Carolina still suffered from political instability and the economic hardship of rebuilding after the Yamasee War. Charleston remained vulnerable to attack from the Spanish at St. Augustine and from hostile tribes influenced by the Spanish or the French. The Creeks and the Cherokee were the largest and most organized tribes, and thus the most dangerous. The growing importance of the Indian trade on the South Carolina economy and the role that the Cherokee could play as a buffer against the French in the Mississippi Valley enhanced the importance of their continued friendship. The Creeks insisted that they could get along without the English since the Spanish and the French would keep them armed.

They even allowed the French to build Fort Toulouse in the midst of their territory. The Creeks were not afraid of the Cherokee and saw them as a continuing source of slaves. At one point South Carolina considered asking the Cherokee to ally with them against the Creeks, but eventually peace would prevail and a treaty with the Creek was inked.

Soon after Nicholson's treaty with the Cherokee was signed, tribal leaders met with the commissioners to establish fair weights and measures. The Committee on Indian Affairs in Charleston asked the legislature for permission to arrest unlicensed traders among the Cherokee, including a French trader known to live among them. Colonel George Chicken, the new trade commissioner, was allowed to travel at will among the Cherokee towns, receiving complaints about abuses by whites and by other Indians trading among them. Many of the Overhill Towns were leaning more heavily toward the French, whose establishments on the Mississippi threatened their downstream trade routes. Relations between England and the Cherokee actually had never been better, and would be encouraged even further after the brutal French defeat of the Natchez (1729–1731) and by the bizarre escapades of Alexander Cuming.

Figure 1 — Leaders in England

1730

Alexander Cuming Takes Cherokees to England

The actions of Alexander Cuming were so bold as to be difficult to believe. The impoverished English nobleman arrived in Charleston in 1729 with hopes of quick financial gains. Whether he acted alone or served as a secret agent for King George II is unclear, but the results of his exploits did benefit his mother country. On March 23, 1730, Alexander Cuming marched into Keowee and spoke to an assembly of Cherokee leaders. Breaking with local custom, he entered the town house heavily armed and went on to demand Cherokee loyalty to the English crown. The group respected his bravery and amazingly agreed to his demands.

Cuming went on to other towns, apparently enlisting the friendship of the powerful medicine men *(Adawehis)* before making the same demands as before. At Great Tellico, Cuming received Chief Moytoy's pledge of loyalty to King George and then arranged for his election as principal chief in Nequassee (in the Middle Towns), calling him "Emperor Moytoy of the Cherokee." This action may have angered the people of Chota, the traditional capital of the Overhill Towns, but it was a brilliant move in that it countered the influence of the French, who had been fomenting anti-English sentiment at Tellico. At the meeting in Nequassee, the assembled leaders held a great feast, which included a ceremony in which the leaders laid down their feathers, scalps, and other regalia, symbolizing their loyalty to King George and their acceptance of Moytoy as their representative.

Cuming was anxious to prove his diplomatic success to King George. He had secured Cherokee loyalty to the Crown and he was willing to demonstrate his own personal confidence by living among them as the king's representative. In another bold move, he arranged for seven Cherokee leaders to accompany him to England for an audience with the King. (See Figure 1, page 29.) Emperor Moytoy chose to stay behind with his ailing wife, and appointed Oukah-Ulah in his place. The young Oukandekah (later to be known as Attakullakulla or Little Carpenter) was the only other chief to accompany Cuming, but five other prominent Cherokee also made the voyage. The old trader, Eleazer Wiggan (Old Rabbit), was brought along as an interpreter. The party boarded the man-of-war *Fox* at Charleston on May 4 and arrived at Dover, England, on June 5, 1730.

The King realized the importance of a tribe that could muster over three thousand warriors on his behalf, and so agreed to meet with the delegation and sign a treaty with them. Arrangements were made for an audience and for a celebratory feast, during which the Cherokee crown of scalps and feathers was presented to the King. While the Cherokee were given a spectacular tour of London, the Lords Commissioners drafted the Articles of Friendship and Commerce (Treaty of Dover). The treaty gave the English exclusive trading rights and would require military assistance from the Cherokee for the next thirty years. The document guaranteed that Englishmen who committed crimes in Cherokee territory would be granted trials in English courts. The Cherokee would be given weapons and other gifts. A ceremony followed the presentation and discussion of the agreement, during which Oukandekah served as spokesman (since he spoke some English). He pledged loyalty to King George II, laying before the commissioners all of the chiefs' feathers surrendered at Nequassee. The actual document was signed on

September 23, at the lodgings of Alexander Cuming in Winchester, in the presence of Robert Johnson, the newly appointed first royal governor of South Carolina. Although Cuming was well respected by the Cherokee and the government did pay off his expenses, he was detained in England to answer to charges of fraud filed against him by colonists in Charleston. Governor Johnson accompanied the entourage of Indians back to Charleston, and Alexander Cuming faded into obscurity.

1731–1739

Small Pox, New Leadership, and The New Alliance

Over the next several years the new royal government of South Carolina continued the rebuilding of its infrastructure and established new townships in the recently acquired Indian lands. In 1731 the government considered invoking the new Treaty of Dover to obtain Cherokee help in ousting the Tuscarora remnant (who were stealing slaves). Carolina backed down, however, fearing severe reprisals from its Iroquois allies. Meanwhile Colonel James Oglethorpe established the new colony of Georgia on the south shore of the Savannah River, thus creating a buffer between Charleston and St. Augustine. The colonists occupied lands once claimed by the Yamasee and Guales, but which were still claimed by the Creeks. The Creek leader Tomochichi negotiated a treaty with Oglethorpe, ceding the land in question and establishing a trade relationship. Tomochichi must have seen the English as potential allies against the Spanish in Florida or the increasingly aggressive French on the Gulf Coast.

By 1734 South Carolina began to doubt the value of the treaty of 1730. The Cherokee were becoming increasingly disgruntled about the high prices of trade goods, while Virginian traders were undercutting the official prices. Charleston accused the Cherokee of stealing and then suspended trade until they made restitution. South Carolina claimed to have exclusive rights to the Cherokee trade and thus asked Georgia not to allow trade with the Cherokee there. The Cherokee had been battling with the Talapoosa and the Alibamu, and it was expected that their need for ammunition would force them to capitulate. Eventually it was decided that the best way to win back and maintain Cherokee loyalty would be to establish forts in their territory, and that a new tax on the traders would pay for them. There was concern that the traders would bypass the taxes by moving into Georgia territory, but again South Carolina warned Georgia that the kings favored their exclusive trade relationship. South Carolina passed a free trade ordinance in 1736 that would allow trade with Cherokee, Creeks, and other friendly tribes, but the King's Board of Trade, which admonished the colonies to settle their differences, rejected it.

Meanwhile the French were increasing their influence among the southern tribes, by sending emissaries to invite them to trade at Fort Toulouse. Even the Cherokee became regular customers, despite objections from Attakullakulla. There was a general fear that the French were organizing the Choctaw and Creeks to attack and overrun Charleston. The concern was that if the Creeks joined the French, the Cherokee would back away from their Treaty of Dover commitments. These concerns pressured Charleston to settle the trade dispute with the Cherokee. The government of South Carolina was plagued by its inability to control its own citizens and by the lack of a coordinated Indian policy with neighboring colonies. Some disgruntled traders from South Carolina were probably responsible for fomenting the Creeks to attack St. Augustine, and possibly even Georgia. Governor Oglethorpe successfully negotiated an understanding with the governor of St. Augustine that both colonies would try to prevent Indian attacks against the other.

During the 1730s the French used the native peoples as proxies in their aggression against the English. French influence among the Cherokee was relatively limited at this time because of their geographical proximity to the English colonies and relative distance from French establishments. The French built Fort Toulouse in Creek territory, not too far from the Cherokee villages, but the Cherokee often viewed Muskogean Creeks as enemies. The French were able to infiltrate the Cherokee villages with traders, despite objections from the English. The erratic Jesuit missionary Christian Priber arrived among the Cherokee in 1736 and claimed to have been sanctioned by Chief Moytoy. He preached a strange socialistic philosophy alien to Indian and European alike. He gained influence over Chief Oconostota, promoting a pro-French policy, but when war broke out between France and England in 1743, he would pay with his life.

In 1736 French aggression was focused on the Chickasaw, English allies who commanded a long stretch of the Mississippi River below the Ohio River. The Chickasaw interfered with French river traffic between the Gulf of Mexico settlements and the Great Lakes. The Cherokee remained allied with the Chickasaw and participated with them in joint operations along the Ohio River. These northern expeditions were withdrawn, however, because their over-extended positions were determined to be indefensible against the Iroquois, Mascoutah, and Kickapoo. The French aggression against the Chickasaw was not successful in 1736, but in 1739 their campaign was at least partially successful. The Chickasaw were weakened, but the French would have to give up their hopes of conquering them for the time being.

And 1739 was a year of holocaust for the Cherokee. Small pox had been brought to the colony aboard a slave ship in 1738 and it soon spread inland. The mortality rate for the Cherokee may have approached fifty percent. Some deaths were attributable to suicides, the shame of disfigurement being unbearable. The devastation shook the foundations of the culture. Traditional medicine was a failure against the epidemic, and many of the priest-doctors died of the disease themselves. At one point all of the traditional medical paraphernalia were destroyed since they had lost their powers. The priests felt that the disease was divine retribution for the rejection of traditional beliefs and for bad behavior of the younger people. The War Chief Oconostota, who was disfigured by the disease, blamed the English. One consequence of the epidemic was a relative loss of esteem for the priests and an increase in power for the young warriors. Although it would take twenty years for the population to recover, Cherokee warriors would be participants in military campaigns within the next year.

In fact over the next decade the Cherokee continued to spar with French-allied tribes (mostly to the north) while becoming more closely entwined with the economy of the English colonies. Although South Carolina had enjoyed relative peace in the 1730s, as the decade came to an end it was clear that the colony was still vulnerable to attack. Friendship with both the Creeks and the Cherokee remained vitally important to Charleston, as these nations were the main buffers between them and the French. The Indians also were seen as potential allies in helping the colonists deal with slave uprisings after the Stono Rebellion sent shock waves through South Carolina. Furthermore, the fledgling colony of Georgia would require the cooperation of these Indians against the looming threat of the Spanish.

Under the Peace of Utrecht of 1713, British merchants were entitled to the *asiento*, the right to supply African slaves to the Spanish colonies, plus the right to one delivery of British goods annually. The British merchants had been violating the terms of the *asiento* for years, and smuggling by British colonists was rampant. The Spanish coast guard intensified its efforts to enforce the trade laws, and ultimately some of their detainees were mistreated. The alleged amputation of the ear of one Captain Jenkins incensed the British Parliament to declare war against Spain in 1739, the so-called War of Jenkin's Ear. Georgia immediately became involved in the war, which eventually would involve the Cherokee and other tribes with them. Within a few years a more general war erupted in Europe, and once again England and France competed for empire on the North American continent.

1739–1748

The War of the Austrian Succession

The Cherokee–South Carolina Alliance

When the War of Jenkin's Ear began in 1739, the colonists mainly were concerned about the Spanish at St. Augustine, but also were aware that the French were arousing the Indians against them as well. The missionary Christian Priber was fomenting anti-British sentiment among the Cherokee and had Oconostota convinced that the colonists were responsible for the small pox epidemic and other social problems of the tribe. Georgia Governor James Oglethorpe hastily countered by promising supplies and other support for the Cherokee. Within a month of the declaration of war the Spanish had killed some Englishmen on Amelia Island, Georgia. Quickly, Oglethorpe enlisted the help of the Cherokee, Chickasaw, Creek, Yuchi, and Yamacraw.

The next spring Oglethorpe and his allies attacked the Spanish and captured Fort Picolata and Fort San Francisco de Pupa. Chief Kalanu

(The Raven) led the Cherokee delegation. The Georgians failed to receive support from the South Carolinians or England and soon withdrew back to Savannah. The British fleet inflicted a great defeat against the Spanish at Cartagena (now Colombia), in 1741, but in 1742 St. Augustine was capable of launching an overland attack against the Georgians at Frederica. The Georgians prevailed at the Battle of Bloody Swamp and the following year they were able to march into St. Augustine virtually without a fight. The Spanish would have no further role in the American phase of the conflict.

There had been an uneasy peace in Europe since the ratification of the Treaty of Utrecht in 1713. The death of the Holy Roman Emperor Charles VI in October 1740 left the Habsburg dynasty without a male heir. The Pragmatic Sanction, devised in 1713, would have ensured that all of the Habsburg lands remain united under one sovereign. Within two months of Charles' death, however, the Elector of Prussia, Frederick "The Great", invaded Silesia, triggering the War of the Austrian Succession. Spain was drawn into the conflict, seeking to regain lands ceded to Italy in 1713. The French entered the war in 1744, hoping to wrest control of Belgium from Austria. Naturally the British were motivated to protect their overseas commerce and to support their protestant allies in Holland. Ironically, the great French victory at Fontenoy, Belgium, in 1745 was followed by their greatest loss in the New World, the Battle of Louisbourg.

The French, who were more fully committed in Europe, were less capable of fighting in the New World than the British. The British colonists fought cooperatively as "Americans" for the first time, but did not receive the support they felt was needed for adequate prosecution of the war. Most of the war was fought in New England and the coastal areas of Canada, where the great fisheries were at stake. The colonists complained that their military efforts in that region were not backed by British naval support, and indeed the British Navy was called into service in Europe and shunted away from New England. Parliament repeatedly questioned the high financial costs of supplying the colonists with arms and provisions. The legislators were especially reluctant to continue supplying "gifts" for the Indian allies. The colonists, on the other hand, especially those from Georgia and the Carolinas, realized that they were utterly dependent on the goodwill of the neighboring Indian tribes. It became the policy of colonies to try to attain peace among all of the Indian nations friendly to the English. The task was complicated by the persistence of traditional tribal rivalries, the constant interference by the French and their allies, the inflammation caused by unfair trading practices, and the lack of central coordination of colonial Indian policies.

The French strategy in North America was aimed toward uniting Canada with Louisiana, making the Mississippi a French river. From the west and north they would rival the English trading relationships with the Indians and even threaten the survival of the English colonies if they could turn English allies against them. To achieve their goals the French needed to turn the Iroquois against the British or at least neutralize them. In the south they would have to either subjugate the Chickasaw or make them allies. The Cherokee had been allied with the Chickasaw since 1715 and helped defend them against French attacks in the 1730s. The French tried to gain the support of the Cherokee in order to get to the Chickasaw, and thus launched a series of attacks against them by surrogate Indian tribes, coupled with diplomatic attempts to gain their friendship. They met with limited success. In 1740 the Cherokee, along with some Natchez and perhaps some Chickasaw, attacked a party of Frenchmen on the Wabash River, thus opposing the French strategic desire for free navigation between Canada and Louisiana. Over the next several years the French decided that they would have to build a fort in the area if peace could not be made with the Cherokee. They also realized that to do that they would have to restrain their Canadian Indian allies and push them to make peace with the Cherokee also. By 1743, however, the Cherokee had become engaged in warfare with French-allied tribes to the south, such as the Talapoosa, and they were talking peace with the English-allied tribes to the north.

In 1742 the Iroquois signed the Treaty of Easton with Pennsylvania, confirming the fraudulent sale of traditional Delaware lands to the English in 1737. The sale placed the Iroquois as the sole bargaining agent between Pennsylvania and the Ohio Indians, and forced the Delawares out of their homeland into lands occupied by Shawnee. This action aroused hostility among these tribes to both the Iroquois and white settlers. Two years later the Six Nations of the Iroquois met with representatives from Pennsylvania, Maryland, and Virginia and signed the Treaty of Lancaster. The Iroquois received money, and all three colonies recognized their suzerainty over the southern tribes, much as they had over the Shawnee and Delawares. Virginia recognized the right of Iroquois warriors to pass through to fight the Catawba and Cherokee, and agreed to provision the war parties in transit. Canasatego, the Iroquois leader, apparently thought he was giving up a section of hunting grounds that the tribe claimed by virtue of military conquest, but he actually ceded the entire Ohio Valley. The English negotiators did not tell him that Virginia claimed lands all the way to the Pacific.

After a period of minimal diplomatic contact between the Cherokee and Charleston, a delegation of two hundred Cherokee visited Governor James Glen in October 1744. Unfair debts to traders had caused a chilling of relations. The most reliable ally of the English, Attakullakulla, had been captured by the French-allied Ottawas in 1740 and was still being held. The Cherokee had been without an "Emperor" since the death of Moytoy in 1741, so Governor Glen appointed Ammouskossittee (Moytoy's teenage son) to succeed him. After a pompous coronation ceremony, Glen showed Ammouskossittee a copy of the 1730 Treaty of Dover to remind him of the obligations of the Cherokee. The Emperor was satisfied with Glen's efforts to address trade issues and thus offered the assistance of the Cherokee against the Spanish.

In 1746 France was winning on the battlefield in Europe but was losing in New England. The French turned their attention once again to the south. If they could achieve peace with the Cherokee, they could avoid having to build a costly fort on the Wabash. Perhaps they could build one among the Cherokee themselves, asserting pressure on the Carolinas and Georgia. They recruited the Shawnee to help them broker a peace with the Cherokee and other southern tribes. A party of Frenchmen and French-allied Indians (led by the Shawnee) met at Chota seeking a general peace. The Shawnee, for their part, wanted Cherokee permission to build settlements near the Cherokee (Tennessee) River. The Cherokee leadership did not commit to the French but used the French initiative to put more pressure on the English.

Connecorte of Chota (Old Hop) traveled to Charleston and reported that the French were negotiating for a fort among the Overhill Towns. Governor Glen would not allow this French fort under any circumstances and sought financial backing to build an English fort instead. The governor supported further financial assistance for the Cherokee, but he also pressured them to stop allowing the Shawnee or other northern tribes safe passage for the purpose of raiding the Catawba. Glen expected that the Cherokee should behave more as allies with the English and pro-English tribes.

Over the next two years very little was accomplished, and neither the French nor the English built a fort among the Cherokee. In an incident in South Carolina, a Cherokee had murdered an English trader named James Butler. The legislature would not give Glen approval for funds to build a fort unless the Cherokee prosecuted and punished the murderer. The guilty Cherokee eventually was executed but by then the war in Europe had come to a halt. The European powers had tired of war and had agreed more or less to revert to the *status quo antebellum* with the signing of the Treaty of Aix-la-Chapelle in October 1748. Louisbourg, the major British territorial gain of the war, was returned to the French. Glen still wanted South Carolina to build a fort among the Cherokee, but there was less urgency.

1748–1754

Between World Wars

South Carolina, Virginia, and the French Compete for Cherokee Loyalty

The founding of the Ohio Company of Virginia and the "discovery" of the Cumberland Gap in 1748 opened up new opportunities for English settlement in the interior. During the 1750s the American colonies grew in population and in economic importance to England, but they remained vulnerable to attacks by Indians and the French, so a general peace was desirable. The English aggressively asserted their new rights to the Ohio area (granted by the Treaty of Lancaster) by establishing trading posts on the southern shore of Lake Erie and further west at Pickawillany. The English tried to undermine French influence with the northern tribes by undercutting their prices. The mere presence of the English in this area taunted the French, whose strategic interest mandated unencumbered navigation of the area's rivers and exclusion of the British.

In 1752 Christopher Gist, representing the Ohio Company, and George Croghan (supposedly representing Pennsylvania) met at the Mingo, Shawnee, and Delaware settlement at Logstown (fifteen miles downstream from the forks of the Ohio). The Iroquois Half-King Tanaghrisson agreed to the establishment of a fortified trade post at the forks, which would allow the Indians access to inexpensive English goods. The fort's location offered a strategic advantage to the English against French navigation, but it also threatened the Indians with the possibility of a permanent English settlement in their territory. Tanaghrisson was offered grand reassurances about the English intentions and was given a fortune in gifts. Although the English would not negotiate with other leaders, Tanaghrisson was compelled to recognize Shingas as "King" of the Delawares in order to secure the cooperation of his people. Tanaghrisson maintained that his dealings would have to be approved by the Grand Council at Onondaga, but in reality the Delawares were emerging as an independent tribe any way.

In 1752 the French appointed a new governor-general, the Marquis de Duquesne, and he was determined to enforce French hegemony over the Ohio Valley. On June 21, 1752, a party of French, Chippewa, and Ottawa warriors, under the leadership of Charles-Michel Mouet de Langlade, captured the trade post at Pickawillany. The post was inadequately defended as most of the men were out hunting. The defenders and women captives were ransomed for Indian traders, of whom two were tortured and cannibalized as an example to the others. After the raid, the Miami chiefs at Pickawillany petitioned Pennsylvania and Virginia for help, but Virginia felt that the Miamis were too far away to be of any concern to them. Likewise the Quaker-dominated Pennsylvania Assembly refused to get involved. The Miamis quietly returned to the French fold, and English influence on the southern shore of Lake Erie was nearly eliminated.

Despite the loss of Pickawillany, the Ohio Company continued with its plans to settle the forks of the Ohio, but took the precaution of erecting the Red Stone Fort, thirty-seven miles upstream from the forks. Settlement of the area was retarded by conflicting claims between Pennsylvania and Virginia (brought before the Board of Trade) and by internal divisions in Virginia between the Ohio Company and the Loyal Company. The Loyal Company, which had claims to the territory south of the Ohio, was able to thwart its northern counterpart until 1749, when the newly appointed lieutenant governor, Robert Dinwiddie became a shareholder of the Ohio Company. His policies would promote the settlement of the area and encourage its defense.

Meanwhile, Governor-General Duquesne was under orders to preserve communication between Canada and the Illinois settlements via the Ohio and to make every effort to drive the British from French lands. He would allow the Indians to visit the English colonies to trade but not to trade with the English while on French soil.

Duquesne prepared the eleven thousand men of the Canadian militia for war and set out to build four forts in the Ohio Valley. By the end of 1753, a fort was established at Presque Isle on the south shore of Lake Erie, connected by a post road to a second fort at Riviere aux Boeufs. Fort Machault was built at the Delaware village of Venango on the Allegheny River. Fort Duquesne was to be built at the forks of the Ohio in 1754—at the site already chosen for a fort by the English. The French had lost more than four hundred men building the forts and had spent an enormous amount of money as well. They felt that the English threat justified the costs and the possibility of provoking a war.

Between 1748 and 1754, as war with France loomed on the horizon, it became apparent that the colonies would have to secure the loyalty of the tribes along the western borders. With the Ohio Valley shaping up as the battle ground between the French and the English, peace with the Iroquois was obviously the top priority. The English worked to create an alliance of friendship among all tribes loyal to the King, but the project was hampered by the persistence of old rivalries. Negotiations with the larger nations were complicated by the fact that they were confederations, whose constituent tribes had varying traditional enemies. The King's Board of Trade coordinated colonial Indian trade policy in such a loose way that the individual colonies saw each other as competitors as well.

To the south, the English continued to put pressure on the Cherokee to make peace with both the Catawba and the Creeks. The Cherokee agreed to help the Creeks oust the Nottaways and other northern tribes and agreed to stop allowing northern warriors safe passage into Catawba territory. South Carolina discouraged the Indians from attacking the French after 1748 but recognized that the French were still actively seeking to influence the Indians and derail the peace process. In Charleston, Governor Glen worked to secure the friendship of both the Creeks and the Cherokee, but was hampered by domestic political squabbles. The Council and the House of Commons (the upper and lower houses of the legislature) contested each other's right to determine fiscal policy and thus drove the government into gridlock. Recent Scots-Irish immigration into the sandhill region created a new rivalry between them and the coastal inhabitants. The new settlements also increased tension with the Cherokee since the new arrivals tended to encroach into Cherokee territory and did not respect trading regulations.

The Creek/Cherokee War flared up in 1750 after the French at Fort Toulouse incited the Creeks to destroy a few Cherokee villages. Governor Glen tried to mediate between the two tribes, but both groups were internally divided and were thus incapable of reaching a consensus. Glen obtained permission from some of the Lower Cherokee to buy land for the erection of a fort near Keowee, but other Cherokee felt that the land could not be sold unless agreed to by leaders from the Middle and Overhill towns as well. Many of the Overhill Cherokee clearly favored the French and continued to allow French-allied Indians safe passage through their territory in order to attack the Creeks and Catawba, despite earlier agreements.

By spring 1751 the South Carolina legislature had become increasingly hostile toward the Cherokee. It favored trade sanctions against them as long as they were allowing northern Indians safe passage. After a party of Cherokee killed some settlers on the southern branch of the Santee, the legislature even proposed organizing an army to chastise the tribe. That summer, even Attakullakulla, the last surviving member of Cuming's delegation to Windsor, was speaking against the British. The Chickasaw defeated the Choctaw in 1750, and in 1751 they attacked French hunters near Fort Prud'homme with Cherokee help. The French were therefore wary of Cherokee friendship and encouraged the Iroquois to attack them.

By the end of the year a Cherokee diplomatic mission, led by The Raven, was sent to Charleston. Governor Glen reiterated South Carolina's desire that the Cherokee stop allowing hostile Indians safe passage through their lands. Despite Cherokee objections that the Creeks were the aggressors, Glen asked them to aid the Creeks against any invasion by the Iroquois. The Cherokee were willing to have a fort built among the Lower Towns but denied permission to build one in the Overhill region. As the Cherokee delegation left Charleston in the spring, a group of Lower Creeks led by Acorn Whistler murdered some of them. Also, Creek raiders entered Cherokee villages to harass the English traders. Governor Glen tried to gain sympathy for the Cherokee by claiming that the Creek actions were insulting to the British, but the legislature was still upset that the Cherokees had never been brought to justice for murdering some settlers in 1751. The legislature proposed pushing the Cherokee to relinquish lands between the Keowee River and the Long Canes Creek.

By the summer of 1752 the Nottaways had entered into war against the Cherokee. The French, still hoping to build forts along the Cherokee (Tennessee) River, attempted to exploit an incident in which Cherokees murdered some Iroquois. The French pressured the Iroquois to seek revenge, but this attempt to drive a wedge between the two English allies failed. The English prestige with the Iroquois was at a peak as they were agreeing to terms at Logstown. Late in 1752 the Creek relented to pressures from Charleston by apprehending and executing Acorn Whistler. Nonetheless Glen would not support further Creek attacks on the Cherokee and actually interceded to prevent a new wave of Creek attacks. At the same time the Catawba ignored Glen's warnings not to attack the Cherokee, but within weeks they were asking for peace.

In 1751 Emperor Ammouskossittee led a delegation to Williamsburg, Virginia, to negotiate a new trade relationship. The Cherokee had suffered under South Carolina's recent embargo and were looking for another venue for commerce. Governor Dinwiddie was mindful of South Carolina's claim to an exclusive right to the Cherokee trade and tactfully declined to sign an agreement, saying that the distances between the two nations was prohibitive. Diplomatic relations between the Cherokee and Virginia were established, however, and would deepen over the next few years. Virginia was preoccupied with plans to exploit its new western claims secured by the Treaty of Logstown. Dinwiddie planned to build forts in the territory, and a friendly relationship with the Cherokee might be useful later.

The ineffective Emperor was attacked and apparently injured on his way back from Williamsburg. Virginia claimed that he had been attacked by French Indians, but South Carolina accused Virginian settlers of the deed. In fact, John Watts, the emperor's translator, named the settlers involved in the attack! The whole incident strained relations between the two colonies.

Meanwhile a rivalry had emerged between Old Hop of Chota and his inexperienced nephew, Ammouskossittee of Tellico. Taking advantage of rumors that the Emperor had sold valuable hunting grounds to Virginia, Old Hop led his own delegation to Williamsburg and met with Colonel Lewis Burrell, the president of the Council. With Ammouskossittee injured and apparently untrustworthy, Governor Glen appointed Old Hop Emperor. Not only was Old Hop the uncle of Ammouskossittee, but as the brother of Moytoy he was also the uncle of the influential Attakullakulla. The Little Carpenter had been released by the French at the end of the war and had regained his leadership position. Although he was friendly with the French, Old Hop was expected to unite the tribe and bring them closer to the English. The Cherokee were deeply divided, as the French-leaning Overhill Towns still rejected the legality of the sale of the land for Fort Prince George, which had been erected at Keowee that summer.

As tensions mounted between the French and the English in the Ohio area, hostilities among the various tribes escalated and became somewhat chaotic. The Chickasaw/Cherokee alliance stepped up its attacks against the French on the Mississippi and Wabash rivers. About the time the Cherokee were reconciling with the Wyandot (to the north), the Iroquois and Delaware joined the French at the Winchester Conference and revoked the Treaty of Logstown. The stage was set for war.

Both Virginia and South Carolina stepped up pressure on the Creeks to reconcile with the Cherokee (and Chickasaw). Governor Glen met with a delegation led by Attakullakulla and suggested that the Cherokee were obligated by the Treaty of Dover to make peace with the Creeks. Attakullakulla replied that the treaty had obliged South Carolina to provide them with arms and other supplies that were never delivered. He also indicated that Virginia would meet their needs if South Carolina could not. Finally Glen released some goods for the Cherokee and promised to build a fort in the Overhills to protect the dependents during times of war. Attakullakulla agreed to take the governor's requests back to Old Hop for consideration.

Lieutenant Governor Dinwiddie petitioned the English for assistance in countering French aggressions in North America. On August 21, 1753, the cabinet responded favorably to his request by ordering the governors of the colonies to build defensive forts in their western territories. The Mohawks, angry over a fraudulent land deal, broke off diplomatic relations with New York, revoking the Covenant Chain. Lord Halifax, First Commissioner of the Board of Trade, instructed the colonies to negotiate a new unified treaty with the Indians. Dinwiddie claimed the Ohio Valley as part of Virginia (whether the English government agreed with this claim is uncertain) and interpreted communications from the cabinet as supporting his plans to fortify the forks of the Ohio. He did not send a delegation to the Albany Congress and thus sidestepped having to deal with Pennsylvania.

In 1753 Dinwiddie was politically weakened by his contention with the House of Burgesses over the right to impose a fee for signing land patents. He would be incapable of asking the legislature to grant funds to raise an army to force the French out of Ohio. Instead, he commissioned twenty-one year-old Major George Washington to act as an emissary to the French in the Ohio regions, representing King George II's desire that they leave. Washington went on a diplomatic mission to Fort Le Boeuf near Lake Erie, but the commander of the French forces rebuffed Virginia's demands to abandon the area and suggested that Washington should present his requests to the governor of Canada in Québec. Washington returned instead to Williamsburg and reported to Dinwiddie that the French would not budge unless forced. The governor ordered that a fort be erected at the forks of the Ohio. At Washington's urging, Dinwiddie sent Nathaniel Gist as an envoy to the Cherokee and Catawba, asking for assistance against any possible attack by the French. Ostenaco, advisor to Old Hop, agreed to send men if Virginia would develop a bigger trade relationship with the Cherokee and if the colony would build a fort in the Overhill area to help protect the women and children while the warriors were away. South Carolina, which had seldom received help in the past from Virginia, refused to send many of its men since they were tied up garrisoning Fort Prince George.

In April 1754 the French occupied the unfinished British fort at the confluence of the Allegheny and Monongahela rivers, renaming it Fort Duquesne. By this time the French were allied with the Chippewa and the Ottawa and were negotiating with Old Hop to build a fort in the Overhill area. Dinwiddie invited the Iroquois, the Ohio tribes, and the southern tribes to a conference. Meanwhile he dispatched Washington on a military mission to attack Fort Duquesne. Washington's men surprised a small party of French soldiers outside their fort, killing their commander and taking some prisoners. A larger French army counter-attacked and the British were forced to retreat, hastily building Fort Necessity. The fort was poorly situated, however, and within a few weeks Washington was forced to surrender. The French and Indian War (The Seven Years War) had begun on American soil.

Chapter Three

1754–1761

The Seven Years War and the Cherokee War

The Seven Years War was the final act in the struggle between Britain and France for the control of North America, and the Cherokee War was among its final scenes. (See Map 4, page 47.) The Treaty of Dover of 1730 had solemnized an alliance between the British and the Cherokee, but this conflict strained it and broke it. In the end the British won control of eastern North America, and France never again posed a serious threat on the continent. The Cherokee, although divided among themselves, were dragged into an unnecessary war against the British as the Seven Years War was ending. After humiliating the British the first year of the war, the Cherokee were in turn subjected to near-genocidal destruction the next. In the end the British gained little if anything by the fighting while the Cherokee suffered casualties of war, the destruction of numerous villages, and the disruption of their economy.

1754

The Cherokee Consent to More British Forts

While George Washington and his men were struggling to hold on to Fort Necessity, delegates from the northern and mid-Atlantic col-

Map 4

onies were conferring with Indian delegates at Albany. Benjamin Franklin proposed a plan for colonial unity at the Albany Congress, but it was watered down later by the Board of Trade. Joint military leadership and common Indian policies were also adopted, despite South Carolina's objection to Dinwiddie's interference with Cherokee affairs. The central government intended to be responsible for regulating the Indian trade, and would purchase Indian lands, erect forts, and pay for them. In fact there was continued disagreement among the colonial governments over Indian relationships and increasing conflict between the colonial governments and the Board of Trade over Indian policy and over fiscal responsibility for the building of forts and organization of militias.

The colonial governments did agree that it was desirable to build forts near and among the Cherokee. Governor James Glen of South Carolina visited the Cherokee in the summer of 1754 and negotiated to build the long-awaited Overhill fort. A few months later Virginia Lieutenant Governor Robert Dinwiddie also expressed his desire to build a fort among the Cherokee, citing the ineffectiveness of Fort Prince George. These competing proposals were a source of friction between

Dinwiddie and Glen over the next year. Meanwhile, North Carolina, whose backcountry population had increased dramatically, found it desirable to establish friendly (and hopefully commercially profitable) relations with the Cherokee. Governor Arthur Dobbs obtained the approval of Attakullakulla for the construction of a new fort located northeast of Fort Prince George. Fort Dobbs would protect North Carolina's backcountry settlers and the Cherokee from French-allied tribes.

The French had plans to build forts along the Wabash and elsewhere. They wanted to build a fort on the Cherokee (Tennessee) River but could not afford to at that time. The French hoped that if the Choctaw and the Cherokee were turned against the Chickasaw, the proposed new forts would be unnecessary. The Cherokee were only able to offer the French neutrality if the French could restrain the northern Indians from attacking them.

1755

The Cherokee Defeat the Creeks at Taliwa

When 1755 began the colonies were scarcely unified. Governors Glen and Dinwiddie continued their personal feud and squabbled over payments to build the proposed Overhill fort. North and South Carolina discussed boundary issues, but South Carolina clung to its demand for exclusive rights to the Cherokee trade and North Carolina sent only a token force to help defend Charleston's frontier. The newly appointed commander in chief of the colonial army, Major General Edward Braddock, arrived in America early in the year and embarked on an expedition to attack the Fort Duquesne. While General Monckton was scoring victories against the French around the Bay of Fundy, the French eluded the British naval blockade and delayed further attacks into Canada. Within months of his arrival, Braddock was mortally wounded at the Battle of the Wilderness near Duquesne, forcing his second in command, Colonel George Washington, to organize a retreat. Massachusetts' Governor Shirley was appointed to replace General Braddock.

While the British and French were engaged to the north, the Cherokee engaged the French and their allies in the Wabash-Illinois area. They also helped protect the Virginia frontier from the Shawnees. Despite British attempts to establish peace between the Creeks and the Cherokee, the two rivals renewed their hostilities. The War Chief Oconostota led a large contingent of warriors and confronted the Creeks at Taliwa. The battle was one of the bloodiest in the history of the southern Indians and would be remembered as one of the greatest victories in Cherokee history. The Creeks suffered great losses and were pushed out of northern Georgia. The Cherokee gained a large tract of land that would compensate for lands in South Carolina that were becoming increasingly depleted of game and encroached upon by whites. The battle would be remembered also for the heroics of a young woman named Nan-ye-hi (Nancy Ward), the niece of Attakullakulla. Nan-ye-hi accompanied her husband, Kingfisher, to the battle as an assistant (which was a Cherokee custom). While she was preparing bullets for him, Kingfisher was shot and killed. Nan-ye-hi picked up his weapon and began firing at the Creeks. Legend has it that the Cherokee were on the verge of losing when her heroics spurred the sagging warriors on to victory. At any rate, Nan-ye-hi was later honored by her people with the title *Ghigau*, or "Beloved Woman." The *Ghigau* was awarded enormous political powers in the Cherokee government, including the right to veto executions of military prisoners. Her moderating influence would be important in the years to come.

After the Cherokee victory, which was probably in part owed to restraints placed on the Creeks by South Carolina, a delegation was invited to Charleston. Old Hop refused to travel to Charleston, citing infirmities, but declared his willingness to cede to South Carolina lands that were no longer inhabited by Cherokees. Governor Glen accepted the compromise and met with the Cherokee delegation half way at the town of Saluda. Old Hop attended but chose the more eloquent Attakullakulla to be his spokesman. A treaty was finalized by which the Cherokee ceded a large tract of land from Cane Creek northeastward to the North Carolina border. South Carolina promised to build a fort in the Overhill area. The cession became official on November 24, 1755. (See Map 3 #2, page 26.) The exact intention of this treaty was quickly disputed. Was it a land cession, or did the Cherokee merely pledge loyalty to the King of England? Whatever the intention, the result was a land cession and a legacy of misunderstanding. This accomplishment was one of the last major acts of James Glen as governor. The South Carolina legislature had been crippled by a constitutional conflict between the upper and lower houses, which had left the government deadlocked for years. Governor Glen was seen by the Crown as being unable to solve the domestic problem and unwilling to cooperate with the other governors of the southern colonies. William Henry Lyttleton was appointed to replace him in 1756. Although the King instructed the new governor to maintain friendly relations with the Cherokee, his task would not be easy.

1756

South Carolina and Virginia Build Forts Near Chota

France still Courts the Overhills

In January 1756 the English signed a pact with Prussia, setting the stage for war in Europe. A few months later, after France formally allied with Austria, England officially declared war on its traditional foe. The French had already anticipated the onset of war by sending Louis Joseph, Marquis de Montcalm, to command their troops in Canada. Montcalm proved himself promptly and disgraced Shirley by capturing both Fort Oswego and Fort George. English influence in the Ohio area was further eroded by France's successful negotiations with the Shawnee. Not only did they promise to help build a fort at the mouth of the Wabash, the Shawnee also helped influence other Indians, including the Cherokees, to favor the French. Governor Louis de Kelérec in New Orleans hoped to influence the Cherokee by bestowing gifts and perhaps by inviting a delegation to visit Paris. The extent of French influence among the Cherokee was demonstrated in the autumn when a secret meeting was held with some of the Overhill leaders at Fort Toulouse. The French built Fort de l'Ascencion at the mouth of the Tennessee River and promised to build a fort in the Overhill area, utilizing the river as a trade route. In return they expected the Cherokee to drive the English out of their territory. France would not ratify the agreement until the Indians had proven their loyalty by attacking South Carolina.

Even before the loss of the forts on Lake Ontario, Shirley had not demonstrated competency as a commander and had developed a reputation as a meddler in Indian affairs. Lord Halifax secured his replacement as commander in chief with John Campbell, Earl of Loudoun. Furthermore, William Johnson was appointed Colonel of the Six Nations and Superintendent of Indians Affairs for the northern colonies. Edmund Atkin, a trader from South Carolina, was appointed Indian Superintendent for the southern colonies. The English Indian policy was to become more centralized under these new leaders. The colonies were encouraged to maintain peaceful relations with the Indians. Trade was to be enhanced while land purchases were to be forbidden except as approved by the commissioners.

The Cherokee remained interested in establishing relations with Virginia, and continued to supply small numbers of warriors to help fight the Shawnee. In March 1756 they even signed a treaty with Virginia and the Catawba. Despite these closer ties, violent incidents were reported involving Cherokee warriors and backcountry settlers in Virginia and North Carolina. Such events threatened to undermine Cherokee relations with the English colonies if they continued, but for the moment they were contained. In truth, the Cherokee were a divided people. Otacitie (Ostenaco) and Skiagunsta were loyal to Virginia and distrustful of South Carolina. The Emperor Old Hop and Attakullakulla professed loyalty to England, while tolerating increasing pro-French sentiments among their following.

The treaty with Williamsburg allowed Virginia to build a fort among the Overhill Towns in return for the services of 400 Cherokee warriors. Presumably the fort would protect the Cherokee women and children from attack while the warriors were away. Governor Dinwiddie had heard that South Carolina was planning to build a fort in the area, but he had not had direct communications with Charleston. Dinwiddie sent Major Andrew Lewis to the Overhill area, hopefully to find the South Carolina party and combine efforts. Lewis arrived before the South Carolinians did and at the insistence of the Cherokee he reluctantly agreed to begin building a fort on the north bank of the Little Tennessee River. The Cherokee asked the South Carolinians to build a second fort on the south bank later.

While the Virginians were building the fort the Cherokee began to have second thoughts about having so many white people living so close to them. Even Attakullakulla had misgivings about it. The Great Council at Chota recommended that work on the fort be halted. Meanwhile Lewis refused to garrison the new fort until the Cherokee delivered on their promise to supply troops. Ostenaco did lead some troops to Virginia, but much fewer than had been promised. Lewis heard of the ongoing conspiracy between the French and some of the Overhill Cherokee at Fort Toulouse and was furious. The Virginian fort was abandoned before the South Carolinians had even begun building theirs.

The South Carolina legislature approved funding for the new fort in the summer and in September a party led by Captain Raymond Demeré left Fort Prince George for the Overhill country. The expedition followed the Hiwassee River and then cut across to the Tellico River, where Attakullakulla greeted them warmly. Engineer William De Brahn chose the site for the fort on the south side of the Little Tennessee River, near the mouth of the Tellico. It was partly on a ridge and surrounded by a moat, which was then planted with locust trees. Four corner bastions were fitted with three small cannon each. Semintorium had surrounding palisades fifteen feet tall. By the end of December rumors of an imminent attack by the French nearly led to a mutiny among the troops. De Brahm fled before the fort had been completed, forcing Demeré to supervise the completion of the fort himself. Once completed, the fort was renamed Fort Loudoun, to honor the new commander in chief.

1757

The Diplomacy of Attakullakulla— The Cherokee Assert Their Rights

In 1757 the pompous Earl of Loudoun proved unpopular among those he was supposed to lead and did not achieve the military success expected of him either. Montcalm routed the English at Fort William Henry on Lake George. William Pitt became Secretary of State in June, declaring all-out war against the French. Pitt's policies were very popular in the colonies, but his meddling in strategic planning annoyed Loudoun. The raising of taxes in England to support Pitt's war effort became a source of friction between the mother country and the colonies—an issue that would worsen over the next twenty years and ultimately lead to the American Revolution.

In 1757 the French success in the north strengthened their alliance with the Shawnee. They completed the new fort on the mouth of the Wabash but did not make any significant inroads into Cherokee territory. Many of the Cherokee were undoubtedly influenced by the French successes, and would have been willing to switch allegiance to the French. The French hoped that the Cherokee would attack the Chickasaw, drive the English out of their fort, return prisoners, and provide escorts for French travelers in return for ammunition, increased trade, and strengthened diplomatic ties with New France. The Cherokee for their part did attack the Chickasaw the following month, but they found that the French could not deliver on their promises. At a conference at Chota in July the French tried to regain their momentum with the Cherokee, but by that time only the pro-Shawnee group in Tellico seemed to be interested. A few weeks later Captain Demeré was invited to attend the Ripe Green Corn Dance in Chota, where Emperor Old Hop and other chiefs officially declared their support for the English. Governor Kelérec was left to complain to the French foreign minister that he could not influence the Cherokee and other southern Indians without trade goods and gifts.

Relations with Virginia were improved by increased Cherokee commitment to the military effort to defend the frontier against the Shawnee and others. The Cherokee made peace with the Tuscarora, Catawba, Nottaways, and others who also agreed to fight with the Virginians. Keerarustikee and Second Yellowbird were among the leaders of the Cherokee efforts there. Old Hop continued to complain that Virginia never garrisoned the Overhill fort and failed to establish new trade activities, but Superintendent Atkin did arrange for the delivery of gifts in Virginia. Reports of violent acts committed by dissident Cherokee against backcountry settlers prompted Atkin to imprison ten innocent Cherokee, but for the moment Williamsburg enjoyed a relatively cooperative and friendly relationship with the Cherokee. By the end of the year societies were established in Virginia to provide Christian missionaries and English schools among the Cherokee.

Relations between South Carolina and the Cherokee were more strained. The Cherokee claimed that they were still waiting for gifts and ammunition promised by the 1755 treaty. They also believed that the trader John Elliot was dishonest, but he was one of the few British willing to work within Cherokee territory. Fort Loudoun was completed and Captain Demeré was replaced by his brother, Paul. Despite pro-French sentiment among the Overhill men and another trip by Attakullakulla to the French fort, John Stuart reported that Cherokee at Chota remained friendly. Governor Lyttleton did not trust the Cherokee and warned Demeré to consider them spies for the French. He petitioned the legislature in Charleston for funds to reinforce Fort Prince George, recognizing that the older fort would be vital for communications with the newer one. Frontier incidents occurred in South Carolina as well as in Virginia, and they also contributed to the sense of discomfort.

Cherokee diplomatic relations with the Iroquois improved in 1757, as they were both signatories to a treaty of friendship with the English. The Iroquois were among the tribes committed to fighting alongside the Virginians. The Cherokee maintained an awkward peace with the Creeks, whom they had defeated in 1755. The French had been trying to influence the Creeks to attack the English, but to no avail. Relations became strained with the Chickasaw, of course, after the Cherokee murdered some of their men as part of their deal with France. Superintendent Atkin, who had read captured letters from Kelérec, was aware of the French deal, and he considered Attakullakulla to be an agent of the French and friend of the Shawnee. It was Attakullakulla, though, who brokered a peace with the Chickasaw, thus avoiding war with them for the moment.

1758

Cherokee Warriors Assist Virginia at Fort Dusquesne

Relations Sour

The year 1758 witnessed a reversal in the struggle between France and England, but an increase in tensions between the English and the Cherokee. Early in the summer Loudoun was forced to abandon his attack against Louisbourg. Prime Minister William Pitt replaced Loudoun as commander in chief with General James Abercromby, but he failed in his attack against Montcalm's forces at Fort Ticonderoga in July. The tide turned later that month when British forces under the command of Major General Jeffrey Amherst captured Louisbourg, thus commanding the mouth of the St. Lawrence River. Within weeks Amherst had been appointed to replace Abercromby.

The French Fort

Frontenac fell to Colonel John Bradstreet in August and on November 25, 1758, the French blew up Fort Duquesne rather than surrender it to Brigadier General John Forbes and his assembly of British soldiers and Indian warriors. The biggest British setback of the last half of the year was the loss of badly needed reinforcements who were shipwrecked by a hurricane in September.

The French were relatively quiet on the southern front in 1758. Governor Kelérec complained again that he could not hope to maintain friendly relationships with the Indians without a generous supply of gifts. Indeed, a small group of Cherokee warriors led by Attakullakulla actually attacked Fort de l'Ascencion on the Ohio River during the winter of 1757–1758. This failed expedition was orchestrated by the Little Carpenter to demonstrate his loyalty to the English at this critical time, but it did not have the support of most of the Cherokee. During the summer, when the Cherokee were deserting the British forces under General Forbes, the French had an opportunity to gain influence with them. The Cherokee weren't gravitating toward the French so much as they were pulling away from the English.

Early in the year General Loudoun tried to capitalize on Virginia's relationship with the Cherokee by asking them to organize a large party of warriors to assist General Forbes, who planned to attack Fort Duquesne from his headquarters at Winchester. Loudoun ordered Superintendent Atkin to organize a party of warriors at Keowee and arranged for North Carolina to provision them during their passage to Winchester. Atkin was unable to attend to the matter personally because of failing health, but Colonel William Byrd was dispatched in his place to lead them to Virginia.

The Cherokee/Virginia alliance proved to be extremely fragile. The Cherokee were still deeply divided in their opinions of the English. There was lingering discontent over the failure of Virginia to garrison the new fort and to open up trade. Many warriors refused to fight because they had not received gifts, and at the same time the English did not want to give them anything until they had fought. Despite reassurances from Old Hop, relatively few of the Cherokee in the Overhill area were persuaded to join Byrd's party.

In the early summer Attakullakulla and other leaders met with Governor Lyttleton at Fort Prince George. Captain Demeré had informed the governor that Attakullakulla was completely dependent on the fort for supplies since he had had no time for hunting. Both Old Hop and Attakullakulla were apologetic, claiming that the Cherokee were indeed the aggressors in Virginia, blaming young warriors who were disrespectful of the tribal leadership. Even though the Little Carpenter had led the brief expedition to Fort De l'Ascencion, he did not hasten to help Virginia.

The Cherokee people were still upset about the incidents in Virginia, Charleston's tardiness in granting presents, ongoing trade abuses, and the failure of the British to reward the Cherokee for enemy scalps. In order for the warriors to join Forbes, they would have to travel through areas of Virginia where the settlers were hostile, and the men would have to be provided with arms. With so little support shown for the British, Attakullakulla could hardly expect to find much enthusiasm for the expedition to Virginia. He tried to save face with the English by claiming that the conjuror predicted defeat for the expedition, and thus many warriors decided to stay home, as was their right. According to ancient customs, the priest or conjuror would divine omens after the war council had decided upon an attack. If the omens predicted defeat, the warriors could choose not to fight without losing face. For their part, the British were reluctant to fully arm the Cherokee anyway for fear that they might stockpile the ammunition for use against them later.

Meanwhile the Cherokee warriors who had already joined the Forbes campaign were becoming disenchanted with the insulting manner of the commander and his seeming reluctance to attack. The warriors had shown good faith by traveling hundreds of miles from their homes just to be frustrated by his insensitivity to their expectations. By the end of the summer nearly all of the Cherokee abandoned the expedition, taking their arms home with them through the Virginia and North Carolina backcountry. A number of incidents occurred that inflamed hostilities between the colonists and the Cherokee. Apparently some white settlers stole horses from a party of warriors. The warriors took revenge (as is consistent with their code of ethics) by stealing back some horses and perhaps killing livestock. The settlers escalated the conflict by killing at least thirty Cherokee, including three Overhill chiefs.

By the end of the summer Virginia's Governor Fauquier asked his counterpart in South Carolina for help. Governor Lyttleton asked the Cherokee not to seek revenge in Virginia, but rather to accept gifts instead. The Lower and Middle Town leadership was apparently not fully convinced, and all-out war was still looming. Attakullakulla, against Old Hop's wishes, led a group of mostly Overhill Cherokee toward Williamsburg on a diplomatic initiative. He was induced while en route to join the attack on Fort Duquesne, but then deserted Forbes when he learned that the French were already abandoning the fort anyway. Forbes was enraged at the chief and so ordered his arrest for treason, sending him in chains, humiliated, to Williamsburg.

1759

The English Gain Québec

Governor Lyttleton Pushes the Cherokee Toward War

The next few months witnessed the climax of the French and Indian War and a sequence of events leading to the Cherokee War. As preparations for an assault on Québec were unfolding at the mouth of the St. Lawrence River, the British were already enjoying victories in New England. Sir William Johnson captured Fort Niagara in July and General Amherst led attacks forcing the French to abandon and destroy both Fort Ticonderoga and Fort St. Frederic. On September 13, 1759, General James Wolfe defeated Montcalm (although both men lost their lives) in the famous Battle of the Plains of Abraham, assuring the fall of Québec. British victory in Canada was inevitable.

Although Amherst had considered a southern attack as well, Governor Lyttleton explained that it would not be feasible for South Carolina to attack the French fort on the Mississippi via Fort Loudoun. He did suggest attacking the French at Fort Toulouse as a possibility. Although South Carolina and Georgia were afraid that the French would influence the Cherokee and Creeks to attack them, in truth Louisiana was inadequately supplied to support alliances with the southern Indians. The Chickasaw resumed their attacks upon the French fortifications along the Ohio and Wabash rivers. Furthermore, English victories in the north eroded French influence with the Ohio Indians, further weakening any possibility of new alliances. The Cherokee would turn to the French only out of necessity, as their relations with the English deteriorated.

At the beginning of 1759 the Cherokee were deeply divided. Old Hop and Standing Turkey tended to favor the French whereas Ostenaco and Willinawa favored the English. The leaders from Settico demanded revenge against the Virginians while another faction preferred to do battle against South Carolina. The Lower and Middle Towns were more or less friendly toward Charleston, but they were increasingly influenced by Mortar, the Creek leader who favored the French. Attakullakulla, despite his humiliating treatment in Virginia, was the most powerful chief and he wished to maintain peace with the English. Successful negotiations with South Carolina and Virginia would enhance his prestige among his own people at a time when some were considering his assassination. The Cherokee political system was approaching a state of crisis as the young warriors (born after Attakullakulla's trip to England and perhaps the small pox crisis of 1738) failed to heed the tempering influences of the elders. The deterioration of the traditional balance of power between generations would continue to destabilize the Cherokee government for years to come.

After being abused by Forbes' men, Attakullakulla explained to the governor that his departure had been delayed by the conjuror's warning and that he had abandoned Fort Duquesne only when it became obvious that the French were destroying it. He reiterated his desire for an expanded commercial relationship with Virginia and asked that the Overhill fort be manned. Attakullakulla left with a mild chastisement and a promise of gifts for Old Hop and himself.

Attakullakulla arrived in Charleston in the spring and met with

Governor Lyttleton, once again explaining his actions of the previous year. The native diplomat argued that since South Carolina enjoyed a trade monopoly with the Cherokee, better trading terms from the colony would lower the level of tension between the two peoples. Even though the chief agreed to fight the French in his own territory, Lyttleton refused to grant him presents or any trade concessions. Such gifts would have increased the domestic prestige of the one moderate Cherokee leader capable of preventing a war. It is possible that Lyttleton, who was losing a battle for power with the South Carolina legislature, actually wanted a war to rescue his failing reputation. Unfortunately, while the Little Carpenter was in Charleston, news arrived that Moytoy of Settico and his war party had murdered over twenty settlers in western North Carolina. The enraged governor demanded that Attakullakulla arrest the murderers and turn them over to South Carolina authorities.

Captain Demeré realized that Lyttleton had placed Attakullakulla in an impossible situation. Although the chief was able to convince Willinawa of Toqua to stop raiding settlers, it would be politically impossible for him to arrest a relative of The Great Warrior Oconostota, and many of the others were in hiding. Besides, in Cherokee eyes the warriors were guilty of no crime; they were fulfilling their clan obligations of avenging the murders of their clansmen the year before. Demeré tried to reassure the governor that Attakullakulla was fighting the French and to warn him that the towns of Settico and Tellico were becoming increasingly hostile. Lyttleton had already decided to ask the legislature to approve the raising of a militia for the purpose chastising the Cherokee, citing their increasing complicity with the French. Colonel Byrd reported rumors that the Cherokee were secretly conspiring with Ohio Indians to attack the English. Furthermore Lieutenant Richard Coytmore reported from Fort Prince George that the Creeks and Cherokee were planning to cut communications with Fort Loudoun. The South Carolina Council voted to forbid any further sales of ammunition to the Cherokee. Governor Henry Ellis of Georgia was concerned since his colony was particularly vulnerable to attack from an alliance of Creek and Cherokee warriors, but when the South Carolina Council learned that Wawhatchee had approached Ellis for help, the legislators angrily asserted Charleston's exclusive rights to negotiate with the Cherokee.

As Québec was falling into British hands, the South Carolina forts were becoming more and more imperiled. Demeré reported that the ammunition ban had angered the Cherokee at Fort Loudoun and that he was anxiously awaiting the arrival of Attakullakulla to calm them down. Attakullakulla suggested that the supply of ammunition be resumed and that the bounties for scalps be discontinued (since this was a source of abuse). His requests were ignored. Coytmore reported from Fort Prince George that although Keowee was neutral, all of the other Lower Towns had become hostile. Only the Middle Towns appeared to remain friendly. Further abuse by the traders provoked attacks from the Cherokee, forcing the surviving traders to seek refuge at the fort.

Meanwhile the legislature in Charleston was divided. The Council gave Lyttleton permission to declare war against the Cherokee (for violating the Treaty of Dover) when he saw fit, although the more conservative Assembly wanted to pursue a peaceful accommodation. Georgia was clearly against the war, and Virginia and North Carolina offered minimal help. The Council petitioned Superintendent Atkin to push the Creek into attacking the Overhill Towns. Lyttleton asked the Chickasaw and the Catawba for help, even though the Cherokee and the Catawba had signed a peace agreement as recently as four months earlier. The legislature did approve the raising of a militia under Governor Lyttleton, although five hundred men smaller than he had requested.

While Lyttleton readied his men for a march into Cherokee territory, a delegation of moderate Cherokees, mostly from the Lower Towns but including Oconostota and Ostenaco from the Overhill Towns, arrived in Charleston. The Indians, travelling under terms of safe passage, wished to re-establish peace with South Carolina and secure ammunition for the winter hunting season. Attakullakulla, who had continued to spy on the French on behalf of the British, sent a letter to the governor reminding him that Forts Loudoun and Prince George were built to protect the Cherokee against their enemies. The governor reminded the chiefs of the Cherokee's responsibility under the 1730 Treaty of Dover to extradite to South Carolina any Indian guilty of murdering a white man. The visiting Cherokees were then forced to march to Fort Prince George, virtually as prisoners. Although most of the Cherokee delegation was released at Fort Prince George, the chiefs signed a treaty under duress, agreeing that one chief would be held as a hostage at the fort for each of the accused murderers. They would be released only when exchanged for the fugitives.

Attakullakulla, the last remaining moderate leader with any influence at all (Old Hop had already turned away from the British), was able to persuade his fellow chiefs to turn over two suspected murderers in exchange for the release of Oconostota and a few others. South Carolina and its neighbors were already preparing for war, but many colonists still favored a peaceful solution. When the English refused to release the other twenty-two hostages, all hope for peace was lost.

As the end of the year approached, the morale was very bad among Lyttleton's soldiers. Most of the soldiers' tours of duty would be completed on January 1, 1760, and there was an outbreak of small pox in the vicinity of Keowee and Fort Prince George. Lyttleton left the fort for Charleston on New Year's Eve, 1759, taking the two extradited murderers with him and most of the militia. The twenty-two hostages were left behind, along with a large supply of gunpowder, in case the Cherokee actually did turn over the remaining fugitives. The Cherokee War, one of the last phases of the Seven Years War, had begun.

1760

The Hostage Crisis Leads to War

The British Humiliated

At the beginning of 1760 the French were losing the war in North America. They had lost Québec and were unable to reinforce the interior of Canada because of the British naval blockade. The Iroquois had abandoned their neutrality in favor of the British, and the other northern tribes were becoming increasingly dissatisfied with the paternalistic style of General Montcalm. After the surrender of Montreal on September 8, France had lost the North American phase of the war, although the southern colonies still feared that Louisiana would organize an alliance of southern tribes capable of destroying Georgia and South Carolina. France's inability to ship supplies to New Orleans, however, doomed any real chances of influencing the southern Indians. Unless they could supply the Cherokee with arms, the French would have little credibility with them or their neighbors. The British had no obvious strategic advantage to pursue a war with the Cherokee or any of the other southern tribes, prolonging the need for the King's troops in North America and needlessly endangering the colonists.

By holding innocent Cherokees as hostages, Governor Lyttleton had either blundered into a conflict with the Cherokee, or selfishly engineered one for personal glory. Old Hop, who was openly hostile to the British, ordered the other chiefs not to trade suspected "murderers" for hostages. Attakullakulla openly criticized the Emperor and proposed that the Cherokee attack the French in return for the release of the hostages. Conditions inside Fort Prince George became more desperate after one of the hostages escaped and another contracted small pox. Captain Demeré found it nearly impossible to get mail to Charleston as white men found outside of the fort were being killed. Within a month of being forced to sign Lyttleton's treaty, the Cherokee staged an attack on Fort Prince George. Although the attack was not immediately successful, Oconostota and his warriors began a siege. Communications with Fort Loudoun were cut off and intense border raids were launched against the Carolinas and Virginia. The South Carolina backcountry settlers were swept from their homes and forced to live in stockades such as the one at Ninety-six. Fort Prince George was even forced to seek help from Virginia.

The Cherokee continued to offer small numbers of prisoners in exchange for the hostages, but were frustrated by the inflexibility of the fort's commanders. On February 16, Oconostota lured Lieutenant Richard Coytmore outside the protection of the fort to negotiate once more. Upon the chief's signal, warriors who had been lying in ambush arose and killed the white commander. The soldiers inside immediately retaliated by murdering the twenty-two Indian hostages.

Governor Lyttleton was not prepared for this unexpected turn of events, or the state of panic it precipitated. The provincial regiment had been disbanded, so there was only a weak militia to protect Charleston. The town was suffering from a small pox epidemic (brought back by the soldiers from Fort Prince George) and there were constant rumors of slave uprisings. Lyttleton desperately pleaded to the Council to authorize new troops, and although the legislature obliged, he knew that outside help was needed. He asked Virginia's Governor Fauquier to help relieve Fort Loudoun and requested troops from General Amherst to defend Charleston and relieve Fort Prince George. Amherst was angered by Lyttleton's ineptitude but did agree to send troops. Ironically, Lyttleton was promoted to become governor of Jamaica and was gone by the time the troops arrived.

Meanwhile, Governor Ellis of Georgia was furious that Lyttleton had dealt so severely with the Cherokee. His blunder had placed Georgia at the mercy of the Indians: Only the continued friendliness of the Creek could save Savannah from destruction. Fortunately, the Creeks refused to aid the Cherokee, and the French were unable to provide them with munitions. The northern Indians had recently come to terms with the English and were not willing to help the Cherokee either. The Cherokee were politically isolated and were still divided internally, with the Overhill Towns less interested in war. They refrained from attacking the two English forts in anticipation of a possible diplomatic resolution to the conflict.

Just as the French were repelling the English at the Second Battle of the Plains of Abraham, Amherst was forced to send more than thirteen hundred regulars from the 1st and 77th Regiments of Foot under Colonel Archibald Montgomery to South Carolina. Lieutenant Colonel James Grant was named as Montgomery's second in command. The colonels were furious when they arrived in Charleston early in April to find that there had been very little preparation for them. The South Carolina Council conceded that they had been unable to obtain the wagons needed for the impending march. The Catawba agreed to join Montgomery in return for protection of their dependents and for the return of some of their land taken by settlers. Montgomery led about fifty Catawbas, three hundred rangers, and his own troops to Congarees to wait for supplies. By May 24 they had reached the stockade at Ninety-six.

As the invasion force loomed at their doorstep, the Cherokee continued to seek political means to settle the conflict. The Emperor Old Hop, who had become outspoken against the English, died in March. Captain Demeré smuggled a letter from Attakullakulla out of Fort Loudoun via a Negro slave named Abraham. Attakullakulla reported that the Overhill Towns did not support the aggressive actions of the Lower Towns and even wanted them to be punished. They continued to search in vain for allies, asking both the Ottawas and the Creeks for help. Even though some Creeks attacked British positions, most of them remained neutral and some of them even joined the Chickasaw in attacking the towns of Estatoe and Keowee as a diverting tactic. Montgomery had been waiting for Byrd to get ready in Virginia so that they could attack the Overhills simultaneously. Byrd was delayed so long that finally General Amherst insisted that Montgomery proceed alone.

On June 1 Montgomery attacked and destroyed five of the Lower Towns, killing over one hundred warriors and burning everything to the ground. Montgomery rested his men while offering the Cherokee a chance to negotiate. By this time it was too late. The leaders of the Lower Towns were in hiding or had taken refuge in other towns, and none had any interest in talking peace.

After ten days elapsed without word of negotiations, Montgomery's Scotsmen began the preparations for an attack against the Middle Towns. The trail to the northwest was so rugged that all wagons had to be abandoned. They began marching on June 23, but four days later Montgomery's men encountered stiff resistance near the town of Echoe. As Captain Morrison led an advance guard of rangers through a deep valley, Cherokee warriors with superior rifled-barreled guns fired upon them from above, killing the leader and several more. Several hours into the battle and after incurring the loss of one hundred men and many of their pack animals, the Scotsmen prevailed by marching toward the left. By the time they reached the village, however, it had been deserted. Unable to proceed to relieve Fort Loudoun, Montgomery ordered the abandonment of unnecessary equipment and headed back to Fort Prince George. After dropping off supplies and men too sick to travel, Montgomery beat it back to Charleston. His commission was to chastise the Cherokee, he insisted, not to relieve Fort Loudoun. By August Montgomery was making plans to sail to New York while General Amherst praised the expedition as the "greatest stroke the Indians have ever felt." The South Carolinians saw his retreat as a humiliating defeat and realized that the forts and the colony were still in danger. Perhaps Amherst realized Montgomery's failure too when in September the colonel was ordered to sail to Halifax (considered a difficult assignment).

The garrison at Fort Loudoun had been isolated for weeks, but had survived on provisions brought in by Cherokee women, some of whom had married soldiers. Attakullakulla, who did not support a siege, actually moved his family inside the fort at one point to dispel rumors of an impending attack. Friendly relations were nearly impossible, however, after news arrived of the devastation of the Lower Towns. A closed siege was begun on June 3, and by August the starving soldiers threatened desertion if the officers did not agree to capitulate. On August 7 Captain Demeré surrendered the fort and its contents in return for safe passage to Fort Prince George. The soldiers set out for Fort Prince George under the protection of a Cherokee escort. The next day, however, a group of seven hundred dissident warriors ambushed the whites, killing twenty-five people: one man for each murdered Cherokee hostage plus three women. Captain Demeré was tortured by being scalped alive and being forced to dance until dead. The only officer to survive was Captain John Stuart, a former Scots merchant who had become a close friend of Attakullakulla. His life was spared because he was well-liked by the Cherokee, and they hoped that he could be forced to help them use the captured cannon against Fort Prince George. The Little Carpenter, however, purchased Stuart and two other men who were married to Cherokee women from Oconostota (by custom the War Chief was entitled to any captives from battle). Attakullakulla escorted Stuart to Byrd's camp in southwestern Virginia, hoping to resume diplomatic discussions with Williamsburg. The other two hundred survivors of Fort Loudoun were imprisoned in the Overhill Towns.

The lull in fighting after Montgomery's retreat created an opportunity for diplomacy. The Middle Towns were in favor of peace but were afraid to negotiate. Attitudes were polarized and once again Attakullakulla was in danger of being assassinated by more radicalized warriors. Oconostota and Ostenaco led an assembly of over two thousand Cherokee at Nequasee in September, which gave them a mandate for seeking peace. The Cherokee had saved face through their performance at Echoe and by capturing Fort Loudoun. Amherst, on the other hand, was furious that for the first time in British history, his majesty's troops had yielded to the savages. George III (for whom Fort Prince George had been named) became King on October 26, 1760, and Amherst swore on his behalf that the Cherokee would be punished.

As winter approached, the Cherokee situation became increasingly desperate. The weather was bad and little ammunition was available for hunting. Montgomery had destroyed much of the harvest from the Lower and Middle Towns so the refugees were faced with hunger as well as homelessness. Although discussions with the French continued, no ammunition could be delivered past the British blockade and the Chickasaw obstruction of the Mississippi. The French were too weak to offer any substantial assistance to the Cherokee if warfare was renewed. Attakullakulla succeeded in opening discussions with Virginia after his rescue of Captain Stuart, but they would be of little use. Governor Fauquier wrote to General Amherst that maltreatment of the Indians was the root cause of the war, but agreed to continue work on the road leading toward the Overhill Towns and to prepare troops for a spring offensive. Governor Dobbs of North Carolina offered peace terms, but he was afraid that since the French had lost Canada, they would organize a general attack in the south. Dobbs petitioned Amherst to maintain troops in the area and urged him to crush the Cherokee, punish their leaders, and even *remove* them from the area!

Governor William Bull in Charleston likewise made some conciliatory gestures while recognizing that South Carolina and neighboring Georgia were still vulnerable to attack by the Cherokee and the Creeks. Fort Prince George remained isolated and would be difficult to defend if the Cherokee were to besiege it, but both sides showed restraint. There was discussion of an exchange of prisoners at Fort Prince George and the Cherokee even allowed safe passage to the fort for the delivery of provisions. Governor Bull was aware of ongoing discussions with the French, however, and continued efforts to enlist a new provincial regiment. The Warrior of Settico had gone to Fort Toulouse with Antoine Lantagnac, who posing as a trader actually served as an agent for the French. Rumors said that Ostenaco was negotiating at Fort L'Assomption (near modern-day Memphis) and that another French fort was being built near the Overhill Towns. The French were reportedly prodding the Choctaw to attack the Chickasaw, who had remained faithful to the English. Meanwhile Superintendent Atkin, who insisted on a policy of keeping the Creeks neutral, resigned in disgust when he learned that Governor Bull and Governor Ellis of Georgia had been secretly trying to buy Creek allegiance. With or without Creek help, the die had been cast. Amherst had appointed Colonel James Grant to replace Montgomery, and in January the new commander arrived in Charleston with fresh troops committed to punishing the Cherokee.

1761

The Cherokee Defeated

When Grant arrived in Charleston he found the South Carolina provincial troops under Lieutenant Colonel Henry Laurens unready for battle. He reported back to Amherst that not only had Bull lied about the readiness of the troops, Charleston was virtually helpless. Grant suggested that the expedition be delayed until spring when the emerging grass would provide food for the support animals. By the time nice weather arrived the army could be properly provisioned. Amherst agreed. He ordered Grant to have his troops at Fort Prince George in May and he told Byrd to have the Virginian troops at Chota at the same time.

Byrd was in a bit of a bind. Attakullakulla had negotiated a peace treaty with Virginia, and Governor Fauquier was giving it serious consideration. To sign the treaty would be a betrayal to South Carolina and yet to attack the Cherokee would be a breach of faith with the Little Carpenter. Fauquier decided that the treaty could not be accepted because it represented the wishes of the Overhill Towns and did not have the support of the Lower or Middle Towns. General Amherst wrote to Fauquier that no separate peace between Virginia and the Cherokee would be allowed; the Cherokee were to be chastised and made to beg for peace.

As spring arrived Attakullakulla focused his diplomatic efforts on South Carolina. He began delivering prisoners taken at Fort Loudoun to Lieutenant Lachlan McIntosh, the new commander at Fort Prince George. Ironically, as more prisoners were released, the easier it would be for Grant to attack. He had been concerned that all of the remaining prisoners would be executed as the battle began, but when more than a hundred people were returned, the risk of attacking became more acceptable. The attack was not delayed by negotiations, but rather by bad weather and disorganization.

Colonel Byrd's party was plagued by poor recruitment, both of Virginians and Indian allies. Governor Dobbs had promised five hundred troops from North Carolina, but he was unable to deliver them on time. Rainy weather and a lack of supplies further slowed them down.

Byrd and his men were able to make camp at Fort Chiswell by early summer, but they were not able to get to Chota in time to launch a battle simultaneously with Grant. Grant for his part also was delayed by poor weather, but on May 27 he arrived at Fort Prince George with 2,250 soldiers, two hundred eleven wagons, and fifty Negro slaves. These men were seasoned and ready for battle in mountainous terrain. Attakullakulla begged for time to consult with his people, but Grant insisted that there would be no negotiations until all of the prisoners were released. He announced his intentions of marching into Cherokee territory and warned the chief that all people found in the villages would be considered friendly but that those in the woods would be enemies.

When Grant's men left Fort Prince George on June 7 and headed toward the Middle Towns, they were followed by a pack train a mile long (with a herd of cattle and a month's worth of food and ammunition). A party of one thousand Cherokee ambushed Grant on June 10 at the pass near Echoe, nearly duplicating the battle fought in 1760. They failed to stop the British advance this time, however, and were not successful in driving off their supplies as they had before. Furthermore, the Cherokee had exhausted their supply of ammunition and were reduced to using bows and arrows. They were helpless as Grant's men destroyed all fifteen Middle Towns and burned all of the crops, killing any Cherokee unlucky enough to be caught.

Grant returned to Fort Prince George on July 9, with his men nearly exhausted, but victorious. They had forced four thousand inhabitants of the Middle Towns to seek refuge in the Overhill Towns and had left the Cherokee economy in shambles. Famine and disease were rampant. The Creeks remained officially neutral, but Catawba, Chickasaw, and Iroquois war parties began raiding the Overhill settlements. Meanwhile, the Virginians had completed a new road from Fort Chiswell to the Holston River. Colonel Byrd had succeeded in leading his party of Virginia provincials and allied Tuscaroras to the Long Island of the Holston, one hundred miles away from the Overhill Towns. Although Byrd was vulnerable because of the lack of supplies, his presence was perceived as yet another threat.

The Cherokee sued for peace in August. The Emperor Old Hop had died, and, with the support of Oconostota and Ostenaco, was replaced by his son Standing Turkey (Cumnacatogue). He sent Attakullakulla, Ostenaco, the Raven of Chota, Old Caesar of Hiwassee, and fifteen minor chiefs to negotiate a treaty with Colonel Grant at Fort Prince George. All white prisoners and captured livestock were to be returned. South Carolina wanted the boundary to be moved to within twenty-six miles of the Keowee River, forcing the Cherokee to cede half of the hunting grounds of the Lower Towns. Grant wanted twenty-two murderers to be turned over as former governor Lyttleton had originally demanded and furthermore wanted four Cherokee leaders to be executed in their hometowns. The Cherokee could not acquiesce to these demands and returned home without signing a treaty. Attakullakulla, however, went on to Charleston, with Grant's permission, for direct talks with Governor Bull. Fortunately for the Cherokee, there had been friction between the local soldiers and the British regulars to the point that Grant became so unpopular in Charleston, he was openly ridiculed on the streets. Bull had known Attakullakulla as a friend for years and was able to negotiate a milder treaty, which he felt would be more able to restore peace. Governor Bull signed the treaty on September 23, 1761, and the chief affixed his seal, declaring that the red men and the white were sons of the same God. The border was placed forty miles east of the Keowee—essentially status quo ante bellum. Lyttleton's demand for the twenty-two murderers was dropped, as was Grant's demand for the executions. Governor Bull allowed the treaty to be signed before Articles of Trade could be completely negotiated, assuming that they could be finished later.

Colonel Byrd had grown frustrated by his inability to obtain the supplies necessary to complete his assignments. Although he had built a new fort at the Long Island of the Holston, he had been unable to launch an attack against the Overhill Cherokee. He resigned his commission in September and was replaced by Colonel Adam Stephen. After North Carolina troops under Colonel Hugh Weddell arrived as reinforcements, Stephen met with a delegation of over four hundred Cherokee, including the new Emperor, who had come to Fort Robinson to sue for peace. A treaty, which was signed on November 19, was negotiated independently of South Carolina. Standing Turkey asked for an officer to be designated as a trade emissary to live among the Cherokee and thus increase the mutual trust and respect between the two peoples. Although Stephen was reluctant to risk an officer's life, the young Ensign Henry Timberlake volunteered. He returned with the Cherokees to their towns and lived with them for several months, developing strong personal friendships with Ostenaco and other chiefs. His work succeeded in increasing trade and friendship with the English and his influence would continue for years.

As the Seven Years War came to a conclusion, the victorious British found that keeping the peace was a challenge. Further Indian wars would require either increasing taxes on the British citizens or finding new sources of revenues in the colonies. A united British Indian policy would be the key to maintaining the peace. By the end of 1761 Thomas Boone had replaced Bull as governor of South Carolina. Although Boone was a member of the Colleton family and seen as an insider, his charge from the Board of Trade was to weaken the legislature's independence. Meanwhile, Superintendent Atkin had died and had been replaced by John Stuart. Although Stuart had strong ties to Attakullakulla, he was also a committed imperialist. He was determined that the governor of South Carolina would never again be able to exert the kind of influence on the Cherokee as Governor Lyttleton had.

During the Cherokee War, Governor Fauquier continued to allow settlement of western lands claimed by Virginia in violation of the Treaty of Easton. In December Lord Egremont, the Secretary of State, announced that royal approval would be required for all land purchases from Indians. King George III wrote Amherst that all settlement on Indian lands would be forbidden. Amherst wished to supervise Indian traders more carefully and thus restricted trade to the posts and forbade it the villages. Furthermore he limited the amount of gunpowder that could be bought at any one time and banned the sale of liquor outright. The policies of King George and General Amherst, although intended to minimize the risk of new wars, antagonized the Indians and gave them a common grievance against the British. The same policies were irritating to the colonists and would lead to new problems. As the Cherokee struggled to recover from the holocaust of 1761, they found themselves once again caught between two great white powers—the British and the Americans!

Chapter Four

1762–1768

Reconstruction and Reconciliation

Fair Trade and Defined Boundaries

After the war the Cherokee were in desperate shape, with many from the Lower and Middle Towns homeless. The destruction of crops and the lack of ammunition for hunting led to famine. Restrictive new trading regulations—designed to prevent war-provoking abuses by traders—hampered efforts to rebuild the Lower Towns. With Keowee in ruins, Chota became the political capital of the nation. The leadership was divided between the followers of Oconostota, who had been distrustful of the British even before the war, and those of Attakullakulla, who saw no other reasonable option but to seek reconciliation with them. Oconostota could not effectively deal with the British at this time and Attakullakulla was distrusted by many of the Cherokee, who blamed him in part for the war. Standing Turkey, a compromise candidate, became Emperor and chief negotiator with the British, but after a nearly disastrous diplomatic visit to London, his influence dwindled. Oconostota, Attakullakulla, and Ostenaco regained their undisputed leadership and were joined by a younger group of leaders such as Saluy (Young Warrior of Estatoe), Kittegunsta (Prince of Chota), Willinawa, Ecuy, Chinisto, The Raven, Tistoe, and others. They sought to rebuild the nation by establishing fair trade and defensible borders with the neighboring colonies. Once peaceful relations were re-established with the British, the fully armed Cherokee nation could then give full attention to its rival tribes.

French influence waned as the Seven Years War came to a conclusion, but the British continued to be troubled by hostile Indians who resented the new trade regulations and white encroachment into the Ohio valley. Facing Pontiac's Rebellion in the north, the British were quick to conclude the Treaty of Augusta with the southern tribes in the autumn of 1763. The Proclamation of 1763 likewise was designed to lessen tensions with the Indians by ending the settlement of lands beyond the Alleghenies.

The British government became increasingly frustrated by the increasing costs of maintaining a standing army in North America while the colonists themselves contributed little to their own defense. Furthermore, the colonies either were not able to prevent offenses against the Indians, or actually promoted them by permitting land grants in areas reserved for natives. British attempts to tax the colonists in order to pay for their own defense led to a series of protestations and the threat of outright rebellion. The growing mercantilist class, supported by teachings of the new liberal philosophers, rejected taxation without representation. Although the colonists were able to coordinate their responses to the Stamp Act and the Townsend Acts, they were unable to coordinate their Indian policies. Contradictory policies of adjacent colonies jeopardized diplomatic efforts of the British government.

Sir William Johnson was appointed Commissioner for the northern tribes and John Stuart was appointed Commissioner for the southern tribes. Stuart, now having responsibility for several tribes, appointed two deputies, Alexander Cameron and John McDonald, to serve among the Cherokee. Both Deputy Commissioners married into the tribe and became popular with the chiefs. Stuart was frustrated by his lack of real power to coordinate the Indian policies with the military needs of General Thomas Gage. He reported his concerns to the Board of Trade, and later the Secretary of State, but met with little success. The British found an apparent solution to their problems in 1768 when responsibility for Indian trade regulation was turned over to the colonies. They prepared the way by negotiating peace treaties with the northern tribes at Fort Stanwix and with the Cherokee at Hard Labour. They also brokered peace between the Cherokee and some of the northern tribes at the same time. Although warfare persisted among the various tribes, the groundwork was laid for an alliance between the pro-British Six Nations, Confederation of Canada, and Cherokee. The newly defined borders would be demarcated physically and thus help prevent encroachment and other acts of provocation. But would the colonists be satisfied with the new boundaries for long? Could the colonial governments enforce them or even have the will to do so? Was it really in the British self-interest to have a well-organized Indian alliance just over the mountains?

1762

Emperor Standing Turkey Meets King George III

French Influence Flounders

By the beginning of 1762 the Cherokee War was over but the Seven Years War still dragged on. England declared war on Spain in January after Spain had entered the war as an ally of France. Within a few weeks the British had captured Fort Martinique, St. Lucia, and Grenada. After a siege lasting a few months, Spanish Cuba surrendered to the British on August 12. On November 3 France and England signed a preliminary peace treaty at Fontainebleau, ending the war. On the same day Louis XV secretly ceded all French territory in North America west of the Mississippi and the Isle of Orleans in Louisiana to Spain, in compensation for its losses.

Despite the loss of Canada, Governor Kelérec continued to ask the foreign ministry for supplies for the southern Indians. He had signed a treaty with the Cherokee during their war with England and he needed them to help the Illinois Indians protect French navigation of the Mississippi. Kelérec summoned Antoine Lantagnac to bring several Cherokee chiefs and other native leaders to New Orleans to discuss plans for driving the British out of the area. Kelérec had sent word that supplies would be available, but despite repeated promises from France, the supplies hadn't come. Needless to say, Oconostota and the other chiefs were

The Three Cherokees, came over from the head of the River Savanna to London 1762. & their Interpreter that was Poisoned.

Figure 2 — Three Cherokees in London

upset that they would return to Chota empty-handed. Lantagnac reported to his governor that over fifty unhappy native leaders were planning to come to New Orleans in the fall to express their displeasure. French influence with the Cherokee and the other southern tribes was at a low point just as the war was winding down.

Meanwhile, even though relations between the British and the Cherokee were improving, border incidents were still occurring and there were reports of violent acts committed by Cherokee against whites and vice versa. General Jeffrey Amherst still felt that Fort Loudoun should be maintained but he was disappointed that neither South Carolina nor Virginia had much interest in it. He was likewise upset when the colonies disbanded their militias, even though South Carolina promised to maintain communications with Fort Prince George through the protective services of the rangers.

Both Virginia and South Carolina had new treaties with the Cherokee that promoted the re-establishment of trade relations. The Lower Towns were rebuilt and trade meetings were held at Chota. When Ostenaco arrived at Williamsburg to confirm the new treaty, he was granted the privilege of visiting London to meet with King George III. Ostenaco (Judd's Friend), Pigeon (a former hostage at Fort Prince George), and Standing Turkey (Cunne Shote, Cumnacatogue) were escorted by Lieutenant Henry Timberlake aboard the *Epreuve*. The ship left Hampton Roads on May 15, with high hopes that the visit would not only strengthen the influence of these three moderate leaders, but also enhance the reputation of Attakullakulla, since they would confirm all the things that he reported from his visit in 1730. (See Figure 2, page 74.)

Unfortunately this visit did not fare as well as the earlier one. William Shorey, the interpreter, died en route. Alexander Cuming and a couple of officers were enlisted as substitute interpreters, but communications were not as good as they should have been. Visits by Indians were not as novel as they were in 1730, and it took three weeks to get an audience with the King. In the mean time the Cherokee were not treated well and they made matters worse by getting drunk. Eventually the chiefs met with the King and were satisfied. They set sail for home on August 25, but Timberlake, now out of money, had to remain behind. The *Epreuve* landed at Charleston on October 28. Ostenaco met with Governor Thomas Boone and expressed both his satisfaction and his desire for permanent peace with England. The trip was a success as far as the Cherokee were concerned, but in England it would be seen as an expensive waste.

While the three Cherokee leaders were away, the British trade policies were causing trouble at home. New restrictions meant that the northern tribes would be deprived of goods and ammunition necessary for a successful hunting season. Furthermore, the Iroquois, Shawnee, and Delaware feared that the British would unite the southern tribes against them. Although Governor Francis Fauquier told the Iroquois that the Cherokee were now friends with England and they should be left alone, he did nothing else to keep peace between them. When the Cherokee released prisoners at Fort Prince George, in compliance with treaty obligations, General Amherst was convinced that the trade restrictions had forced the compliance. Consequences of their shortsighted policies would plague the British in North America over the next twenty years.

1763

Pontiac Rebels in the North, Southern Tribes Negotiate in Augusta

On February 10, 1763, the Treaty of Paris officially ended the Seven Years War. Britain retained Canada but returned the Caribbean islands Martinique and Guadeloupe, which were valuable exporters of sugar. France also retained St. Pierre and Miquelon islands south of Newfoundland. Britain traded captured Cuba back to the Spanish in return for East and West Florida, thus completing their conquest of the Atlantic seaboard from Newfoundland to New Orleans. In return for their support during the war, France ceded all of Louisiana to Spain.

The defeat of the French was a major blow to the Indian tribes living in the vicinity of the Great Lakes. These tribes had been able to maintain some degree of independence by playing the two European powers against each other. For the nations who had enjoyed busy trade relations with the French, the new British trade regulations caused economic chaos. The limitation of sales of ammunition endangered the natives' ability to hunt for food and skins. The disreputable traders were guilty of plying the Indians with alcohol so that they could cheat them out of their furs. At the same time costs were rising and the quality of supplies was dropping, General Amherst decided to limit gift giving. He did not understand the cultural significance of this custom, just the immediate costs. He felt that Britain had defeated the savages and owed them nothing, and they needed to learn how to take care of themselves. Unfortunately for the Indians, the war had disrupted their planting cycle as well as the hunting season and without assistance they could face starvation.

Many of the western tribes reluctantly abandoned their French allies toward the end of the war when it became apparent that the English would win. In return for their support, the British promised that after the war they would abandon all forts west of the Alleghenies. After their victory, the British saw no reason to keep that promise. Not only did they maintain the forts, they also allowed new settlements in defiance of the Treaty of Easton. Furthermore, the British pressured the Indians to return all captives, despite the fact that many had been successfully adopted (as was the native custom).

By the spring of 1763 the desperate conditions had sparked Pontiac's Rebellion. Pontiac, an Ottawa chief, responded to the Delaware prophet, Neolin, who urged the Indians to rise up against the Europeans and to reclaim their old lands and old ways. Pontiac inspired many of the tribes to arise and over the spring and summer the alliance captured all of the smaller British posts: Michilimackinac, St. Joseph, Miami, Ouiatenon, LeBoeuf, Sandusky, Presquile, and Venango. They also besieged the major forts (Detroit, Niagara, and Pitt).

The British response to Pontiac's Rebellion was hampered by disunity among the colonies and militias. Many of the regiments had been decommissioned and those that were still intact were concerned with the protection of their own colonies. Troops also were needed to man the newly acquired forts in Florida. At one point General Amherst felt that the situation was so desperate that he considered trying to start a small pox epidemic among the Indians to counter their slaughter of the British garrisons. Amherst and his colonels also considered enlisting the support of the southern tribes against the northern ones, but they did not trust them as allies. They preferred to keep them out of the war by improving diplomatic and trade relations.

Amherst implored Superintendent John Stuart to put an end to trade abuses in South Carolina and other southern colonies. Stuart, however, had no such authority since such matters were up to the individual colonies. In May, however, Charles Wyndham, second Earl of Egremont, Secretary of State for the southern colonies, ordered Stuart to organize a conference of the four southern colonial governors and representatives of the southern tribes. But it would not be so easy. Since the fall of Canada, the Iroquois (supposedly British allies) had renewed raids against their traditional enemies, the Cherokee. The Creeks were upset over what they thought were unfair trade practices in South Carolina that gave an advantage to the Cherokee. The Catawba were upset over the murder of some of their woman and falsely accused the Cherokee of the crime. The Choctaw were allied with the Creeks against the Chickasaw and the Cherokee were constantly squabbling with the Choctaw.

Although the French governor remained at New Orleans until his Spanish successor arrived, his influence with the Cherokee and other southern tribes was limited. Oconostota was resentful of being held prisoner at Fort Prince George and truly hated the English. He had not been impressed by Ostenaco's report of the London visit. Kelérec was able to provide him with a limited amount of ammunition and brandy, but most of the other Cherokee leaders had no affinity for the French. They felt that the French betrayed them by not supporting them during the war. It was obvious to Attakullakulla, Ostenaco, and Standing Turkey that the best way to rebuild was to seek peace with Britain.

Attakullakulla accepted Stuart's invitation to meet at Augusta, although the timing was poor (falling at the beginning of hunting season). Attakullakulla was anxious to meet with the governors to settle some trade issues and to seek help against the continuing Iroquois raids. While Oconostota was in New Orleans, Attakullakulla and Ostenaco showed their good faith by transferring a French prisoner (captured at Fort L'Assomption) to the custody of Thomas Sumter. Sumter, who had accompanied Ostenaco on his trip to England, was in Cherokee territory helping Ostenaco debrief the Cherokee people about the visit.

The Augusta conference took place as scheduled despite hostile acts committed by the Creeks against the Cherokee. Difference between the Cherokee and the Catawba had been patched up. In addition to Superintendent Stuart and the four governors (Georgia, Virginia, the Carolinas), representatives from the Cherokee, Chickasaw, Catawba, Choctaw, and Creeks were in attendance. On November 10, the Treaty of Perfect and Perpetual Peace and Friendship was signed. It proclaimed mutual forgiveness for past offenses. Each race would be responsible for the punishment of its own criminals (ending the offensive practice endorsed by the Treaty of Dover in 1730). The treaty also promoted improved trade practices and called for the demarcation of the boundaries between the tribes and the colonies. The boundary with South Carolina was proclaimed to be forty miles east of Fort Prince George. The Cherokee renounced claims to all lands east of the Holston River to Virginia.

By the end of the year the tide had turned in favor of the British as Pontiac's attacks against Fort Pitt and Fort Detroit had been rebuffed. General Amherst had been recalled and was to be replaced by General Thomas Gage. As part of a reshuffling of the British government, Will Hills, Earl of Hillsborough, replaced Shelburne as president of the Board of Trade. The new government saw that ending the Indian wars would be an economic imperative. On October 7, King George III, in the Proclamation of 1763, forbade the settlement of land west of the Allegheny Mountains. The policy was designed to prevent bloodshed between the Indians and the colonies by placing a buffer between the two. It would show the Indians that the British intended to honor its recent treaties. The barrier also was intended to shunt new population growth to the recently acquired colonies in Canada and Florida, where English-speaking settlers were desperately needed. The British were also concerned that if new colonies were established beyond the coastal regions, they might develop their own manufacturing in competition with the English factories.

Within a month of the proclamation, an incident in western Pennsylvania seemed to underscore its wisdom. In response to a series of raids along the frontier and the government's lack of action to prevent them, a group of settlers from Paxton and Donegal, Pennsylvania, attacked a group of innocent Indians. When the Pennsylvania assembly ordered their arrest, the "Paxton Boys" organized a march on Philadelphia—amounting to a backcountry mutiny. The crisis was defused through the efforts of Benjamin Franklin, and as a result the western settlers attained greater influence in the colonial government.

1764

The Cherokee Rebuff the Creeks and Support the British

Britain Imposes Taxes on the Colonies and Limits Western Expansion

In 1764 the British government was saddled with a large war debt, and it was still incurring expenses defending the American frontiers. It was imperative to prevent further wars with the Indians. At the beginning of the year the British were winning against Pontiac and his followers, but there was growing tension in the south that could erupt into another armed conflict. The British thought that it was better to separate the colonists from the Indians; minimizing contact would minimize misunderstandings. The Proclamation of 1763 and the trade laws enacted at the end of the Seven Years War served this purpose, as did the proposed reorganization of the western lands into three trade districts. The individual colonies suffered under the restrictive trade laws, however, as did the Indian nations. In some areas the Indians merely crossed the Mississippi River to trade with the less restrictive French. The needs and rights of the colonies conflicted with those of the Board of Trade and the British military.

Meanwhile the British Parliament passed a series of revenue acts (the Grenville Acts) designed to make the colonists pay for their own defense and administration. The American Revenue Act (the Sugar Act), passed in April, raised or established import duties on a number of items and forbade the importation of some foreign alcohol products. The act not only served to tax the colonists; it also served to protect British domestic industry. Another act passed the same day established a vice admiralty court in Halifax, Nova Scotia, with jurisdiction over all of the American colonies. The court was charged with the reorganization of the ineffective American customs system and enforcement of the new revenue acts.

The Currency Act, also passed in April 1764, gave British merchants the right to refuse colonial paper money as legal tender. The overproduction of paper currency depreciated its value, but the new act created deflationary pressure and threatened the stability of the colonial economies. The act further served as a common grievance for the colonies and stimulated talk about the legality of taxation without representation. The Grenville Acts inspired the organization of the Committees of Correspondence, which coordinated the reactions of the various colonies. The first such response was a boycott of imported luxury items by merchants in Boston. The seeds of the American Revolution had been planted.

The restrictive trade rules also set the colonies against the British. South Carolina was enjoying good economic growth as the demand for indigo and rice in Europe was high. The backcountry population was growing but the trade with the Cherokee was reduced practically to nothing. The Cherokee economy was still in shambles, as the harsh trade restrictions had hampered them in their attempt to rebuild after the war. The British government also discouraged South Carolina and Virginia from giving presents to the Cherokee and other Indians. Attakullakulla suggested that the trading center be moved from Keowee (in the ruined Lower Towns) to Chota, essentially the capital of the Cherokee, but his request was denied. Attakullakulla also proposed that he and Oconostota (who still harbored anti-English feelings) visit London to discuss trade and the growing tension with the Creeks. Secretary of State Halifax denied the request as too expensive and not likely to be effective. Governor William Bull of South Carolina believed in the sincerity of Cherokee friendship and petitioned the Board of Trade to repeal the Cherokee trade laws. He also saw that reopening the Cherokee trade would bring in revenue and also would help lower tensions between the Creeks and the Cherokee. He also feared the possibility of joint action by the Indians against Charleston. Not only was Governor Bull's request not granted in 1764, he was even asked to provide more funds to repair Fort Prince George!

Despite growing evidence of Cherokee friendliness, General Gage encouraged Superintendent Stuart to exploit the growing hostility between the Creeks and the Cherokee. He feared that the charismatic Creek Chief Mortar could inspire a Creek/Cherokee alliance against the British. Although the peace treaty had been signed in 1763, the murders of Henry Benfield and his family at the Long Canes settlement created a rift between the Creeks and the Cherokee, with each accusing the other of the crime. Apparently some disaffected Creeks living among the Cherokee at Tugaloo committed the murders, but claimed that they did so at the request of the Cherokee leadership. Stuart met with Saluy and the Great Warrior of Estatoe and demanded that the Cherokee prove their innocence. Stuart sent Alexander Cameron (former commander at Fort Prince George) to live in Chota to foment hostility against the Creeks.

Even Oconostota proclaimed the Cherokee to be innocent and expressed his willingness to fight against Britain's enemies. The population of Cherokee warriors still had not recovered from the effects of the war of 1760–1761 and the small pox epidemic of the same time. They could not afford an all-out war against the Creeks and wanted help from the British in case war did erupt. In May Ostenaco reported to Stuart that the Cherokee people valued their favored trade relationship with South Carolina and that they would not honor Mortar's request to remain neutral if the Creeks attacked the colonies. He also reported that Great Warrior of Estatoe had arrested the two guilty Creeks (although one later escaped). By the end of the year the guilty Indian had been executed in South Carolina. As a sign of good faith, Governor Thomas Boone reported that a white man guilty of a similar crime had been executed at the same time.

By the latter half of the year, General Gage seemed less concerned about Cherokee relations with the Creeks and more concerned about ongoing warfare with the tribes along the Ohio and Illinois rivers. Undoubtedly the French were still supplying these tribes with ammunition so it was important to disrupt the supply lines. Since the Cherokee had been continuously fighting the Indians of this territory, it seemed obvious to enlist them to help even further. With the Long Canes murder crisis resolved, and Mortar backing down, Governor Boone was able to request Cherokee help. Although Attakullakulla indicated that they would not be able to help in Illinois until the next spring, Willinawa did lead a successful raid in the vicinity of Fort L'Assomption. By the end of the year Cherokee were engaged against the Shawnee, Delaware, Wabash, and Miamis.

1765

Treaties with South Carolina, Virginia, and the Iroquois

Although Pontiac's Rebellion had been put down by 1765, the English continued to fight against French-allied Indians in the Ohio and Mississippi valleys. Increasing immigration of whites into the backcountry and beyond the Proclamation of 1763 line and other established boundaries with the Cherokee and other nations continued to arouse border conflicts. England's need for a large standing army in North America continued to be a financial burden for the nation. Parliament persisted in its desire to force the colonists to share the costs of their own protection by passing the Stamp Act (the first direct tax upon the colonial merchants). Parliament also passed the Quartering Act, requiring the colonies to provide housing for the army when requested.

The Stamp Act inspired organized opposition by the colonists, including a non-importation pact among New York merchants and a petition to King George III drafted by the Stamp Act Congress (which met in New York in October). By the time the Stamp Act took effect on November 1, all of the agents responsible for its enforcement had been harassed into resigning. In Virginia the fiery speech of Patrick Henry inspired the House of Burgesses to draft the Virginia Resolutions, declaring the colony's right to self-government.

During the year the military was frustrated by the inability of the colonies to provide financial support for the improvement of forts and to provide other supplies and personnel. The colonies were still unable to control the actions of the western settlers and disreputable Indian traders. They were only partially successful in negotiating with the various Indian tribes to prevent direct conflict with the English or causing trouble with other tribes friendly to the English. Since New York was the entry point for many soldiers who were sent west to defend the frontier, General Gage requested that the New York colonial assembly comply with the Quartering Act and provide shelter for his troops. This first use of the Quartering Act in December 1765 set the stage for increasing conflict between the colonies and the mother country in 1766.

In 1765 the French influence on the Cherokee continued to decline. The Cherokee intensified their attacks on the French-allied Illinois Indians, who in turn were led to believe that the British would reward the Cherokee with their lands. French diplomats did meet with Oconostota, Ostenaco, and Kinneteteh (Oconostota's brother) at Hiwasee in the summer, primarily using alcoholic refreshments to help stir up resentment against the British. Ongoing violations of the Treaty of Augusta boundaries and the murder of Standing Turkey's son (Young Fellow) and others in Virginia caused tension between the Cherokee and the British, but neither the French nor the Creek Chief Mortar were able to exploit the situation to their advantage.

Ostenaco, who had never been friendly with the French, led an expedition against the French and their allies during the winter, even though it meant missing out on hunting season. Not only did his warriors successfully interrupt French shipments of arms to the Shawnees and Delawares, they also captured two Frenchmen (and killed others). The incident was an embarrassment for General Gage since the English were not at war with the French and the Cherokee had not been authorized to attack them. On the other hand, he sent orders to Captain Gavin Cochrane at Fort Prince George to interrogate the prisoners carefully before they were released. Both the military and civil leaders saw to it that Ostenaco was rewarded for his accomplishments. A further complication for the British, however, was Oconostota's refusal to release the prisoners. Although Oconostota had reasons to be upset with the British over trade issues and cross-border violence, his refusal to return the prisoners was motivated not by a hatred for the British, but rather by a desire to trade them for Cherokee prisoners being held by the pro-French Illinois Indians. Oconostota's movement away from French influence and turn toward the British was demonstrated by his attendance at meetings at Fort Prince George with Ensign George Price in May and with Governor Bull in July. These were his first visits to the fort since his detention there at the beginning of the Cherokee War.

Cherokee relations with Virginia were strained by the murders of Young Fellow and his associates, probably by the Augusta Boys vigilante gang. The gang was acting in defiance of colonial and British policy and represented a threat not just to peaceful relations with the Indians, but to the stability of the colonial regime. Although Oconostota and Attakullakulla had been denied a visit to London, Henry Timberlake and Aaron Trueheart brought three Cherokee chiefs to London late in 1764. Standing Turkey may have been among them since he did not participate in other diplomatic events in 1765. The government had not approved the trip, so the King did not grant an audience or authorize reimbursement for its costs. Although the King paid for the safe return of the chiefs, Trueheart had died and Timberlake's career was in ruins.

Attakullakulla met with Governor Fauquier early in the winter to discuss the murders, relations with the Iroquois, and trade issues. Although Attakullakulla's long stay in Williamsburg led some to fear that he too had been murdered, he indeed returned safely and apparently satisfied with Virginia's efforts to punish the murderers and compensate the victims' families. Virginia passed a new trade law for dealing with the Cherokee, and Governor Fauquier petitioned Sir William Johnson (at Attakullakulla's request) to help mediate a peace treaty between the Cherokee and the Iroquois. The Iroquois had already ceded all claims to land south of the Ohio River down to the Cherokee (Tennessee) River, and Ostenaco had already agreed to stop fighting the northern Indians. Although Johnson was uncertain that peace between the two tribes would be in Britain's best interest, he nonetheless was successful in getting them to agree to a tentative peace by the end of the year.

South Carolina's diplomatic efforts with the Cherokee were centered on violations of the Augusta Treaty boundary. Terrapin, a warrior from the Lower Towns, was detained after crossing into South Carolina territory. At the same time white settlers were routinely crossing into Cherokee territory to harass hunting parties. They stole horses and set fires to hunting grounds, trying to frame the Cherokee for the crimes. At one point the westerners even destroyed a convoy of supplies intended for the Cherokee near Fort Prince George.

Ensign George Price and Alexander Cameron hosted talks at Fort Prince George in the spring in which Oconostota, Ostenaco, Attakullakulla, and Willinawa represented the Cherokee. The importance of marking off the border was discussed, but the issue was not resolved at that time. The chiefs discussed concerns over the detention of Terrapin, the murders in Virginia, and violent acts committed by Catawbas against Cherokees. Although Ostenaco was rewarded for his efforts against the French, Oconostota refused to release the French prisoners. Oconostota also demanded the execution of one white man for every Cherokee murdered, but was satisfied that Attakullakulla had secured Virginia's cooperation. He even appointed Ostenaco to go to the Middle and Valley Towns to ask them not to try to avenge the murders.

Later in the summer the chiefs met again at Fort Prince George, this time with Governor Bull. It was agreed that the border would not be marked off until Superintendent Stuart was available, but the Cherokee pleaded that the Twelve-Mile River not be suggested as the boundary since the area included lands considered to be vital hunting grounds. The governor was asked to keep white settlers out of the disputed area until the issue was resolved. There was some dissension among the Cherokee in that the chiefs from the Lower Towns did not think that the Overhill leadership had jurisdiction over their territory. Nonetheless an agreement was reached, and in October Ostenaco and the Prince of Chota (Kittegunsta) led a delegation that signed a treaty at Fort Prince George. A strip of land between Dewitt's Corner and the Long Canes Settlement was ceded to South Carolina, but the parties agreed to wait until the next year to mark off the boundary.

By the end of the year the Cherokee had reached agreements with Virginia, South Carolina, and the Iroquois. The British government renewed its commitment to the Proclamation of 1763. Not only did the Board of Trade authorize the use of military force to protect the Cherokee; the colonies were ordered to evacuate illegal settlements west of the

1763 line. But at year's end the western settlers continued to harass the Cherokee and interfere with their hunting parties. The Cherokee feared that war was looming once again.

1766

The Cherokee Help the British Blockade the Mississippi River

Border Incidents Strain Relations with South Carolina and Virginia

Pontiac's Rebellion officially ended in 1766, but the British continued to incur the large costs of maintaining a standing army and upgrading fortresses. Colonial objections to unfair taxation were debated in Parliament, and in March King George III repealed the Stamp Act. This victory for the colonists was offset in part by the revision of the Trade Act. Some of the changes appeared favorable to the colonists but the overall effect would be to raise the tax rate. On another front, New York's refusal to acquiesce to the Quartering Act led to violent skirmishes between British soldiers and colonial protesters. While the King may have been willing to amend the revenue acts, his response to the Quartering Act controversy was to recommend dissolution of New York's legislature.

The French continued to wield some influence with the western and northern Indians in 1766, but a British-led alliance of Chickasaw, Choctaw, and Cherokee warriors successfully blockaded the flow of arms up the Mississippi and Illinois rivers. French influence declined further with the arrival in New Orleans of Don Antonio Ulloa, the first Spanish governor of Louisiana. Although there was no immediate military threat from the Spanish, their traders very quickly began undercutting the prices of the British traders.

British trade policy continued to be unpopular with the Indians anyway, as the traders notoriously used any means they could to cheat them. Attempts to limit the power of the traders by restricting trade to the forts was not successful either, since the Indians resented having to travel long distances to make transactions. In an attempt to improve co-ordination of policies, the government required that all communication from the colonies go through the Secretary of State instead of the Board of Trade. Northern Indian Commissioner Sir William Johnson complained to Secretary Henry Seymour Conway that the lack of coordination of the trade policies of the several colonies, the inherent weakness of the Indian commissioner's position, and the increasing greed of the western settlers doomed British Indian policy to failure. Governor James Wright of Georgia added that the conflicting policies of the various colonies gave the Indians a common grievance against the British.

Although the King had stated unambiguously that it was his wish that peace be maintained with the Indians—especially the Cherokee—the inability of the colonies to enforce the Proclamation of 1763 threatened to provoke wars. Even the Auditor General added fuel to the fire when he suggested that land claims granted before 1763 should be honored. By the middle of the year Governor Fauquier of Virginia at last called for the removal of illegal settlements west of the Alleghenies, but he confided to the Board of Trade that he was not able evict them with military force.

Relations between Virginia and the Cherokee were somewhat strained in 1766. The Augusta murderers had never been brought to justice, and despite Fauquier's promises to Attakullakulla in 1765, the families of the victims had never received compensation. Fauquier's hands were tied by fear of reprisals from the western settlers, whom he saw as threatening the political stability of the entire colony. Virginia did send a trade representative to the Overhill area (a Mr. Ross), who was instructed to negotiate the right to build a factory on the Long Island of the Holston, near Fort Robinson. Oconostota (who still harbored ambitions to go to England with Attakullakulla) denied Virginia's request to build on land sacred to the Cherokee, but did grant the right to build a factory at Chiswell Mines, a little further east. The Cherokee asked all of their neighboring colonies to mark off their boundaries, but Virginia did not reply.

The boundary issue was even more acute with South Carolina. Relations between the Cherokee and Charleston were strained by the continual incursions of white settlers into important hunting grounds. Naturally, violent clashes ensued, including the murder of a settler named Boyd by White Owl and his followers. The diplomats maintained cool heads this time and war was avoided. A Cherokee delegation led by Ostenaco, Kittegunsta, Kenetake, Tistoe of Keowee, and Ecuy met with Alexander Cameron. The Cherokee group agreed to the cession of a small tract of land in exchange for peace, and some of the Lower Town inhabitants decided to move to the Seneca River, a little farther away from the settlers. Cameron assigned Commissioner Edweard Wilkinson to run the line from De Witt's Corner fifty miles southwest to the Savannah River.

The Cherokee hoped that North Carolina and Virginia would agree to the extension of the South Carolina line. Governor William Tryon complained that a large influx of non-English inhabitants into western North Carolina made Fort Dobbs obsolete; settlements extended seventy miles west of the old outpost. Commissioner Stuart persuaded Governor Tryon to negotiate with the Cherokee, citing Creek attempts to exploit Cherokee anger over the Augusta murders. The Cherokee wanted to extend the line with South Carolina into North Carolina, running it from Reedy River (South Carolina) to Chiswell Mines (Virginia). Although the offer represented a concession from the Cherokee, the proposed line would cut through parts of Mecklenburg and Rowan counties, already settled by whites. A compromise line was agreed to that kept the populated mountainous areas under North Carolina's jurisdiction. Because of illnesses and the onset of hunting season, the Cherokee requested that the boundary be marked off the following spring. A meeting at Fort Ninety-six was planned for April 10, 1767.

During 1766 the Cherokee continued to support the British military by participating in the alliance that blockaded the western rivers. Despite William Johnson's peace efforts the previous year, the northern Indians (Nottaways, Kickapoos, Shawnees, and allies) continued to attack the Cherokee and reportedly killed one of Attakullakulla's sons. While negotiating the boundary line at Fort Prince George, the Cherokee asked for British help in ending the war with the northern tribes. Commissioner Stuart doubted if an end of the hostilities was really in the British self-interest, but he conceded to South Carolina's Governor Bull that the Cherokee should be kept strong. The charismatic Creek leader, Mortar, had been trying to exploit differences between the British and the Cherokee in an attempt to form an Indian alliance strong enough to threaten both Georgia and South Carolina. By the end of the year nothing had been done about the northern Indians, but the British in Florida had induced the Chickasaw and the Choctaw to join forces against the Creeks.

1767

Trade Abuses and Border Violations Complicate Boundary Negotiations

In 1767 the British continued to be frustrated by the costs of defending the colonists, who were unable or unwilling to control their traders and western settlers. The behavior of the colonists was greatly increasing the risks of war with the Indians. The British thought that the Americans should shoulder some of the economic burden of their own defense. Chancellor of the Exchequer (and Acting Prime Minister) Charles Townsend denounced William Pitt's distinction between internal and external taxes and announced his plans to override colonial authority and levy new taxes. The Chancellor died and was replaced by Lord North before the Townsend Acts took effect and before the merchants in Boston re-instated the non-importation movement. His legacy was to increase the political tension between the colonies and the mother country.

The Indian trade situation was becoming even more chaotic. The Spanish traders in New Orleans continued to pay more for furs while undercutting British prices and even exerting some political pressure on the southern Indians. They may have supported the Creeks in their fight with West Florida (where the British were allied with the Chickasaw and the Choctaw) and they may have influenced the Cherokee to commit revenge murders in retaliation for the Augusta murders in Virginia. The rising influence of the Spanish was a wake-up call for the British to devise new trade regulations. Commissioner Johnson complained that the colonies failed to comply with his (and Stuart's) recommendations anyway. The merchants were clamoring for the colonies to set their own individual policies at the same time the Board of Trade was considering the abolition of the Indian Department and the withdrawal of the military from Indian territories. In the meantime Johnson lifted restrictions on traders north of the Ottawa River and Lake Huron, perhaps as a prelude to a peace conference with the northern Indians to be held that winter.

The Cherokee continued to have problems with traders in their midst. Governor Charles Montague of South Carolina realized that continuing warfare with the Cherokee could retard the colony's growth. He lamented the fact that traders were out of control and was anxious to work with the Cherokee for a solution. A meeting was held at Hard Labour on Cane Creek in May, as was planned the previous year. Commissioner Stuart met with a large Cherokee delegation including Oconostota, Ostenaco, Attakullakulla, Saluy, Kittegunsta, Tistoe of Keowee, Raven of Nikwasee, Warrior of Cowie, Scalalousky of Nikwasee, and three hundred more. The Cherokee protested that they were unable to spare enough men to run the boundary with North Carolina because of continuing attacks by the northern Indians. They formally requested (again) that the British help bring the Six Nations to the negotiating table. Saluy complained that long hunters from South Carolina continued to encroach into Cherokee hunting grounds, thus depriving the Cherokee of their only means of repaying debts. Stuart warned the traders that the boundaries had royal backing and would be strictly enforced. He also extracted from them price concessions. Stuart sent Commissioner Cameron and a delegation led by Ostenaco to North Carolina while he led Oconostota and a small group of Cherokees to Charleston to attend a large conference of Creeks and traders.

The Cherokee met Governor Tryon at Reedy Creek (not at Salisbury as requested, because of fear of attack from northern warriors). Ostenaco asked that the boundary be continued from the South Carolina line. He said that the Cherokee receive clothes that wear out; the whites get land that lasts forever. Negotiations went smoothly and on June 13 Ostenaco, Ecuy, Saluy, Tistoe, Wolf of Keowee, and Chinisto of Sugar Town signed a new treaty. Tryon announced that settlement beyond the new boundary would be strictly forbidden. The Cherokee honored the governor as "The Wolf of North Carolina."

Cherokee relations with Virginia were much more strained. Virginia had reneged on its promise to punish the perpetrators of the Augusta murders or compensate the families of the victims. Seven Virginian traders were murdered in the vicinity of Fort Prince George early in the year, apparently in retaliation. This incident would make it more difficult for Governor Fauquier to deal with the Cherokee, since he feared an uprising by his own constituents in the western settlements. When pressured by the British government to satisfy the Cherokee needs, Fauquier did agree to provide gifts for the victims, but by then the revenge murders had already occurred. Furthermore, Fauquier refused to run a boundary with the Cherokee without explicit instructions from the King. He went so far as to deny any knowledge of the Proclamation of 1763. Secretary of State Shelburne sent instructions to Fauquier for running the Cherokee boundary, but by the time they arrived, it was too late to proceed in 1767.

The Cherokee maintained peaceful relations with the other southern tribes in 1767, and even met with the Creeks in Charleston. The only major conflict that year was with the northern Indians. The official policy of the British government was to discourage the continuation of the conflict. Although the murder of the seven Virginian traders threatened to disqualify the Cherokee from attending a peace conference with the Six Nations, General Gage concluded that somebody else committed the murders and that the Cherokee should be welcomed to the meeting. Alexander Cameron sailed from Charleston to New York with Oconostota, Attakullakulla, Tistoe of Keowee, and the Raven of Tugaloo (formerly of Nikwasee). They rode to Johnson Hall to meet with Commissioner Johnson and the Six Nations, arriving on December 30. At first the Six Nations did not want to negotiate unless the Cherokee recognized them as their conquerors. The northern Indians were indeed not hurt by the war as much as the Cherokee, but the British would be careful not cede land to them that was also claimed by the Cherokee. Johnson did liberalize trading regulations in the north just prior to the meeting. It was anticipated that in 1768 peace would be concluded in the north and that agreement with Virginia would complete the Cherokee boundary in the south.

1768

Cherokees Sign Treaties at Fort Stanwix and Hard Labour

The Townsend Acts of 1767 triggered a more vigorous response from colonial protestors than had been seen previously. On February 11, 1768, the Massachusetts assembly approved a circular letter drafted by Samuel Adams that protested taxation without representation. The letter intended to communicate to the other colonies the steps that were being taken in Massachusetts and called for united actions by the colonists against British encroachment upon colonial rights. The English Secretary of State for the Colonies, Lord Hillsborough, ordered the governors of the various colonies to make sure that Adam's letter was not approved by their respective legislatures.

Nonetheless several other colonial assemblies approved the circular letter, and violence broke out in Boston. The British frigate *Romney* appeared in Boston harbor to protect the customs commissioners. A few weeks later, a customs official was held against his will in the cabin of the merchant sloop *Liberty* while wine was unloaded illegally. The subsequent seizure of the *Liberty* by the *Romney* set off rioting on shore. While the beleaguered customs officials in Boston dispatched requests for more troops, Governor Bernard finally ordered the assembly to rescind Adams' letter. The assembly denied the governor's order, so he had no choice but to dissolve the Massachusetts general court.

The immediate response of the merchants in Boston was to draft a non-importation pact that banned the importation of all items enumerated in the Townsend Acts and almost all other British goods. New York merchants were the first to join the Bostonians by signing the non-importation agreement. At a town hall meeting in Boston, there was a call to arms (supposedly against a French threat) and a call to Bernard to re-instate the general court (which of course he refused). As representatives from all over Massachusetts met at Faneuil Hall to discuss their grievances, two regiments of British troops and more warships arrived in Boston.

The events in New England overshadowed progress that was made in 1768 toward granting the colonies more power over the Indian trade. The influence of the French and the Spanish continued to decline. By the end of the year the Creole citizens of New Orleans had rebelled against Spanish rule and had forced Governor Antonio de Ulloa to flee for protection. With less foreign interference to worry about, Secretary of State Hillsborough announced early in the year that after peace treaties were concluded with the northern and southern Indians, England would relinquish responsibility for the regulation of the Indian trade to the various colonies. The Indian commissioners would be responsible only for Imperial policies. In response to colonial demands for more land, it was announced that the Proclamation of 1763 line would be moved westward by direct negotiations with the various tribes. The British troops would then be withdrawn from outposts within Indian territories, such as Fort Prince George.

The Cherokee were involved with both of the major British diplomatic efforts of 1768. They participated in the negotiations at Johnson Hall, by which the British were seeking a comprehensive settlement of issues with the northern tribes. Settlement of the war between the Cherokee and the northern tribes was needed in order to resolve the border negotiations with the southern colonies. Secretary Shelburne was anxious to conclude the negotiations quickly so that the British could relinquish control (and expenses) to the colonies. General Gage was anxious to satisfy the needs of the Cherokee so as to keep them from supporting the Creeks in Florida.

Negotiations took place at Johnson Hall near Fort Stanwix, in Mohawk territory. The conference was led by Commissioner Sir William Johnson and was attended by representatives of the Six Nations and the Seven Federated Tribes of Canada.

Attakullakulla, Oconostota, and the Raven of Tugaloo represented the Cherokee. Negotiations between the Cherokee and the Six Nations were made easier by the close personal relationship of Attakullakulla and Chief Taghtaghquisera of the Caughnawaga Mohawks. Attakullakulla had been adopted as his brother after being captured in the 1740s.

The Six Nations claimed land south of the Ohio River, which was considered to be important hunting grounds by the Cherokee. Johnson thought the Cherokee claim was more legitimate, and he was successful in purchasing from the Iroquois their claim to it. He also succeeded in purchasing a large tract of land in western New York. Although the Cherokee delegation visited the Shawnee, Delaware, Susquehanna, and Mingo leaders at Fort Pitt, they were not successful in bringing them into the general agreement. These tribes were no longer directly controlled by the Six Nations, and thought that their lands had been unfairly sold. Even Commissioner Johnson was unable to persuade them. The participating parties finally signed the Treaty of Fort Stanwix on November 5, 1768. The treaty apparently did not include any admission by the Cherokee that they had lost the war with the Iroquois. Neither did the treaty address the conflicting claims over the lands south of the Ohio and beyond the Kanawha Rivers.

In the southern district, negotiations with the Cherokee for completion of their eastern boundary with Virginia had been hampered by Lieutenant Governor Fauquier's unwillingness to act against the wishes of the western inhabitants. Fauquier died early in the year, however, and was succeeded by Colonel John Blair (president of the Council) as Acting Governor. Blair immediately asked Commissioner Stuart for directions on running the boundary. He was concerned that Virginia was being asked to cede lands that had already been purchased from the Six Nations. Stuart assured Blair, however, that the proposed line would give the Cherokee more than enough land and that Virginia could purchase large tracts west of the Kanawha River at a later date. Blair finally agreed to run the line northward from North Carolina border over to Chiswell Mines, and then follow the New and Kanahwa Rivers up to the Ohio.

During the summer, while negotiations were taking place in New York and South Carolina, the Wabash continued to raid the Overhill Towns and the Cherokee were being pressured to join either the Creeks or the Chickasaw/Choctaw alliance. Despite these pressures, General Gage directed Commissioner Stuart to inform the Cherokee leadership that Fort Prince George was about to be abandoned. Stuart asked Captain Louis Fuser of Fort Prince George (who was popular with the Cherokee) to give adequate notice and then also sent Alexander Cameron out to the Overhill Towns and Keowee to distribute presents to soften the blow. Stuart informed Attakullakulla, Oconostota, and Ostenaco about the plans, and they requested that the evacuation be delayed until they could return from the negotiations. Fuser did not receive Stuart's request in time and, with great distrust among the Cherokee, closed down the fort in their absence.

The Treaty of Hard Labour was signed on October 14 in the town on the Long Canes River. (See Map 5 #3, page 95.) The treaty con-

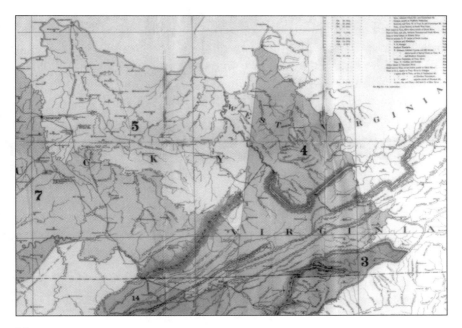

Map 5

firmed the Treaty of Augusta (November 10, 1763) and ratified the
negotiated boundaries between the Cherokee and the three southern
colonies. The Cherokee were officially excused for the murders of the
Virginian traders since Chilhowie had never been compensated for the
Augusta murders of 1765. Ironically, the new Governor-in-Chief of Virginia, Norborne Berkeley, Baron de Botetourt, had gifts available for the
murder victims, but decided to save them for later since the murders had
been avenged and the Cherokee were satisfied. The gifts would be distributed at the marking of the new boundary line, which would proceed
from Chiswell Mines on May 10, 1769. Oconostota, Ostenaco, Willinawa, Tistoe, Saluy, Ecuy, Warrior of Cowie, Wolf of Keowee, Raven
of Tugaloo, Chinisto, Mankiller of Chota, and more signed the treaty.

   The British also negotiated a new boundary with the Creeks that
shifted their boundary with South Carolina westward. It also established
the Ogeechee River as the border with Georgia. Attakullakulla, who had
returned from Fort Stanwix with one of the principal warriors of the Six
Nations, proposed a new round of negotiations to conclude a peace between the Creeks and the Chickasaw.

   At year's end the possibility of a comprehensive peace on all borders seemed possible for the Cherokee. They hoped for friendlier and fairer trade relations with South Carolina and a resumption of trade with Virginia. The end of the northern war and improved relations with the southern neighbors would allow them to recover more fully from the devastation of the war of 1760-1761. Before the ink was dry on the treaties of 1768, however, Virginia's Botetourt was already promising his followers that the Cherokee would have to give up more land.

Chapter Five

1769–1774

Colonies on the Brink of Rebellion Against Britain

Encroachment on the Frontiers Strains
Anglo/Cherokee Relations

During the 1760s the British were frustrated by the cost of defending colonies whose policies threatened to provoke more Indian wars. In 1768 the treaties of Fort Stanwix and Hard Labour secured the purchase of lands west of the Proclamation of 1763 line in order to set defined boundaries with the Six Nations and the Cherokee, and thus limit the possibility of a border dispute triggering a larger war. At the same time, the British government turned Indian trade regulatory authority over to the colonies. Although the colonies were never able to coordinate their Indian trade policies for their mutual good, deterioration of relations with Great Britain would unite them in a different common cause.

The Townsend Acts had been issued by Parliament to force the colonists to pay for some of the costs of their own defense. Opposition to the acts began with the non-importation movement and culminated in the Boston Massacre. The elevation to power of Lord North, who was more conciliatory than his predecessor, led to the repeal of almost all of the Townsend Acts and the subsequent collapse of the non-importation movement, but British over-reaction to the *Gaspée* incident ended a year of good feelings. Parliament proclaimed that those who attacked the customs ship would be deported to England for trial. This infringement on the right of colonials aroused widespread opposition and led to the restoration of the Committees of Correspondence.

During this time of heightened sensitivity, economies were decaying on both sides of the Atlantic. Then Parliament passed the New Tea Act, subjecting the colonies to new import duties and giving the economically weakened East India Tea Company a virtual monopoly on the tea trade. Angry merchants in Boston refused to pay import duties on tea and reacted by throwing cases of tea into the harbor before it could be unloaded. Parliament responded to the Boston Tea Party with a new set of laws designed to force the colonies to comply with the Tea Act and to force Massachusetts to pay compensation for the destroyed tea. These Coercive Acts were so offensive that the rebellious colonial leaders organized the First Continental Congress in 1774. By the end of the year the opposition to the King's policies led not only to civil disobedience, but also to acts of war.

The disintegration of British authority eventually affected relations with the native peoples, but in the early 1770s the biggest threat to peace was the colonists' insatiable greed for land. The ink was scarcely dry on the Treaty of Hard Labour before Virginia pressed claims to more land. Governor John Murray, Earl of Dunmore, who undoubtedly would gain financially from the sale of western lands, asserted that all of Kentucky was purchased at Fort Stanwix and that he was prepared to make Virginia land grants good. The Cherokee, impoverished and indebted, also were pressured by traders to sell tracts of land to private investors. Although the British government forbade such private land sales, Oconostota proclaimed that the Cherokee were free to do whatever they wished with their own land. The Cherokee also dealt with encroaching settlers by either selling or leasing them the lands they had cleared.

Conflicting claims to land were the root of most serious disputes between whites and Indians and among the tribes. A war between the Creeks and the Cherokee nearly erupted after the Cherokee sold land also claimed by the Creeks. Similarly, the Cherokee and the Six Nations sold land in Kentucky (coveted by Dunmore), but the Shawnee and their allies had the best claim to them. The Shawnee attempted to form a large alliance of tribes to counter British claims. They were never able, however, to pull the Cherokee away from their alliance with the Six Nations, or turn them against the British.

The Shawnee and their allies stepped up attacks along the western frontier, threatening any attempt at new settlement. Virginia's victory in Dunmore's War in 1774 destroyed Shawnee opposition in Kentucky, leaving the Cherokee isolated from their allies to the north. British fear that the Cherokee would join the Shawnee (or perhaps form a southern alliance with the increasingly more hostile Creeks), prompted them to provide less and less ammunition for Chota. The deterioration of colonial authority further limited the availability of arms for the Cherokee, as the American patriots feared that the British would arouse the Indians to attack them. The rebellious colonials therefore seized for their own use goods intended for the Cherokee.

Just as the British authority over the colonies was being questioned, the regime of Skiagunsta Oconostota and Uku Attakullakulla was also beginning to crumble. These two aging leaders, the War Chief of Chota and the Peace Chief of Chota, respectively, had dominated Cherokee foreign policy for a quarter of a century. The younger warriors, who still needed large tracts of land for hunting, resented all sales of land to the British. Technically Cherokee tradition required unanimous consent of all present for ratification of treaties. Increasingly young opposition leaders would no longer keep quiet or leave the proceedings to allow unanimity. Rather they were beginning openly to question the authority of the elders and defy them by forming their own war parties. Much as the colonial governors could not control the actions of the western settlers, Oconostota and Attakullakulla could not prevent groups of young warriors from joining the Shawnee in Kentucky.

1769

Virginia Needs More Cherokee Lands

During 1769 several more colonies joined the non-importation movement to protest the Townsend Acts. After George Washington introduced a non-importation proposal and a protestation against taxation without representation, Governor Norborne Berkeley, Baron de Botetourt, responded by temporarily dissolving the House of Burgesses. The Virginian representatives met unofficially the next day and approved the proposals anyway. The Board of Trade informed the colonies that the government was considering a repeal or revision of the Townsend Acts, but the colonial assemblies continued to sign non-importation and boycott pacts.

After the control of Indian trade regulation had been turned over to the colonies, Commissioner Stuart became more and more frustrated with his lack of authority. He requested and was granted the right to be appointed to the colonial councils in order to help draft Indian legislation. Georgia's legislature acted responsibly when it acceded to Governor Wright's request for a law condemning encroachment on Indian lands. The situation was much more complicated to the north, where Virginia and Pennsylvania residents interpreted the Treaty of Fort Stanwix as authorizing the purchase of lands north of the Ohio River and west of the Kanawha River. In April settlers hoping to apply for western land grants swamped the land office in Pittsburgh. The newly organized Vandalia Company petitioned King George III for the right to purchase over two million acres of western lands, but he rejected any settlement of lands beyond the Kanawha River at that time. Despite royal policies, Daniel Boone's exploration beyond Cumberland Gap into Kentucky helped spur more interest in the settlement of that territory.

Secretary of State Hillsborough was angry that Commissioner Johnson did not follow his orders for the negotiations at Fort Stanwix. The boundary dispute between the Cherokee and the Six Nations had not been resolved so that any settlement of the disputed lands would surely arouse hostilities. Even as Johnson allowed the sale of lands beyond the Kanawha, Hillsborough reminded him that the treaties of Fort Stanwix and Hard Labour had not been officially accepted and ratified by the British government. Johnson warned Hillsborough that not all of the northern tribes agreed to a peace with the Cherokee and that further inter-tribal warfare could be expected.

Although the Treaty of Hard Labour had supposedly resolved the Virginia/Cherokee border dispute, the Virginians requested further negotiations before the actual marking of the boundary. Doctor Thomas Walker argued to Stuart that the line he negotiated was a disservice to the nation. Stuart explained that the boundary was negotiated carefully over a five-year period, despite Governor Fauquier's intransigence. Governor Botetourt explained that Fauquier did the best he could, considering the circumstances. Oconostota, Attakullakulla, and Ostenaco were persuaded by the Virginians to reopen the negotiations, but swore that any new land cessions would come at a dear price. Furthermore, they refused to relinquish land between the Kanawha and Holston Rivers, as those lands were vitally important hunting grounds. The Cherokee wanted to keep a good distance between their villages and any settlements of Virginians, whom they considered to be bad neighbors. Indeed, during the negotiations the Virginians continued to encroach upon Cherokee territory, including the sacred Long Island of the Holston. There were reports of Cherokee aggressions committed against Virginian settlers, but many of the reports were probably fabrications.

King George III gave his approval for the new negotiations, on the condition thatno settlement be established beyond the Kanawha River and that Virginia pay for the costs of the negotiations and boundary marking. Commissioner Stuart delivered an ultimatum to Governor Botetourt that he accept the King's conditions or otherwise acquiesce to the boundary agreed to in the Treaty of Hard Labour. Botetourt had already dismissed the House of Burgesses, but he agreed to ask for the funds required for the re-negotiation of the boundary as soon as the assembly reconvened in November. The House of Burgesses did approve of the plan in December, but requested that even more land be purchased!

Inter-tribal relations remained complicated despite the détente between the Six Nations and the Cherokee. Some of the Caughnagawa chiefs accompanied Attakullakulla back from Fort Stanwix and served as goodwill ambassadors.

Attakullakulla hoped to negotiate the formation of a large alliance of northern and southern Indians to confront common enemies. The Cherokee refused to interfere with northern warriors passing through to attack the Catawbas, but they did join the Creeks in inviting the Catawba to come and live within their territories. Relations with the Creeks were strained when the Coweta Chief Etchoby quoted Saluy as claiming that Virginia wanted the Cherokee to help in a surprise offensive against the Creeks. While Saluy denied ever saying such a thing, Stuart also denied that Virginia had any such plans to attack the Creeks. After a party of Cowetas killed some Cherokees, Creek Chief Mortar denied responsibility and invited the Cherokee to seek revenge against the Cowetas. Apparently the Cherokee attacked the Chickasaw at the Chickasaw Old Fields (near modern Tupelo, Mississippi) without provocation in 1769, but their lack of ammunition led to a stunning defeat for the Cherokee. The Cherokee had hoped to compensate for lands lost to negotiations in the east by seizing lands in the west. This battle left the Cherokee less capable of evicting illegal white settlers and less likely to resist pressures for more land sales.

1770

The Treaty of Lochaber Revises the Boundary

Cherokees Cooperate with the Iroquois but Avoid an Alliance

Relations between the colonists and the mother country were sinking even lower in January 1770 when the Sons of Liberty provoked a skirmish with British soldiers at Golden Hill in New York. In an incident known as the Boston Massacre, soldiers fired point-blank into an angry mob, killing three people. Governor Thomas Hutchinson took the advice of Samuel Adams and withdrew the soldiers back to the islands in Boston Harbor, so as to lessen the risk of further confrontation. The elevation of Lord Frederick North to the office of Prime Minister, however, signaled the beginning of a period of less conflict. King George approved North's policy of repealing all of the Townsend Acts except for the tax on imported tea. A complete repeal would have appeared weak. The Quartering Act was allowed to lapse without renewal. Over the rest of the year several of the colonies revoked their non-importation pacts (except for tea). In December, the leader of the Sons of Liberty in New York were convicted and placed in jail.

Governor Wright of Georgia and Governor John Penn of Pennsylvania recognized that the colonies would have to coordinate their various trade regulations. Otherwise, they would never be able to enforce sanctions against offending tribes and traders, or prevent unfavorable price wars. A trade conference was held in New York during the summer including representatives from most of the colonies. Without unanimous attendance, the conference was unable to accomplish any significant coordination of policy. The colonies would pursue their own Indian policies independently for the moment. Interestingly, Governor Bull of South Carolina proposed the possibility of employing Cherokee women in the manufacture of silk. This was the first serious consideration ever given to include the Cherokee in the economy of the colony.

The British leadership wanted to maintain peaceful relations with all of the Indian nations in eastern North America, and thought that the delineation of boundaries would serve that purpose. General Gage thought that if the settlers would stay on their own side of the boundaries then the Indians could be left in peace. Secretary of State Hillsborough, however, saw that the lack of cooperation of the governors and the insatiable greed of the land speculators were making the negotiated boundaries ineffective. He also feared that while the colonial policies remained fragmented, the native tribes were becoming more organized. Several new alliances or confederations were taking shape that could lead to military danger for the British. The focus of the Indian policy in 1770 was to avoid provoking wars against Indian tribes, to finish the border negotiations with the Cherokee, and to prevent any new confederation of Indian tribes.

While Governor Botetourt waited for the King's approval of Virginia's aggressive border proposal, Commissioner Stuart argued that the Cherokee could never agree to its terms. The Cherokee would not cede the sacred Long Island of the Holston. Stuart also argued to Hillsborough that placing the borders so far west would put the settlers well out of the reach of their own government. Despite Botetourt's promise to restrain new settlement, westerners already were encroaching onto Cherokee territory and otherwise behaving provocatively. General Gage echoed Stuart's concerns and insisted that the northern Indians were not likely to agree to any revision of their borders either.

A congress was held at Congarees, South Carolina, in early April. Alexander Cameron and interpreter David McDonald met with representatives of the Overhill and Lower Towns: Oconostota, Kittegunsta, Ostenaco, Saluy, Ecuy, Tistoe, the Wolf, Chinisto, Corunna, and other male and female leaders. Oconostota reassured Cameron that the Cherokee would not join a confederation of northern and western tribes, but he insisted that something had to be done to prevent encroachment across borders. The problem of issuing land grants to private citizens also was discussed.

Stuart reported to General Gage that the congress at Congarees underscored the danger in Virginia's arrogance. He quoted Doctor Thomas Walker as telling Young Warrior of Estatoe that he had already bought land west of the line negotiated at Hard Labour, and that he was going to settle it one way or another. After word came that the King had approved Virginia's request for border negotiations, the governor immediately wanted to know which lands could be settled by virtue of the Treaty of Fort Stanwix. When warned by Hillsborough that Virginia should stop land grants that violated the Proclamation of 1763, Colonel William Nelson, president of the Council (who had replaced Botetourt), replied that all grants made before 1763 were legal. Even before the negotiations were completed, surveyor George Washington reported that nearly all of the nine thousand square miles requested had already been claimed by the Greenbrier and Loyal companies.

Border negotiations were further complicated by private efforts to purchase land from the Cherokee. The Cherokee usually were motivated by a need to settle private debts to traders, and had no other means to bargain. Jacob Hite and Richard Pearis visited the Lower Towns to buy land. They offered weapons and goods and even promised to take Young Warrior of Estatoe to London. Oconostota declared that he was in favor of the sale and that he wanted to open direct negotiations with Virginia, but Governor Botetourt told him that only Commissioner Stuart was allowed to negotiate with the Cherokee.

Once King George gave his approval, Hillsborough encouraged Stuart to complete the border talks quickly. Cherokee refusal to join any confederations proved their loyalty to Britain and thus they should be kept happy. There was also concern that Western Florida was vulnerable to attack by the Choctaw and Creeks (perhaps with Spanish support), so Stuart's attention was needed there. Stuart established a meeting at Lochaber, South Carolina, to be held in October. Virginia authorized almost three thousand pounds to cover the costs and sent John Donelson and Major Lacy to represent the colony. Alexander Cameron and James Simpson represented South Carolina. Three interpreters assisted Commissioner Stuart: John Watts, Joseph Vann, and David McDonald. Oconostota, Attakullakulla, Oukah Ulah, Kittegunsta, Tistoe, Terrapin, Ecuy, Chinisto, Otacitie of Hiwasee, the Rat of Keowee, and others represented the Cherokee. Attakullakulla complained that the white men continued to encroach upon Cherokee lands and didn't even obey their own laws. He reiterated concern that the Cherokee received goods that eventually wear out, while the whites received land that lasted forever. Oconostota warned that there were bad omens and that many of the young warriors wanted to go to war against Virginia. Even while the talks were going on the Virginians used underhanded methods to try to sabotage the efforts. They apparently lied, stole horses from the Cherokee, misrepresented Young Warrior of Estatoe, and tried bribery. A treaty was signed on October 18 and in the end the line was placed six miles east of Virginia's requested boundary: The Cherokee would not give up Long Island. (See Map 5 #4, page 95.)

Once again, the ink was scarcely dry on the treaty before there was further talk of revisions. Oconostota requested permission from Stuart to sell a tract of land between the Broad and Saluda rivers in South Carolina to Edward Wilkinson in order to pay back debts. Even Stuart was criticized when it became known that Alexander Cameron's son had received a private grant from the Cherokee. Governor Bull announced that he was pleased for the moment, but when the planters ran out of land he would want to purchase lands west of Keowee.

Inter-tribal relations were very complicated in 1770. The Shawnees and Delawares were attempting to transcend traditional rivalries to organize a confederation of tribes willing and able to fight white encroachment onto Indian lands. The Cherokee did not join the alliance and turned down peace overtures from the western tribes (although they did reconcile with the Wabash). They allowed the Shawnee free passage to fight the Choctaw, but Oconostota threatened to kill any Chilhowie Cherokee who joined them against the English.

Good feelings existed among the Six Nations, Confederation of Canada, and Cherokees during 1770, and they signed a mutual friendship agreement in July. The British feared such an alliance but did see the value of having them oppose common foes of the English. The Six Nations could help keep the Shawnee and Delaware at bay in the Ohio area while the Cherokee shielded South Carolina from the north. The Cherokee downplayed their relationship with the Six Nations when talking with the British, but within a few months of signing the treaty, the Six Nations were helping the Cherokee fight the Choctaw.

The Creeks, who had also been fighting the Choctaw, were more problematic for Georgia and Western Florida. There were concerns that the Creeks and Choctaw were reconciling and might represent a military threat to the British posts at Mobile and Pensacola. The Creeks had

been more or less ignored while Stuart was negotiating with the Cherokee. Coweta warriors had killed a couple of Georgians and escaped into
Cherokee territory. Governor Wright met with leaders of the Cowetas, Selichees, and Lower Creeks to demand satisfaction, per the terms
of the Treaty of Augusta. Governor Wright received no satisfaction and
found that it was impossible to punish the Creeks by levying trade sanctions, since they could simply trade elsewhere. Certainly Georgia could
see the need for a united colonial trade policy and for a strong alliance
with the Cherokee.

1771

*White Encroachment and Sales of Disputed Lands
Threaten to Trigger a New Creek/Cherokee War*

The year 1771 saw the end of the non-importation movement, and
no new taxes were levied against the colonists. King George III made it
clear that preserving the peace with the Indians would be a top priority—England could not afford a new war in North America. England's
hold on peace was tenuous, as there were numerous threats, internal and
external.

The British feared the formation of powerful Indian alliances, such
as the one the Shawnees were trying to engineer. Much of the land sold
by the Six Nations at Fort Stanwix, although claimed by the Cherokee,
was actually traditional hunting ground of the Shawnee. The Shawnee
saw that the real enemies were the whites, not the Indians. Fortunately
for the colonies, the Six Nations and the Cherokee maintained their
previous alliance and resisted overtures from the Shawnee. Northern
colonies were concerned about the potential strength of the Iroquois/
Cherokee alliance, and Georgia feared the military threat of a Creek/
Cherokee alliance.

Although the French tried to influence some of the western and
southern tribes against the English, they were not very successful. The
Spanish, on the other hand, may have had a little more success with the
southern tribes, particularly the Creeks. Although Spanish emissaries

visited the Upper Creeks and invited their chiefs to visit both New Orleans and Havana, their real opportunity came when the Creek/Cherokee dispute over land titles threatened to erupt into a war. Spain was the natural ally of the Creeks. The very presence of the Spanish in Louisiana limited Georgia's ability to pressure the Creeks by withholding trade.

The use of trade as a weapon wasn't limited just by the presence of Spanish competitors. The colonies continued to pursue their own independent Indian trade regulations without real coordination, despite plans to convene another pan-colonial trade conference by the year's end. Internal politics or special circumstances often inhibited the enactment of effective trade regulations. When the King approved the Treaty of Lochaber, Virginia's president of the Council Colonel William Nelson was given specific instructions to establish new trade laws to prevent provocative violations. Later, the newly appointed Governor-in-Chief John Murray, Earl of Dunmore, promised to enact the regulations that his predecessor had failed to produce.

The tidewater-piedmont rivalry came to a boiling point in North Carolina after the assembly passed the "Bloody Act" by which rioting was made an act of treason, punishable by death. The law was directed toward the Regulators, an organization of western settlers who were angry about abuses by county court officers appointed by the governor. They were also disturbed by under-representation in the legislature, inadequate infrastructure development, mandatory support for the Anglican Church, and wasteful spending by the governor. After peaceful attempts to address their grievances failed, the Regulators resorted to violence. The new law gave Governor William Tryon the legal support for launching a military initiative against them. On May 16 a militia twelve hundred strong led by Tryon himself confronted the rebels at Alamance Creek, near the western town of Hillsborough. The loyalist forces trounced the Regulators at the Battle of Alamance and executed several of the treasonous leaders the next day. Other captured Regulators and the entire western population were asked to swear an oath of allegiance to the government of North Carolina. Although the movement was crushed, no more than five percent of the Regulators reconciled with the colonial government. Many of them fled further westward, where they could live safely beyond the reaches of the law—in land belonging to the Cherokee, especially along the Holston River and its branches.

Encroachment by white settlers onto Indian lands remained the most serious threat to peaceful relations between the races, and was in fact the driving force behind the Shawnee attempt to form a confederation of diverse tribes. Encroachment was not limited to the backwaters of North Carolina, but was a problem across the boundaries with virtually every tribe. Nor was the phenomenon limited to lawless rebels fleeing colonial authority. On a hunting expedition sponsored by North Carolina judge Richard Henderson, Commissioner John Stuart personally escorted Daniel Boone through the Cumberland Gap into Kentucky. Nonetheless, the Cherokee leadership respected the Treaty of Lochaber and sent representatives to Virginia to mark off the new boundary.

Ironically, encroachment seems to have provoked more hostility between the tribes than against the whites. Tribes that had ceded land to the British attempted to compensate by asserting rights to lands claimed by other tribes. The Iroquois, for example, had ceded tracts of western lands that were claimed by the Choctaw. Fighting erupted between the Choctaw and the Six Nations, and the Cherokee were dragged into the conflict as allies of the Iroquois. Cherokee military involvement against the Choctaw was limited (supported mostly by younger warriors). A large-scale war with the Creeks, however, became a real threat in the fall.

A different type of encroachment inflamed the conflict with the Creeks: private land sales to traders and settlers. After the Cherokee War of 1760–1761 the nation incurred tremendous debts. The only currency the Cherokee had was peltry, but hunting was limited by white encroachment into the hunting grounds. Furthermore, only the British could provide the ammunition needed for hunting and self-defense. Unfair trading practices contributed to the imbalance as well. While the Middle Town Chief Towecke of Cowee could offer gold and silver in exchange for debt relief, the Overhill and Lower Towns could offer only land. Even though private land sales to colonists were prohibited by royal decree, Oconostota declared that the Cherokee were free to sell their lands as they pleased. The Upper Creek Chief Emistisiguo discovered, however, that the Cherokee were selling lands claimed by the Creeks. Georgia Governor Wright thought that the land claimed by the Creeks and Cherokee could be bought by the colony and sold at a profit to settlers. The profit would be used to establish a new fort on the Oconee and to provide for the defense of the settlers. Settlement of the crisis would require reconciliation between the two tribes; as winter drew near there were reports that Chief Mortar was en route to Chota.

As war loomed with the Creeks, the Cherokee leadership began to show serious strains. For years Oconostota and Attakullakulla had dominated the council house at Chota and effectively determined national policy. The younger warriors resented the concessions granted at Lochaber by the aging leaders and wanted the boundary line moved back to Chiswell Mines. Alexander Cameron met with the chiefs in March at a trader's house and reported that many of the younger warriors (especially Terrapin, Mankiller of Little Chota, Tistoe, and the Wolf of Keowee) were anxious to go to war, especially against the Choctaw or Chickasaw. Although some of the warriors assisted the Iroquois against the Choctaw, by and large their influence was still. For now the elders remained in control, but their grip on power was eroding.

1772

Virginia Presses for More Land

War with the Creeks Averted

In 1772 John Stuart complained to General Gage that the colonies were interested only in land grants, not in boundaries. Even as the Georgian and South Carolinian merchants struggled to resolve the land sales dispute between the Cherokee and the Creeks, lawless settlers invaded Cherokee lands along all frontiers. Governor Dunmore did his part to complicate matters by insisting that the Cherokee cede more land than had been approved by the Secretary of State. Further pressure to settle lands ceded at Fort Stanwix accelerated encroachment and made it more difficult to resist offers from the Shawnee to form a large alliance directed against the British.

Financial problems in England triggered a recession in the colonies, adding to the government's woes. Then the relative peace of 1771 was shattered on June 9. A British customs schooner, the *Gaspée*, ran aground while chasing another ship in Narragansett Bay. While it was disabled, boatloads of men from Providence attacked and destroyed the ship while placing the wounded captain and his men ashore. The British over-reaction to the incident rekindled the radical flames that had been suppressed the year before. The British insisted that the guilty parties be deported to England for trial. This new attack on the rights of colonials alarmed not only the radicals, but also the moderates. Once again Samuel Adams called forth a new Committee of Correspondence that quickly adopted proposals with the most aggressive wording. The Revolutionary movement had picked up unstoppable momentum.

Relations between the colonies and the mother country also were strained over the interpretation of the negotiations at Fort Stanwix and through private land sales. The British Attorney General added fuel to the flames when he decreed in April that Indian land sales could take place without royal patents. Within weeks petitions poured in for grants along the Ohio, Holston, and New rivers. The Earl of Eglintoune argued that the establishment of settlements on the Mississippi River itself would act as buffer to protect the colonies from attack by Spanish or French colonials and their Indian allies, and actually petitioned the King for such a grant. The dangers of such a plan were evidenced by several incidents in which Cherokees killed Englishmen along the Ohio and Mississippi rivers. Some attacks were carried out by such dissidents as Mankiller and his brother Kenneteta and were not sanctioned by the Cherokee leadership. Even though the worst offenders were punished by banishment, Lord Dartmouth, the new Secretary of State, commanded Commissioner Stuart and General Gage to get satisfaction for the murders. Yet another frontier with the British became an irritant with the Cherokee.

The actions of Governor Dunmore threatened to make the Virginia border more volatile than ever. John Donelson, who had represented Virginia at Lochaber, supervised the running of the border with the Cherokee, establishing the South Fork of the Holston as the boundary. (Later surveys would place some of that territory in North Carolina.) The controversy came when Dunmore insisted that the boundary be run over the mountains and include all land between the Kentucky and Ohio rivers. (See Map 5 #5, page 95.) He based his claim on the Treaty of Fort Stanwix. Secretary Hillsborough was deeply disturbed by this unilateral action of Virginia, foreseeing that it would lead only to more trouble.

Meanwhile Superintendent Stuart visited the Holston settlements and insisted that all settlers move north of the South Fork. A group of settlers along the Watauga River were reluctant to move and thus abandon the cabins and crops that they had worked so hard to build. Some of the settlers had been Regulators, and although they found themselves technically in North Carolina again instead of Virginia, they felt that it would be safer to stay where they were. The North Carolina government was unable to enforce its laws there, and the Cherokee seemed reasonably friendly. The Wataugans actually negotiated a ten-year lease with the Cherokee for the right to live on their land. Being within no legal jurisdiction, the group established the Watauga Association—heralded as the first self-governing body of white men in North America. Stories are told of good relations with the Cherokee, but episodes of violence did occur and were well-known to Stuart and to General Gage.

The Cherokee/Creek land sale controversy continued in Georgia and South Carolina. President Habersham of Georgia felt that the land in question would be valuable for the burgeoning silk industry, but that the sales should be coordinated through Stuart's office. Secretary Hillsborough felt that the Cherokee land sales were improper but thought that the Board of Trade would approve them if the Creeks did not dispute them. Stuart told the Creeks that he was unaware of the sales and that they were not officially sanctioned. He instructed Alexander Cameron to tell the traders that the King thought that the sales were in violation of the Proclamation of 1763. By that time a group of merchants from Augusta, led by David Taitt, had been sent as emissaries to the Upper and Lower Creeks to discuss the problem. The traders agreed to compensate the Creeks for land bought from the Cherokee and were successful in gaining their consent for the sale of lands between the forks of Savannah. The Creeks in reality were giving up lands that were nearly useless as hunting grounds. Besides, the Creeks had been driven out of the area in 1755 when the Cherokee won the Battle of Taliwa. Habersham discovered that the lands in question were being settled illegally by fugitive Regulators and others, and with Hillsborough's consent issued a proclamation calling for their eviction. By the end of the year, the new Secretary of State, Lord Dartmouth, told Stuart that the Creeks had sanctioned the land sales and that the tribal leaders should meet in Augusta to finish the deal.

The Cherokee continued to coordinate their inter-tribal policy with the Six Nations and resisted joining the Shawnee alliance. The Cherokee continued to fight against the Wabash, who were interfering with British navigation of the Ohio and disturbing outposts in the Illinois country. Captain John Thomas at Fort Bute negotiated with the Spanish governor in Louisiana to organize the Cherokee, Chickasaw, Shawnee, and Arkansas Indians to fight against the Osages and the Kickapoos. Stuart had not approved of the negotiations with the Spanish and responded by dismissing Thomas from his duties. The incidents were cited as reasons that the Kickapoos, Wabash, and others did not attend Superintendent Johnson's annual conference at Scioto.

Although the Cherokee had attacked the Chickasaw in the spring and had been on the verge of war with the Creeks, by the end of the year the Chickasaw were sending peace delegations to the Creeks and the Cherokees. The British suspected that the Shawnee were trying to reconcile the southern tribes to unite them against the northern tribes, or even against the colonies. Despite reassurances from Oconostota, Ostenaco, Willinawa, and Old Tassel. Gage and Johnson were concerned about the possibility of a new war.

1773

Troubles with Virginia and an Unsatisfactory Agreement in Georgia

During 1773 British diplomatic successes with the Indians were overshadowed by rising tensions with the colonial merchants. Even as the colonies were organizing new committees of correspondence to counter the British reaction to the *Gaspée* incident, the new Tea Act aroused even more ire. The colonial embargo of tea and the financial recession had led the East India Tea Company nearly to bankruptcy. The company's influential lobbyists procured the passage of the new Tea Act, maintaining the colonial import fees. Furthermore, the East India Tea Company was a granted a virtual monopoly in North America and was allowed to designate consignees as soul distributors. When the ship *Dartmouth* arrived in Boston harbor the merchants called for the resignation of the consignees, who happened to be relatives of Governor Thomas Hutchinson. When it was decided that the ship would be turned back to England without unloading its cargo, Hutchinson refused to allow the ship to leave until all import fees were collected. Samuel Adams spoke to a rally of eight thousand Bostonians about the governor's demands on December 16. That night men dressed as Mohawk Indians boarded the *Dartmouth* and dumped all of the casks of tea overboard—the Boston Tea Party. A few days later, after some embarrassing letters written by Hutchinson to a Member of Parliament were made public, the Massachusetts assembly petitioned the King to remove him as governor.

While relations between the colonials and the mother country were becoming more strained, General Gage and Secretary Dartmouth saw that the relations between the Indians and the British were likewise more strained. Settlement of western lands and persistent demands for more land cessions provided the various tribes with a common grievance against the white men. The Shawnee continued their efforts to reconcile warring tribes in an attempt to build a confederation, and they increased attacks along their part of the frontier.

In 1773 the Cherokee dealt with the British on two fronts: the South Carolina/Georgia/Creek border dispute, and the establishment of a stable border with the ever-expanding colony of Virginia. (See Map 3 #6, page 26.) The land sale debate in the south was seen as vitally important for the economic development of Georgia. It was clear that the private land sales were not to be respected, but rather an officially sanctioned cession from the two tribes was in order. Superintendent Stuart met at Augusta in June with representatives from the Cherokee (led by Ostenaco) and the Creeks (led by Mortar). The Creeks balked at some of the demands, but the Cherokee compensated by giving up more of their lands—with the new border nearly at the doorsteps of the Lower Towns. The traders were upset because they had closed the books on sales they thought were final, and now had no way of being sure about their accounts.

The apparent success of the conference was marred by the murder of two Cherokees, the sons of chiefs, who were assigned to help mark off the new boundaries. John and Hezekiah Collins were identified as the guilty parties. The official colonial response was to denounce the action, offer rewards for their capture, and to give gifts to the families of the victims. Hezekiah was captured but he escaped before he could be tried and sentenced. Although the chiefs in Keowee, Chinisto and Ecuy, promised Alexander Cameron that they would not seek blood revenge, Second Man of Chota murdered a white man in the Overhill region about the same time.

While these deadly incidents were handled in such a way as to defuse their explosiveness, similar incidents in Virginia were not. Governor Dunmore had forced the Cherokee to accept the Kentucky River as a natural border, thus nullifying the negotiations at Lochaber. Even while Superintendent Stuart was promising the Creeks and Cherokee that there would be limited settlement of the Ohio area, the Board of Trade petitioned the King for new land grants in the area. The claim to the land was asserted later in the year when Daniel Boone attempted to cross into Kentucky with a party of settlers. The murder of William Russell's son, allegedly by Cherokees, prompted Governor Dunmore to warn Stuart that the deaths would have to be avenged. Meanwhile General Frederick Haldimand demanded that Stuart press the Cherokee for compensation for the murders of Virginians in the Holston area the year before.

The settlement of the Kentucky and Ohio lands were particularly offensive to the Shawnee, Delaware, and Mingos, who perhaps had the best claim to them. All the while the Shawnees were pushing the Cherokee for a reconciliation, the Six Nations pressured them to resist. Oconostota conducted the negotiations with the Shawnee at Chota while Cold Weather met with leaders in the north. After the Kickapoos rejected Attakullakulla's offer of peaceful relations, the Little Carpenter led a war party against them. Negotiations also were held with the Wabash, and a conference was planned for the next year.

The Creek Chief Mortar returned home from Augusta disgusted with the British demands for more land, and was motivated to push for reconciliation with the Cherokee. He asked them to join the Creeks and the Chickasaw against the Choctaw (who were perhaps the most dependent on the British). The Cherokee countered with a suggestion that the Creeks join them in a meeting with the Shawnee and the Nottaways. Oconostota told Stuart that the Cherokee were interested in forming an alliance strong enough to force the western Indians to seek peace.

1774

Dunmore Defeats the Shawnee and Weakens the Cherokee Position

The Creeks Remain Volatile

The year 1774 witnessed an extreme deterioration in relations between the British and the colonials, further eroding the possibility of having any unified approach to Indian policy. The British Parliament, angered by the rebellion of Massachusetts, passed the Coercive Acts to force the colonials to compensate for the losses associated with the Boston Tea Party. The Boston Port Bill effectively shut down the port until restitution for unpaid duties had been made. The colonials' demand for Governor Hutchinson's removal was answered with his replacement by Commander in Chief General Thomas Gage, who marched into Boston accompanied by four regiments of troops. Subsequently the Massachusetts Regulatory Act altered the structure of Massachusetts' government so as to place more authority in the hands of the Crown. The Administration of Justice Act immunized the royal authorities from civil trials within the jurisdiction of the colonies. The Quartering Act was revived and strengthened, and in response to the increasing costs associated with the defense of the colonial frontier, the Québec Act extended the southern border of Canada to the Ohio River.

The colonial response to the Coercive Acts was the opposite of what was intended. Not only was the non-importation movement revived, the First Continental Congress met in Philadelphia on September 5. Proclaiming the right to life, liberty, and property, the Congress passed a series of resolutions, including the Suffolk Acts. The Suffolk Acts declared the Coercive Acts to be illegal and not to be obeyed. After General Gage seized the arsenal at Charlestown, Massachusetts, the Congress called for the formation of local militias. When Paul Revere warned that the British planned to station troops at Portsmouth, New Hampshire, a Massachusetts militia attacked and captured the arsenal at Fort William and Mary. This successful and bloodless act was the first military campaign of the Revolution by the American colonials.

With the colonies on the brink of rebellion, the British were in no position to defend against any concerted military effort by an alliance of Indian tribes, and were hardly capable of dealing with individual colonial needs. The Shawnees and their allies were escalating their attacks on the frontier from Pennsylvania to Virginia, and the Creeks and Cherokees were causing problems in the south.

The Cherokee remained the most populated and the most "civilized" of the southern tribes, but the Creek were also a large confederation and were capable of inflicting significant damage to Georgia and South Carolina. Stuart had successfully negotiated the Cherokee/Creek land cession the year before, but neither tribe was completely satisfied. Creek and Cherokee leadership alike was vexed by dissension. Although Chief Emistisiguo asserted that the Creek remained friendly, the Cowetas clearly were hostile to the Georgians. While Oconostota and the leaders from the Lower and Middle Towns, including Chinisto of Sugar Town and Wolf of Seneca, insisted on their loyalty to the British, many of the younger warriors, including the Raven of Tugaloo, were defiantly joining forces with the Cowetas.

The British feared the Creeks the most because they seemed the most volatile and were in a position to make the newly bought lands uninhabitable and worthless. They continued to supply arms and supplies to the Choctaw (who were fighting the Creeks already) and the Chickasaw (traditional allies). The Cherokee were granted some supplies but the flow of ammunition to them was limited because of fear that it might wind up in the hands of the Creeks. Both the Creeks and the Cherokee had received some provisions already as part of the land cession deal the year before. Commissioner Cameron, who had been instructed by Stuart to try to turn the Cherokee against the Creeks, asked how that could be done without acknowledging that the colonies were too weak to defend themselves against the Creeks. Although Cameron feared an offensive from the Cherokee enough to fortify Lochaber, he bravely moved to Keowee as instructed. Although the Cherokee remained friendly, a series of murders and revenge murders involving Cowetas, Cherokees, and whites had highly charged the atmosphere. Governor Wright of Georgia complained that the first white family to settle in the new cession was murdered. Georgia's inability to track down and punish whites guilty of murdering Indians continued to keep the Indians inflamed, and the inability of the Creeks to limit raids by Cowetas and to punish offenders kept the colonists wary of settling the new lands. Governor Wright requested that General Gage send troops to maintain order in the area and to chastise the Creeks if needed, much as British troops had been brought in to help South Carolina against the Cherokee in 1760. Secretary Dartmouth assured Wright that the Crown fully supported his efforts, but the military leadership complained that his plan to allow settlers to select and survey their own claims would be inflammatory. No troops were sent: The Georgian would have to rely on diplomatic means.

Governor Wright met with leaders of the Upper and Lower Creeks and declared that murders had been committed on both sides and that enough was enough. Many of the Creek leaders did not attend the conference because they were worried that they would be imprisoned just as the Cherokee leaders had been in 1759. Emistisiguo complained that the Cherokee had tried to sabotage the conference by scaring away some of the leaders, and insisted that they were encouraging them to attack Georgia. Emistisiguo also complained that the Cherokee had been meeting all summer long with Indian dignitaries at Chota, including Chickasaws, Arkansas, Shawnee, Delaware, and Illinois. He feared that the Cherokee were organizing a coalition against both the whites and the Creeks. By the time the Creeks signed a treaty with Georgia in October, the colonials weren't sure who could be trusted. Stuart discounted accounts of friction between the Creeks and the Cherokee and feared that they were secretly joining forces. While the British control over the colonies was faltering, the South Carolina Council met without Governor Bull's consent and approved funds to provide arms to western settlers. Once again, as diplomacy seemed to be successful, external circumstances threatened to make the results meaningless.

The Cherokee's northern frontier with Virginia also threatened to explode in 1774, mostly in response to two incidents involving murders. The Shawnee had been attacking western settlements with vehemence and were trying to enlist the Cherokee as allies. Although in the end the Cherokee leadership maintained their alliance with the Six Nations and the British, some of the younger warriors joined the Shawnee. A group of Delaware warriors (joined by Cherokee Elk Warrior among others) killed a party led by the son of Captain William Russell. Dunmore assumed that the Cherokee were guilty and demanded satisfaction.

The other incident happened at a horse race in the Watauga settlement that was part of a celebration of the new lease from the Cherokee. Relations with the Cherokee had been good and thus many of them were present at the festivities. The drunken William Crabtree shot Cherokee Billie in cold blood, sending the other Indians home in a panic. The incident threatened to push the Cherokee toward the Shawnee, but cooler heads prevailed. A party of settlers including William Falling and James Robertson traveled to Chota to apologize for the murder and to promise satisfaction. Captain Andrew Lewis also apologized to Oconostota, but reminded him that the Russell murders demanded satisfaction as well.

Governor Dunmore saw the Shawnee as the main threat to western expansion and did not want to leave Cherokee behavior unpunished, but also did not want to drive them into the Shawnee camp. Although the Holston settlement was his responsibility, the Wataugans were technically in North Carolina and were mere irritants in his eyes. He discouraged expansion in the Watauga region for the moment, although he did express the desire to obtain more land in the area later. Dunmore had political problems of his own—he dissolved the House of Burgesses after they passed a resolution denouncing the Boston Port Bill—but he was still able to muster a functional militia to attack the Shawnee. On October 10, at the mouth of the Kanawha, in the Battle of Point Pleasant, the Virginians routed the Shawnees. The only major battle of Dunmore's War resulted in the opening of Virginia's western lands to settlement without fear of the Shawnee alliance.

The Virginian victory weakened Cherokee complaints about the Watauga incident. The Cherokee still had some clout when they could threaten to assist the Shawnee, but after Point Pleasant the Cherokee leaders sent an emissary to Virginia to apologize for the rash actions of those young men who supported the Shawnee. Shortly thereafter the Cherokee executed a man convicted of killing Russell and another guilty Cherokee fled to the Chickasaw.

On August 27 Judge Richard Henderson from North Carolina founded the Transylvania Company, intending to obtain land in the Kentucky region for settlement. During the course of Dunmore's War, the land speculator himself visited Chota to discuss his proposal with the Cherokee leaders. After the Shawnee defeat, Henderson and his party escorted Attakullakulla to Watauga, where the aging chief gave assurances that peace would be maintained as long as there were no more serious provocations. Henderson took Attakullakulla to Cross Creek,

North Carolina, to show him a great warehouse of supplies, with which he hoped to purchase the desired land in Kentucky. The party would travel back to the Long Island and early in 1775 a dramatic meeting would be held to consider the Transylvania Company's offer. That meeting would have profound consequences for the Cherokee people, dividing them generation against generation, and leading ultimately to war.

Chapter Six

1775–1783

Sycamore Shoals, The American Revolution, and the Second Cherokee War

When the Revolutionary War began the Cherokee were in a state of poverty and weakness, having never fully recovered from the war of 1760–1761. The aging leaders of the tribe grew more conciliatory toward the encroachment of the white settlers and favored selling more land in return for material goods and peace. The tide was rising, however, for a younger generation of warriors, bent on preserving territory and traditions. The disintegration of British authority along the frontier brought complications in the relations between the whites and the Indians, and the generation gap widened. Before the French and Indian War, the Cherokee were courted by the French to the west but generally remained loyal to the British until pushed to war by Governor Lyttleton's incompetence. During the Revolution they remained mostly loyal to the British but were forced by circumstances to treat with the Americans to the east and north. While the peace faction in the Overhills was quick to bend to the American dominance, the war-like Chickamauga faction of refugees continually attacked American posts throughout the Revolutionary War.

At the end of the war the Cherokee were impoverished to the point of being unable even to procure enough ammunition to hunt for food and trade. Small pox was rampant and shelter and clothing were in short supply. The newly victorious Americans pushed the tribe into selling more and more land to cover debts. The Cherokee were divided into two camps, the Old Towns and the Chickamauga. Old Tassel took over as leader of the Overhills after the deaths of Attakullakulla and Oconostota, and Dragging Canoe emerged as the leader of the Chickamauga. The Chickamauga, having lost the British as an ally, found a potential new friend in the Spanish, who had gained control of Florida from the British. When the British deserted the Cherokee, many of them joined Dragging Canoe rather than cooperate with the hated conquering Americans.

1775

The Treaty of Sycamore Shoals

The year 1775 was a watershed year in Cherokee history as well as in American history. At a meeting at Sycamore Shoals, Attakullakulla, Oconostota, and some of the other older leaders sold an enormous tract of land encompassing much of modern Kentucky and middle Tennessee. Their actions so offended the younger warriors (led incidentally by Attakullakulla's son, Dragging Canoe) that the old regime could no longer maintain governing control. Although the schism among the Cherokee did not lead to civil war, it did eventually allow the more aggressive younger warriors to determine policy and wage war. This dramatic change in Cherokee politics took place in parallel with the disintegration of British control over the American colonies.

By the beginning of the year the Declarations and Resolves of the First Continental Congress had been presented to Parliament. All of the colonies supported the non-importation movement and trade embargo to protest the Coercive Acts, and military skirmishes already had occurred in Massachusetts and New Hampshire. While some voices in Parliament called for restraint and reconciliation, King George III endorsed the New England Restraining Act—severely restricting economic activities in New England. Secretary Dartmouth gave General Thomas Gage, Governor of Massachusetts, orders to use all force necessary to enforce British laws. The escalation in rhetoric was followed by a series of military actions including the battles of Lexington and Concord and the seizure of Fort Ticonderoga. By the time the Second Continental Congress met in May and declared a "state of defense," Parliament had already declared Massachusetts to be in a state of rebellion. The British and the colonists organized for an impending war while still trying to find diplomatic means to prevent it. The King rejected the last compromise proposal from the colonies and had imposed harsher restrictions on colonial trade. Several generals were sent to Boston to help Gage prepare for war. The colonists appointed George Washington as Commander in Chief of the seventeen thousand-man colonial militia and took steps to secure foreign support in the event of war.

The deterioration of the colonial government created a power vacuum along the frontier. Western settlers, never firmly under the control of the mostly coastal governing class, were emboldened by the circumstances. Frontiersmen coveting rich new lands were even less likely to care if the King's representatives considered their actions legal. Traders cared less about selling ammunition to the Indians for profit, but worried more about having weapons to fight the British Army. Rebel actions forced North Carolina's Governor Josiah Martin to govern from aboard a ship in the Cape Fear River. Governor Dunmore declared martial law in Virginia and had offended the planters when he promised freedom to slaves willing to fight for the King. A small militia of volunteers humiliated the Virginians at Great Bridge in December. The decline of royal authority in Virginia destroyed its ability to counter the illegal land purchase of the Transylvania Company and to control western settlers bent on seizing Indian lands.

While Governor Dunmore paved the way for safe settlement beyond the Kanawha River by defeating the Shawnee at Point Pleasant, it was Judge Richard Henderson of North Carolina who was prepared to exploit it. Henderson had organized the Transylvania Company, and had begun negotiations with the Overhill chiefs during the summer of 1774. The Transylvania Company had amassed a large supply of arms and goods (worth approximately ten thousand pounds) with which to purchase the land, and, with the help of Daniel Boone, had started organizing settlers for immediate occupation. After Henderson escorted Attakullakulla to North Carolina to inspect the goods, the Cherokee leader called for a meeting to be held at Sycamore Shoals, near Long Island of the Holston. While Dunmore objected to Henderson's activity as a violation of the royal policy against the private purchase of land from Indians, the judge found justification in a law that actually pertained to the purchase of land in India! Governor Martin (whose colony also stood to lose land and profits from Henderson's scheme) forbade the purchase and later called for Henderson's arrest. Meanwhile, the savvy judge played both sides. Knowing that the royal governments were weak, he threatened to establish his own independent colony if the Crown rejected his petition. Furthermore, the proprietors of the Company addressed a memorial to the Second Continental Congress requesting that Transylvania be considered a member of the United Colonies.

Officially the negotiations between the Transylvania Company and the Cherokee began on March 13, 1775, although the day was spent mostly in ceremonies such as the passing of the peace pipe. The twelve hundred Cherokee men and women participants were represented by Oconostota and his nephew Savanooka (Raven of Chota), Attakullakulla, and Old Tassel. Although Ostenaco expressed his disapproval of the negotiations by staying home, Dragging Canoe and other young warriors chose to attend the meeting in order to try to defeat the proposals. Several hundred white men also were present, including Henderson and the main investors, representatives of the Holston and Watauga settlements, Daniel Boone, and numerous surveyors, traders, interpreters, and others. What took place over the next few days will forever be considered among the most controversial negotiations in Cherokee history. Because the Cherokee did not yet have a written language, it is impossible to determine what the Cherokee negotiators understood about the treaty and what their motivations were.

On March 14 Henderson opened the negotiations by declaring his intent to purchase lands south of the Ohio River, from Point Pleasant at the mouth of the Great Kanawha to the mouth of the Tennessee River. The southern boundary of the purchase was to be the Cumberland River. Virginia had in 1770 already negotiated the purchase of the tract north of the Kentucky River, which emptied into the Ohio about two hundred miles west of the Kanawha, so that part of the request was already claimed. The Cherokee confirmed that they indeed had title to the lands otherwise requested. The Cherokee had hunted these lands for generations and had claimed title to them since they forced the Shawnee out of the Cumberland region in 1715. Cherokee warriors had fought Shawnee and Iroquois for generations over the right to hunt these lands, and young men continued to hunt them at that time. The negotiators parted for the day for internal deliberations.

The next day witnessed one of the most dramatic orations ever delivered by a Cherokee. Dragging Canoe offered a counterproposal to sell the tract of land north of the Kentucky River, east to the Kanawha. This was the tract of land that Virginia acquired after the signing of the Treaty of Lochaber. The Cherokee could sell this land in good faith since they had never received payment for it. Henderson, on the other hand, had no real interest in buying Virginia's claim and clarified his intention to buy the land south of the Kentucky River. Dragging Canoe summarized the history of white encroachment onto Cherokee lands and the subsequent weakening of the nation. He ended by predicting the eventual removal of the Cherokee from their ancestral homeland and their ultimate extinction when there would be no place else to go. Henderson must have been dumbfounded that a lower-ranking Indian, much less the son of Attakullakulla, could have been allowed to give such a speech, but it was Cherokee custom that all be allowed to speak. It was up to the leaders to persuade the participants to agree with their points of view, or otherwise lose the respect of everyone. After Dragging Canoe and some of his followers withdrew from the meeting, Oconostota and Attakullakulla decided that there would be no more talks that day.

The next day Oconostota warned Henderson that he was asking for lands that were extremely important to the younger generation of Cherokee, and that he could never promise the safety of white settlers in the area. He went on to complain that the small amount of goods offered by Transylvania did not adequately compensate the Cherokee for this large tract of fine hunting land. Henderson countered by pointing out that he was offering a warehouse full of supplies and that he could offer no more. The sides retired for the night. The Cherokee feasted on Henderson's beef and drank his rum as they considered their own pitiful lack of ammunition, hardware, and food.

The events of March 17 remain shrouded in mystery. Henderson presented the chiefs with several copies of the "Great Deed" by which the Cherokee would agree to sell the large tract of land south of the Kentucky River for the warehouse of supplies presented to them. (See Map 6 #7, page 125.) Despite warnings from Joseph Vann (the interpreter), Oconostota, Savanooka, Old Tassel, and Attakullakulla signed them. All but Attakullakulla later retracted, claiming that they thought they were

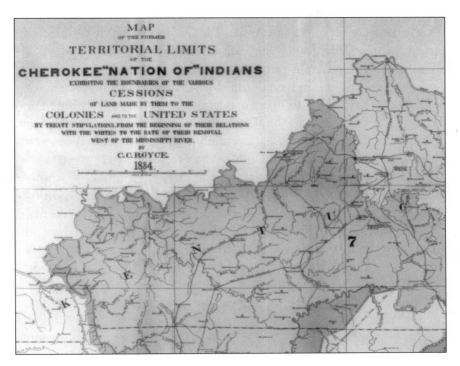

Map 6

agreeing only to a lease arrangement. It is not clear if Attakullakulla believed that or if any of them truthfully did not intend to sell the land. Dragging Canoe was present as the deeds were passed around and rose in protest. Saying that a dark cloud hung over the lands, he pointed out that the land was interposed between the Cherokee and some of their enemies to the northwest (such as the Kickapoos) and that the blood of both white and red men would be spilled there. Oconostota waved off Dragging Canoe's protests and the deal was done.

Not yet satisfied, Henderson immediately proposed another purchase. It would not be possible for the Transylvanian settlers to reach their new land without travelling across Cherokee territory, so he wanted to buy the land required for the pathway connecting the Holston settlements with the headlands of the Kentucky River. He pointed out that the Cherokee owed the settlers of Carter's Valley (within the tract) compensation for crimes committed against them, but he did offer more ammunition and supplies (which he had claimed he did not have the day before). Dragging Canoe stomped his feet on the ground in protest and left the meeting for good, but Attakullakulla (and probably Oconostota) signed the new treaty, called the Path Deed. Over the next few days, Attakullakulla (and others) agreed to a few more private land cessions, including the outright purchase of the Watauga lease. The division among the Cherokee was further deepened as the goods were distributed and the individual warriors saw how little they received. Many had not been informed of the new purchases. Certainly they could obtain more as individuals merely hunting the lands that were sold. There were immediate incriminations and denials, but the deals were done. Within six months over a thousand white people were settled on the Kentucky River, despite reports of killings there and in the Holston settlements.

Where was John Stuart? As the King's agents, Superintendent Stuart and his deputy, Alexander Cameron, were opposed to the Transylvania Company's dealings with the Cherokee, and they issued warnings to both parties. Neither of them was in attendance at Sycamore Shoals and thus was in no position to prevent the signing of the treaty. Despite his disagreement with Attakullakulla on this issue, John Stuart was still held in high esteem among the Cherokee. But he was in deep trouble with the southern colonies. Revolutionaries who had seized power in Charleston accused Stuart of inciting the Cherokee and Catawbas to attack them. Although he denied the accusations, the revolutionary Committee of Charleston declared that Stuart's home would be confiscated and held as bond against the good behavior of the Indians. Although some members of his family were detained, Stuart was able to flee to safety in St. Augustine where he would continue to act as superintendent with the help of intermediaries, such as his brother Henry.

Cameron reported that the Cherokee were ready to take up arms in defense of their friend, Superintendent Stuart. For the revolutionaries, this was another excuse to organize a militia, but their immediate response was diplomatic. William Henry Drayton, chairman of the Secret Committee of the South Carolina Council of Safety, met with Cherokee leaders in August and explained to them that Cameron had not been told the truth about their intentions. He explained the issues behind the colonial rebellion and asserted that the revolutionaries had no intention of attacking the Cherokee or other Indian tribes. He concluded by inviting the Cherokee to visit with Richard Pearis in South Carolina for further talks.

Stuart sent word to the Overhill chiefs imploring them to remain neutral and not to interfere with the colonial political troubles. He explained that the rebels had stolen ammunition intended for them but that there would be more coming to them later. He also asked that they refrain from murdering settlers along the frontier so as to avoid provocations.

Neither side continued to plead for Cherokee neutrality for very long. Within a month of Stuart's message to Oconostota and Attakullakulla, General Gage sent instructions for Stuart to encourage the Indians to attack the rebels and to keep them supplied with arms. Likewise, at a meeting at Congarees, Drayton offered assistance to the Cherokee if they would join the struggle against the British. Drayton unsuccessfully tried to get Cameron to leave the vicinity of the Cherokee, so the rebels tried to counter his influence by appointing their own agents to the Cherokee: Edward Wilkinson, George Galphin, and Robert Rea. Stuart sent his brother Henry, John MacIntosh, and Alexander Cameron on missions to the Upper Creeks, Cherokee, and Chickasaw to encourage them to join forces and fight against the rebels. The Creeks were engaged in a war with the Choctaw and were not available. The Cherokee were destitute and without sufficient ammunition to be effective partners. They also told Cameron that it would difficult for many of them to fight against men whom they had known as traders when they had no personal grudge against them. A few months earlier, perhaps the Cherokee and the Creek alike may have gladly fought for the British, but as winter approached their enthusiasm waned.

1776

The Second Cherokee War: A Nation Defeated and Divided

Americans Declare Independence

Although 1776 will forever be remembered for the birth of the United States, it should also be remembered as the year in which the Cherokee nation was nearly destroyed. By the time the Declaration of Independence was signed in July, revolutionary councils controlled the colonial governments, and their militias had already had some successes. The Continental Congress declared that the Americans would strive to maintain Indian neutrality, but the British leaders were divided among those who favored Indian neutrality, those who favored a limited role for the native tribes, and those who hoped to inflame the tribes into full-scale hostility against the Americans.

The Cherokee were in a difficult position. The revolution had disrupted the usual supply lines and so left them with a relative lack of ammunition and other supplies. They were vulnerable to attack from hostile tribes as well as from the Transylvanian and Wataugan settlers. Although the Americans were in a better position to provide ammunition than the British, the Cherokee recognized that those western settlers guilty of encroachment were supporters of the new regime. Whereas the British might see possible Cherokee involvement in the war as a diversionary tactic, the war party of the Cherokee envisioned war as necessary for revenge, honor, and survival. The Americans would fight them for defense if needed and conquest if provoked. But the Americans used diplomacy to avoid war with the southern Indians at first.

The Americans feared that a concerted attack by the Creeks and the Cherokee would pose a significant military threat to Georgia and South Carolina. The Cherokee were invited to meet with the American representatives at Fort Charlotte on April 16, but only a small number actually attended, and none was from the Overhill Towns. Dragging Canoe and other leaders had already solidified relations with John and Henry Stuart and had no interest in the American offers. The Cherokee delegation, led by Ecuy, hoped to attain ammunition at Fort Charlotte and was willing to agree to the American requests for neutrality even though they expressed concern that the Americans were rebuilding old Fort Prince George. The Americans failed to deliver gifts, and the Cherokee would fail to maintain their neutrality. The Americans met with the Creeks on May 1 and likewise made promises in return for neutrality. The Creeks were already entangled in a war against the Choctaw and were in no position to enter into a war with the white men.

For Dragging Canoe the question was not whether the Cherokee would fight the Americans, but rather when. The ink was scarcely dry on the illegal Treaty of Sycamore Shoals before settlers began moving onto land outside of the purchased territory.

Dragging Canoe's first priority was to procure ammunition. He led a party of sixty-two Cherokee to St. Augustine in January to meet with John Stuart. Stuart knew that the Cherokee would eventually be drawn into the war, but he hoped their involvement could be delayed so as to coordinate their military operations with the British. He recognized the desperate situation of the Cherokee and authorized the release of ammunition for them in return for loyalty to the King.

Unable to go himself, Superintendent Stuart sent his brother Henry on a mission to the Cherokee, Chickasaw, and Creeks. Henry left Pensacola in March to meet with Dragging Canoe at Mobile. Dragging Canoe complained about encroachment along the Virginia and North Carolina borders and about the unacceptable land deals negotiated by "the Old Men." He was patient with Stuart's promises of arms, which would be delivered via the new supply route established from West Florida to the Overhills through Creek territory. Dragging Canoe returned to Chota to wait for the supplies.

When Henry Stuart arrived in Chota with twenty-one horse-loads of ammunition on April 24, the Cherokee honored him with an invitation to an Eagle Tail Dance. This ritual, by which the participants asked for success in upcoming battles, suggested that war was inevitable, even though Oconostota and Attakullakulla did not participate. The young warriors were motivated and now armed. Henry Stuart realized that the least provocation would now trigger a war and that more arms would be needed. While he planned another expedition to Mobile for more arms, Stuart strove to delay the inevitable outbreak of violence by sending letters to the Watauga and Nolichucky settlements. He hoped to appeal to any loyalists who might be living there and encouraged the settlers to avoid conflict by moving to the safety of Florida. Stuart's plan backfired somewhat when Jesse Benton intercepted one of his letters and forged a new one in which Stuart suggested that the British were encouraging the Cherokee to attack the Holston settlements as well as Transylvania. Regardless of Benton's intentions, his forgery did spur the American forces to be better prepared for an attack from the Cherokee.

The last hope for peace faded in May when a delegation of northern Indians arrived in Chota. Representatives from the Six Nations, Mohawks, Ottawas, Nantucas, Delaware, and Shawnee were organizing a united Indian opposition against the encroachment of white settlers. Even while the Indian leaders were relaying news about great injustices being dealt by whites in Kentucky, a Cherokee trader arrived and spoke of rumors that a large army of Americans was preparing to attack. Within a few days a Grand Council meeting was held at Chota, where the northern Indians were given an opportunity to formally ask for a military alliance.

Oconostota and Attakullakulla sat patiently during the meeting as the visiting delegates presented wampum belts signifying friendship. Dragging Canoe and his followers, Doublehead, Young Tassel, Bloody Fellow, and Osiotto, enthusiastically accepted the belts. A turning point came when Savanooka, the Raven of Chota, stood up to accept the belt offered by the Nantucas. His defection from the peace camp to the war faction enhanced the general mood for war. The most dramatic moment came after a rousing speech by the Shawnee representative, calling not just for friendship, but for war. Dragging Canoe, by accepting the Shawnee wampum belt not only agreed to war, he effectively committed a coup d'état. Although he had every right to express his opinion, only the Great Warrior Oconostota could legally accept a war belt. Oconostota and Old Tassel held their tongues.

The next day a meeting was held in Settico where the war strategy was planned. All of the Cherokee men were painted in black and were hot for battle. Dragging Canoe turned his hostility toward traders in the area and even to Henry Stuart. Oconostota warned Stuart to leave Chota for fear that Dragging Canoe would kill him, but he was preparing to leave anyway. He and Attakullakulla had already planned to go to visit John Stuart, but were waiting for the next shipment of ammunition to arrive. Oconostota had promised Stuart to stall any attacks against the Americans, but after the arms arrived he would be powerless to stop Dragging Canoe. Besides, word came that the Lower Towns had already attacked the South Carolina frontier in a concerted action with the British, who were attacking Charleston by sea. The British failed in their attempt to take Fort Moultrie and the Cherokee were forced to withdraw back to the Lower Towns.

Although John Stuart had been given instructions to advise Dragging Canoe to attack the Virginian settlements in concert with the South Carolina attacks, he failed to do so. The Cherokee needed no prompting, however, and were busy preparing for battle. Nan-ye-hi (Nancy Ward) the *ghigau* and niece of Attakullkulla committed an act which might be interpreted as both patriotic and treasonous. As *ghigau* she had access to all the war plans, but as a member of the peace faction she must have been offended by the way her cousin Dragging Canoe had usurped power from Oconostota. Nan-ye-hi was married to Bryant Ward, a white trader, and was not biased against the white race. She also was appalled at the likelihood that a new war would bring on mass destruction of the villages, as had happened in 1760 and 1761. On July 8 she passed secret information on to traders to deliver to Wataugans at Fort Lee. Upon receipt of Ward's warning, Lieutenant John Sevier ordered the evacuation of Fort Caswell (near Sycamore Shoals) and further organized the defense of the area. Without the element of surprise, Dragging Canoe and his warriors would be much less likely to win a confrontation.

Seven hundred Cherokee warriors assembled near Fort Lee around July 17. They were divided into three groups under Dragging Canoe, Old Abram, and Savanooka. Dragging Canoe was to lead about two hundred men to attack the Holston settlements while Savanooka would take a similar number to attack Carter's Valley. A larger number of warriors would besiege Fort Caswell under the leadership of Old Abram. They planned to attack Transylvania after their victories.

On July 20 Old Abram and his men attacked Fort Caswell and, despite Nancy Ward's warning, some people were trapped outside of the structure. Most of those captured were put to death by torture (by custom captives could be either killed or taken as slaves). The *ghigau*, who had the right to veto executions, saved the life of Mrs. William Bean in a famous episode, supposedly for teaching her how to churn butter! The battle has become part of Tennessee folklore and for his actions there, John Sevier became known as a successful Indian fighter. The siege lasted for two weeks until Colonel William Russell arrived with reinforcements.

Dragging Canoe attacked the Holston settlements on July 20 also. His warriors met about one hundred seventy troops near Island Flats, six miles below Eaton's Station. The Virginians seemed to be losing and were seen scurrying back in retreat. Dragging Canoe, unaware of Nancy Ward's treachery, took the bait and chased after the fleeing men. The tides were turned as the Cherokee warriors were assembled in a more organized fashion whereas the Virginians were waiting in ambush, Indian style! Thirteen Cherokees were killed and Dragging Canoe was shot in both legs. Despite having to be carried off the battlefield, Dragging Canoe knew that he could not return to Chota in honor without a scalp for every man lost. He re-organized his warriors and headed off to Virginia to attack the undefended countryside. Although he was clearly routed, Dragging Canoe did succeed in bringing back eighteen scalps and thus saved face with his people.

Savanooka started his attack on Carter's Valley on July 21. Meeting little resistance, his men followed the Clinch River northward toward Virginia. Upon hearing of Dragging Canoe's defeat and Old Abram's lifting of the siege of Fort Caswell, Savanooka likewise retreated to Chota.

The Americans undoubtedly had contingency plans to attack the Cherokee even before the failed attack against the Holston region. They had secured the neutrality of the Creeks and had defeated the British/Cherokee alliance in South Carolina. On July 29 the Continental Congress ordered the North Carolina Council of Safety (and the revolutionary governments of Virginia and South Carolina) to prepare for war. Three armies were organized: Colonel Andrew Williamson led eleven hundred fifty troops from South Carolina; Brigadier General Griffith Rutherford had two thousand men from North Carolina; and eighteen hundred Virginians followed the orders of Colonel William Christian. There were probably no more than two thousand Cherokee warriors altogether.

On August 14 Colonel Williamson began his assault on the Lower Towns. In the face of overwhelming superiority of the American troops, Dragging Canoe ordered the evacuation of the Lower Towns and resettled temporarily in the Overhills. Although Williamson did not have the opportunity to kill many warriors, he did destroy the homes and crops of the Lower Towns. All of the major Lower Towns were torched; even Keowee was destroyed. By the end of September Williamson's job was done so he combined forces with those of Rutherford and assembled three thousand men to attack the Middle and Valley Towns. The Cherokee had little choice but to flee once more. The people from this area fled to the Overhills, to Florida, to the Upper Creeks, or scattered into the woods to face starvation. Their homes and crops were destroyed without a fight.

Colonel William Christian and his troops arrived at the Watauga area on September 21. The settlers were in bad shape and still holed up in their forts. After relieving the settlers, Christian began his march from Fort Patrick Henry on October 1 and headed for the Overhills. The

Overhill leaders knew that they had been beaten and so sent Savanooka to ask for mercy. Christian accepted his pleas to spare Chota, the City of Peace, but declared that he would first destroy Great Island Town, since its leaders had been the instigators of the war. Meanwhile, Dragging Canoe and the militant faction evacuated the threatened towns, knowing that defending them would be suicidal. Dragging Canoe and his followers established new towns to the southwest in the Chickamauga area along the Tennessee River, near the Upper Creeks.

By the end of October the Cherokee were a conquered nation and were at the mercy of the Americans. Ironically, John Stuart reported that he had secured an end to the Creek/Choctaw conflict and that they would support the Cherokee! To secure their western frontier, the Americans had committed a large number of troops who perhaps could have been used to fight the British elsewhere, but they did ensure that they would be able to continue their western expansion even as the Revolutionary War continued. The Cherokee war faction had tried to defend the integrity of the tribal borders but had faced overwhelming opposition. The population of the white men had increased so much that the Cherokee would no longer be able to threaten them seriously. Now they would negotiate with the Americans on the white men's terms, as a vanquished nation. Colonel Christian and Oconostota agreed to a cease-fire on November 29, but a comprehensive treaty conference would be held the next year. Many Cherokee were left to spend the winter of 1776–1777 homeless and without crops.

1777

Overhill Leaders Cede Land to the Americans

Dragging Canoe establishes the Chickamauga Confederation

After the war the Cherokee were truly a divided nation. Oconostota and the peace faction had managed to prevent the destruction of Chota and some of the other Overhill Towns, but much of the nation had been destroyed. Dragging Canoe and his followers established new towns in the Chickamauga area, southwest of the Overhills on the Tennessee River. In addition to the young aggressive warriors, refugees from the destroyed Lower, Middle, and Valley Towns joined him, as did many of the neighboring Upper Creeks. The location was isolated from the white men (although the trader John MacDonald and his Cherokee wife had been there for years) and was known as a meeting place for renegades and outlaws. The Tennessee River gave access to fish for food and navigation for military needs, and the difficult terrain helped defend against attacks by land. While the new community held on to many traditional values, it lacked the traditional political organization. Dragging Canoe was accepted by the Chickamaugans as leader, however, and he succeeded in attracting a diverse confederation opposed to the Americans.

The peace faction in Chota was left to deal with the Americans alone, as Dragging Canoe would have nothing to do with them. In fact, the Chickamaugans staged raids against settlers even while the peace faction was promising neutrality. There were two sets of negotiations taking place: Ostenaco led a delegation to talk with representatives of South Carolina, and Oconostota and Attakullakulla led talks with representatives from Virginia and North Carolina.

A peace treaty was signed at DeWitt's Corner (Due West, South Carolina) on May 20, 1777. (See Map 3 #8, page 26.) At this meeting the Cherokee were forced to cede almost all of their land within the boundaries of South Carolina, including Keowee and most of the Lower Towns. As a conquered nation, there was no exchange of gifts, just reassurances of neutrality. This drastic cession forced the Lower Town Cherokee into permanent exile and allowed expansion of white settlements deep into territory bordering the Creeks. Dragging Canoe did not recognize this treaty, of course, and argued that it was invalid since the Lower Towns had not been represented; the Overhills had no right to cede it.

Nathaniel Gist, whose wife was Cherokee, arrived in Chota as a representative of Virginia to issue an invitation to negotiate at the Long Island of the Holston. This friend of George Washington and recent convert to the rebel cause was well-respected by the Cherokee. Gist warned that 1777 would be worse than the year before if the Cherokee listened to representatives of the British and did not come to terms with the Americans. A group of Cherokee leaders traveled to Long Island and met with William Christian, William Preston, and Evan Shelby.

Oconostota and Old Tassel explained that Dragging Canoe was responsible for the hostilities and that they no longer had any influence over him. They also explained that they were under pressure from the British not to make peace with the Americans. The Americans made few promises but asserted their need to build new forts within Cherokee territory. Oconostota and Attakullakulla went on to Williamsburg to establish friendly relations and to open up trade with the new state.

While the Transylvanian settlements had officially become Kentucky County, Virginia, the territory west of North Carolina's mountainous border became its Washington County. The Overhill Towns as well as the Watauga settlements were now officially part of North Carolina. Governor Richard Caswell appointed Waightstill Avery, Robert Lanier, and Joseph Winston to represent North Carolina at the negotiations at Long Island. The Cherokee had little choice but to agree to the demands of the states. The vanquished leaders ceded to Virginia land north of the Holston River, from near the Long Island to a point at the southern opening of Carter's Valley. From there the boundary extended in a straight line to a point just west of Cumberland Gap. Even though these areas were partially in North Carolina, Virginia was still administering them. The North Carolina boundary was drawn in a straight line from Cloud's Creek (at Carter's Valley and the Holston River) northeast to Chimney Top Mountain, then south to the Nolichucky River and from there southeastward to the Blue Ridge. All lands east of the Blue Ridge were ceded. The sacred Long Island was ceded, but was deeded specifically to Nathaniel Gist. Waightstill Avery proclaimed that they were fixing a line that would remain for generations to come. (See Map 3 #9, page 26.)

Virginia appointed James Robertson and North Carolina appointed Joseph Martin to serve as Commissioners, living among the Cherokee. They were to counter the influence of Cameron and Stuart, who were still trying to create an anti-American alliance of southern Indians. The troubled tribe, for decades used as a pawn in the Franco-English struggle for empire, was now wedged between the British and their American adversaries. The French entered the scene again as the Marquis de Lafayette arrived to help the American war effort, and later France recognized the United States as an independent nation. The French also supplied the southern states with goods intended for the Indians, but very little actually benefited the Cherokee. The Cherokee were destitute and that was fine with the Americans. An impoverished tribe could pose no military threat to them and would serve as an example to other tribes who might consider allying with the British.

Meanwhile the British were trying to organize a large confederation of tribes to attack the American frontier from Pennsylvania to Florida. Lieutenant Governor Henry Hamilton met with several enthusiastic northern and western tribes in March and established a plan to attack Pennsylvania and Virginia. It was not feasible for John Stuart to arrange a similar conference of southern Indians, but he did intensify individual negotiations. The Chickasaw and Choctaw were reliable British allies, and now that Stuart had arranged peace between the Creeks and the Choctaw, he pressed the Creeks to help the Cherokee. The British planned to launch an attack against Georgia from St. Augustine and to use the Creeks to attack from the west. The Creeks were unwilling to help since the Americans were too close to their towns to leave them unguarded, lest they suffer the same fate as the Cherokee. Besides, the British were scarcely able to provide them with provisions needed to wage war. Likewise, the Chickamaugans, who were more than willing to engage the Americans, were silenced by a lack of ammunition.

1778

Desperate Cherokee Reduced to Neutrality

Cherokee Misery serves as an Example to Other Tribes

Horatio Gates' victory over the British at the Second Battle of Saratoga on October 7, 1777, had dramatic repercussions in Europe. The French took notice of the American military success and agreed to treaties of alliance and commerce with the fledgling nation the next February. Lord North responded to the Franco-American alliance by sending a peace delegation to the Continental Congress. The Americans were emboldened by their new alliance with France and anticipated a military victory assuring independence once the French fleet arrived. The Americans were also encouraged by more military gains in

1778. George Rogers Clark was largely successful in routing the British out of the western territories, and the evacuation of Philadelphia by General Henry Clinton (General Howe's replacement as Commander-in-Chief) allowed the Continental Congress to return to its home. The formal declaration of war by France against Britain and the subsequent arrival of the French fleet in America prompted the British peace delegation to withdraw to London.

The British continued their military efforts, of course, during the period of peace negotiations. They had recruited various northern and western tribes to attack frontier settlements from western New York all the way to Kentucky. Two campaigns were planned involving the southern Indians: an attack on South Carolina and Georgia and an attack on Spanish New Orleans. Timing was critical. If the French entered the war and successfully blockaded the southern ports, the British would have no way of supplying their Indian allies. The tribes would have no choice but to become neutral or even ally with the Americans.

Although the Chickamauga Cherokee, Choctaw, Chickasaw, and Creeks all were friendly with the British, each tribe had issues. Commissioner Stuart recognized the desperate plight of the Cherokee and encouraged them to plant their crops to avoid starvation. Although the Cherokee did send warriors to intercept American shipments at the mouth of the Cherokee (Tennessee) River, the tribe would not be able to join any major military crusades until after the Green Corn Festival.

The other southern tribes were well aware of the desperate condition of the Cherokee and were afraid of American retribution. They were suspicious of any promises from John Stuart. Even after a shipment of supplies arrived in Pensacola for the benefit of the four hundred Cherokee refugees and other southern Indians, only the Cherokee were committed to the campaign against New Orleans. Despite the arrival of fresh troops in Pensacola, the other tribes refused to attack unless under direct British leadership. The campaign never materialized.

The British campaign against Georgia and South Carolina called for a coalition of regular troops, loyalist rangers, and allied Indians to attack along the western frontier while more troops pushed northward from St. Augustine. Despite Creek reluctance to overextend themselves and to incur the wrath of the Americans, the British had a flurry of successes along the frontier, and on December 29 they captured Savannah. The push toward Charleston had begun. Meanwhile, British leaders to the north had sent war belts to the Chickasaw and Cherokee asking for help against the Virginian settlements.

1779

Cherokee Diplomacy Rides the Tides of the Revolutionary War

In 1779 the Cherokee nation remained divided between the old towns and the new Chickamauga Confederation, and the welfare of the tribe was dependent on the good graces of the warring white men. The economy was in ruins since the British had been incapable of supplying the population adequately and the Americans had been unwilling.

Many of the towns had been destroyed and the corn crop failed for the second year in a row. The desperate Cherokee could not break out of their deadlocked situation until one or the other protagonist (and potential benefactor) developed a military advantage over the other.

A big break came in January when British forces led by General Augustin Prevost and Lieutenant Colonel Archibald Campbell captured Savannah and then Augusta, Georgia. The British victories put the Savannah River into British hands and thus opened up a reliable supply route to the Cherokee. The renewed flow of goods persuaded many Cherokee to return to the British fold, and to escalate hostilities against the Holston and Nolichucky communities. Despite Waightstill Avery's proclamation in 1777 that the border with the Cherokee would stand for all time, encroachment had continued unabated.

Virginia's representative to the Overhills, Joseph Martin, reported to Governor Patrick Henry that the Chickamauga, at the urging of the British, were committing violent acts against the Americans, despite the objection of the leadership in Chota. Furthermore, Dragging Canoe was recruiting new followers from the Lower Towns and even other tribes. James Robertson, emissary to the Overhill from North Carolina, agreed with Martin's assessment that the best way to put an end to Chickamauga hostility and to prevent dragging the whole Cherokee nation into another war, was to chastise the secessionist group with a pre-emptive military strike. Governor Henry appointed Colonel Evan Shelby to get the job done.

Shelby led a group of several hundred Virginian and North Carolinian volunteers into the Chickamauga towns in April, while the Indian warriors were still fighting in Georgia. With minimal resistance, Shelby and his men destroyed eleven towns, including the crops. They confiscated British ammunition and all of John MacDonald's furs and supplies and sold them later at Sale Creek, near modern Chattanooga. Later Dragging Canoe returned but decided not to rebuild the ruined villages. Rather, the Chickamauga accepted an invitation from the Creeks to build five new towns further down the Tennessee River: Nickajack, Running Water, Long Island, Crow Town, and Lookout Town. The inhabitants of the new towns earned an even worse reputation for hostility toward whites! Dragging Canoe sent a message to Colonel Shelby (through Oconostota) that was conciliatory in tone. At the same time he told the Shawnee that despite their losses, the Chickamauga were still capable (and willing) to go war against the Americans.

Meanwhile, Commissioner John Stuart died, leaving British policy in a confused state. Deputy Alexander Cameron and Stuart's brother Charles volunteered to serve in the position pending a permanent appointment. Cameron had served among the Cherokee for over a decade and had married a Cherokee woman, but Governor Patrick Tonyn in St. Augustine preferred Thomas Brown. Governor Peter Chester in Pensacola accused Cameron of being uneducated and not qualified to be commissioner. He appointed his own commissioners pending notification from authorities in London. Within a few months Secretary George Germain decided to divide the Southern Indian Division into two districts: The Mississippi District included the Chickasaw and Choctaw and would be represented by Cameron; the Atlantic district included the Cherokee, Creek, and Catawba and would be assigned to Brown. Cameron accepted the new position, but he delayed his departure from the Cherokee claiming that they didn't want him to leave and that the tribe might join the Americans in his absence. Truthfully, Cameron's presence in Chota had chased Virginia's Joseph Martin out. He knew no more about the western tribes than Brown knew about the Cherokee, but either way the absence of leadership resulted in confusion and undermined British influence among the Cherokee and the other southern tribes.

By the middle of the summer the Americans had launched counterattacks in Georgia and had defeated an alliance of Iroquois and other northern Indians led by Joseph Brant. Furthermore, Governor Henry Hamilton had been captured at Vincennes, so the British Indian initiative in the north was in shambles. In July the Raven of Chota traveled to Fort Pitt and declared Cherokee friendship with the Americans and the Delawares. The Raven and several other Cherokee leaders signed a treaty with Colonel Daniel Brodhead on July 22. The treaty seemed to be standing up to the test after Spain entered the war against Britain. Spain had actually promised to help the French in America in return for help in regaining Gibraltar from the British. Spain did not enter into an alliance with the United States, but helped indirectly by capturing Baton Rouge and other British holdings in Western Florida. When the British asked for help from the Cherokee, however, they were unwilling to help without substantial assistance up front.

The Cherokee situation became even more desperate, and the British diplomatic mission to the Cherokee lost its credibility. The Chickamauga had fought for the British and wound up having their homes destroyed. Despite Brodhead's treaty, the Cherokee received no significant supplies from Virginia. The crops had failed and there was a new outbreak of small pox. The Six Nations sent an appeal to the Cherokee to remain loyal to the British cause and to band together to fight the Americans. The Spanish Governor General Bernardo de Gálvez in New Orleans likewise made an appeal to the Cherokee (and other Indians) for friendship. Everyone had made promises before but no one had delivered. Again, the fate of the Cherokee would remain clouded as long as the Revolutionary War was undecided.

1780

Thomas Jefferson Chastises the Overhills

In 1780 the British enjoyed significant gains in the southern theater of the Revolutionary War, but the tide turned in favor of the rebels, in no small way thanks to the military efforts of the western settlers. The Cherokee, like the other southern tribes, were used as pawns in the struggle between the Americans and the British, and now between the Spanish and the British. Improved relations between the British and the Cherokee brought more supplies into the Overhills and influenced more Cherokee to fight for the King's cause. Attakullakulla apparently died in 1780 and Oconostota's influence waned just as his nephew (Raven of Chota or Savanooka) rose to power. As the rebels' power grew, military success against the British allowed them to turn their resources toward silencing the Cherokee.

The British successfully defended Savannah and Augusta against patriot guerrilla attacks while the new commissioner Colonel Thomas Brown arrived in Georgia. The British weren't quite sure what to do with the Cherokee at this point. General Clinton arrived off the coast of Charleston with eight thousand British troops in February and went on to capture the city in May. Colonel Brown had put together a militia of over two hundred fifty displaced Cherokee, Creeks, traders, and loyalists who he hoped would be used in the defense of Augusta, the traditional British trade center for the Creeks and the Cherokee. Secretary Germain encouraged Brown to use his Cherokee and Creek forces to help General Cornwallis in his invasion of North Carolina. Brown agreed with the recommendation, but he was having difficulty with Indians taking back their hunting grounds from settlers now well-established. Cornwallis rejected the offer anyway, saying that the Cherokee situation was too complex to sort out and that the British should not use any Indians for military purposes. Brown met the Creeks and Cherokee at a conference in Augusta in September and awarded them supplies and ammunition. Although many of the Indians abandoned the project because of an outbreak of small pox, Brown maintained an effective force of brave warriors, who successfully defended Augusta against American attacks. For the Indians, victory there signaled an opportunity to regain land taken from them in South Carolina after the defeat of 1776 and perhaps to recoup losses in the Holston Valley region later.

Alexander Cameron finally assumed his post to the west in 1780. Governor General de Gálvez of Louisiana proposed that Spain and Britain should renounce the use of Indian allies in their conflict but General Archibald Campbell refused. Spain captured Mobile and enlisted the support of the Choctaw, thus cutting the British off from communication with Indians west of the Mississippi River. Cameron's instructions were to manipulate the Chickasaw, Cherokee, and Creeks so as to force the Choctaw back into the British fold. Although the Cherokee were part of this coalition and did help patrol the Ohio and Mississippi rivers, they did not play a big role against the Spanish. The Cherokee also sent two delegations to a meeting with the Six Nations, Shawnee, Delaware, and others. The Raven of Chota was forced to defend his friendship with the Americans, as the tone of the meeting was pro-British. The Cherokee allowed the Shawnee to construct villages along the Tennessee River between the Chickamauga towns and the Chickasaw territory, but the Cherokee had little interest at this time in the western activities. Their attention was turned to the north, to Virginia.

Early in the year, Virginia Governor Thomas Jefferson gave instructions to Major Joseph Martin, emissary to Chota, to negotiate the right to build a fort at the mouth of the Ohio River and to obtain more land in the Cumberland and Kentucky regions. The population had continued to increase in Kentucky and in the Holston settlements and Fort Nashborough had been founded on the banks of the Cumberland River. At the urging of Judge Richard Henderson, James Robertson had led the original group of settlers overland in 1779. Another group, led by John Donelson, traveled down the Tennessee River from the Holston settlements to Nashborough, arriving in 1780. Predictably, their passage through the Chickamauga area was met with a violent attack. Ironically, the one boat that the Indians captured held a group of immigrants who were under quarantine for small pox. The Chickamaugan village was subsequently decimated by the disease!

The Cherokee attacks were not limited to the extreme western settlements. The increased flow of British goods from Georgia and South Carolina enabled the Cherokee to increase hostilities in the Holston, Watauga, and Nolichucky areas. Governor Jefferson appointed General William Preston to command a campaign to punish the Chickamaugans and destroy their towns. Jefferson emphasized the importance of distinguishing between the rebellious faction and those in Chota who had remained friendly with the Americans. As late as October he even invited Oconostota and other friendly Cherokee to visit him in Virginia.

The situation changed dramatically that autumn. After Colonel Brown's conference at Augusta even the Raven of Chota behaved as an ally of the British. Brown's military success there convinced many of the Overhills that the British offered hope of regaining lost lands in Virginia as well as in South Carolina. The increased frequency of Cherokee raids, launched from the Overhills, against the Holston Valley settlements did not go unnoticed.

What appeared to be a minor skirmish between the British and a group of American militiamen turned out to be a decisive turning point in the Revolutionary War. Major Patrick Ferguson, who had been scouring the countryside, was leading a group of over a thousand British troops back from northwestern South Carolina toward General Cornwallis so as to join his invasion of North Carolina. Ferguson, whose troops had been harassed by small militias from the Holston settlements, boasted that he would march his men across the mountains and lay waste to the area. The Americans decided not to wait for such an attack but rather organized a militia of almost a thousand frontiersmen. Ferguson got wind that the rag-tag group of settlers was approaching so he assumed what he thought was a safe position on a narrow ridge known as King's Mountain. On October 7, Colonel William Campbell led his men in an Indian-style attack and after a one-sided battle, the British troops surrendered and Ferguson was dead. The invasion of North Carolina would have to wait. It was clear that the backcountry could not be held so long as the western settlements remained unconquered.

Meanwhile Jefferson realized that the increase in hostilities against the frontier settlements was not completely the fault of the Chickamauga. Clearly the Overhills also were involved. Indeed, the Cherokee had recently told Thomas Brown that they would agree to increase their attacks against the Americans even further. Jefferson realized that the Cherokee had been alienated against the Americans, who had done little to alleviate their desperate conditions, but he was nonetheless determined to strike them down. He dispatched Arthur Campbell and John Sevier (a hero of the recent King's Mountain victory) on a mission to chastise the Cherokee. The American troops marched southward and then into the Overhills via the Little Tennessee River. They took over Chota, plundering its supplies and forcing Oconostota to leave his important (and perhaps incriminating) papers behind. Chilhowie, which was the only town to offer resistance, was destroyed utterly. After several more towns were similarly razed, Nancy Ward was sent to negotiate a cease-fire with Arthur Campbell. The *ghigau* was rebuffed, as the Americans wanted to punish the towns on the lower Hiwasee River especially. When the American assault ended on New Year's Eve, they had destroyed seventeen towns and all of their provisions. They began their march home the next day.

1781

Americans Raid the Middle Towns

*British Losses Force the Cherokee to Accept
American Ultimatums*

At the end of 1780 Arthur Campbell and his men had destroyed utterly many of the Overhill Towns. As they headed back toward Virginia, Campbell addressed Hai-a-tee of Chota (the only Cherokee that he said he could trust) and issued an ultimatum. The Cherokee would meet American representatives at the Long Island in two months or face further destruction. Hoping for Creek assistance and British aid from South Carolina, perhaps, the Middle Town Cherokee answered by launching a raid into Powell's Valley. Arthur Campbell responded by sending John Sevier to chastise the Middle Towns. Sevier led his men down treacherous mountain trails in March and captured Tuckasegee in a surprise attack. The other towns nearby were destroyed with almost no losses for the Americans. Another American expedition was sent to Cumberland Gap at about the same time to chastise Indians who had been interfering with travelers heading into Kentucky. Further raids by Dragging Canoe's men at Fort Nashborough and an attack on new settlements on the French Broad were met with swift punitive attacks from Virginia. The defeat of the British at Cowpens, South Carolina, and Cornwallis' costly victory at Guilford Courthouse, North Carolina, meant that the British would be less likely to help the Cherokee. The fall of Pensacola to the Spanish in May eliminated any chance the Creek would help. The situation for the Cherokee was desperate: Hundreds of them were homeless and there was inadequate food, clothing, and ammunition. A call for peace was made in the Council in April. Oconostota, Hanging Maw, and Old Tassel sent Horse Leach and Anco of Chota to Joseph Martin to deliver a set of blue and white beads. The beads symbolized that there had been bad times between the Cherokee and the Virginians, but that times were now better. They explained that the Cherokee resented encroachment in the area around Chimney Rock that occurred immediately after the last treaty was signed. They explained further that Colonel Thomas

Brown had encouraged them to seek revenge and that Abram of Chilhowie had taken up the hatchet.

A treaty meeting was held in July. General Nathaniel Greene had appointed a commission composed of William Christian, William Preston, Arthur Campbell, Joseph Martin, Robert Sevier (who had died before being able to serve), Evan Shelby, Joseph Williams, and John Sevier. Old Tassel, the principal speaker for the Cherokee, expressed uncertainty over Sevier's intentions and hope for a peaceful resolution. Sevier explained that the Americans did not hate the Cherokee but were merely trying to defend their territory. He promised that if the Cherokee refrained from attacking farmers, a new boundary would be drawn up that winter, although he did not promise to relocate any whites over the boundary. In other words, the settlers wanted more land. He and Colonel Christian encouraged the Cherokee to remain neutral in the war with Britain and to expel British agents from Cherokee territory. An invitation was extended to the Cherokee to send a delegation to Philadelphia. The most moving speech of the meeting was an impassioned plea by Nancy Ward for peace. She said that although women are looked upon as nothing, they are the mothers of the soldiers. She wished that the American and Cherokee women would accept each other's sons as their own.

Even as Oconostota and two other chiefs traveled to Williamsburg, the Raven of Chota was meeting with British Commissioner Thomas Brown. He insisted that the Cherokee were still loyal to the King's cause and that Oconostota was negotiating with the Americans only to obtain goods and ammunition. The Raven insisted that the Cherokee would be fighting against the rebels with enthusiasm once their situation was less desperate. Within weeks, however, Oconostota and his allies were actually encouraging Virginia to attack the Chickamaugans.

In October 1781 General Cornwallis was forced to surrender his army after the Americans and French besieged his forces for three weeks, with no escape route by sea or land. The failing economy of the young republic got a huge boost when the Netherlands granted the United States a large loan. It now seemed clear that the British could not prevent American independence. Cherokee sentiment remained divided between those who supported the British cause and those who were resigned to dealing with the Americans.

1782

North Carolina Raids the Chickamaugans

Virginia Seeks Peace with the Cherokee

With Cornwallis' defeat at Yorktown, the British military efforts in the American Revolution came to an end. Prime Minister Lord North resigned and Parliament voted to authorize the King's representatives to negotiate peace with the United States. Sir Guy Carleton replaced General Henry Clinton as Commander-in-Chief and was charged with the task of withdrawing British troops from the new nation. A few more skirmishes occurred during 1782, but most of them involved Native Americans, for the British withdrawal did not solve their military and political problems.

The situation was complicated for the Cherokee, not only because of their own internal divisions, but because the American states also were divided. Cherokee representatives met with other tribes at a British-led conference in Detroit where they continued to profess alliance with the Six Nations, even after the British evacuation of Savannah. Although the Treaty of Long Island had put an official end to the hostilities between the Americans and the Cherokee, Dragging Canoe and the Chickamaugans continued to mount terrorist raids against the settlers in the remote Cumberland River settlements around Fort Nashborough and also around Nolichucky. If the Old Town Cherokee played both sides of the fence they were motivated by desperation. The people were impoverished and without means of hunting or producing their own clothes. The Chickamauga remained a force with an ideological axe to grind.

Benjamin Harrison, the new governor of Virginia, was satisfied with the Treaty of Long Island and had no quarrel with the Cherokee. His state had been greatly damaged during the last year of the war and could not afford a continuation of the Cherokee War. By the summer Virginia's emissary to Chota, Joseph Martin, reported to Colonel Arthur Campbell that even the Chickamaugans were ready for peace. They were heading to Chota with twenty prisoners they intended to release. A changing of the guard took place at that time also when the ailing Oconostota resigned his authority in favor of his son Tuckasee, the Terrapin.

British troops did not withdraw from Charleston until December 1782 and until then many of the Middle Towns remained loyal. American Governor John Matthews of South Carolina protested to Governor Harrison that Virginia should not aid the Cherokee with ammunition until after his state was secure. North Carolina had another idea. The Nolichucky settlements were part of North Carolina and deserved to be defended. The state legislature approved a new offensive against the Chickamauga and authorized Governor Alexander Martin to appoint Colonel John Sevier and Colonel John McDowell to lead the mission. McDowell never participated, but Sevier quickly raised a militia of two hundred fifty riflemen from Nolichucky. They arrived in Chota early in September and met with Indians who promised to lead them to the Chickamauga settlements. Sevier wisely didn't trust the guides and decided to take his men through the abandoned Middle Towns toward the Chickamauga. After a lopsided battle at Lookout Mountain they proceeded to destroy abandoned towns, including Spring Frog, Ustenali, Ellijay, and Coosawatie. Sevier did not find the newer Chickamauga towns and instead headed back to Chota. He met with Oconostota, Old Tassel, and Hanging Maw before heading back to Nolichucky.

The leaders at Chota made a plea to Governor Harrison to intervene in North Carolina on their behalf. The Overhills remained helpless since they had never received the ammunition that Virginia promised and North Carolina continued to allow its settlers to encroach upon Cherokee land. The Cherokee especially wanted to preserve their title to the sacred Long Island. Governor Harrison apologized for the delay in shipping ammunition to them and promised that more would come after the Americans and British had signed a formal peace treaty. He kept his word and contacted the governors of both North and South Carolina. He criticized Governor Matthews for expeditions he had launched against the Cherokee and expressed hope that South Carolina would cooperate with the Cherokee, Creeks, and Chickasaw. Harrison asked Governor Martin to make peace with the Old Town Cherokee, suggesting that North Carolina's attacks would put Virginia's western settlers at risk of becoming victims of indiscriminate retaliatory attacks.

Harrison went on to propose a joint commission by which Virginia and the Carolinas could coordinate Indian policy.

By the end of the year the British had evacuated Charleston and the Chickamaugans reportedly were in desperate shape and asking for peace. British influence among the Indians was not gone, however. Thousands of Indians from the north and south, including Cherokee, were on their way to a conference to be held at St. Augustine.

1783

The Aftermath of War: Disease, Poverty, and Political Division

Great Britain signed preliminary peace treaties with France and Spain in January 1783 and shortly thereafter the British Parliament and American Congress mutually declared an end to the military hostilities. The final draft of the Anglo-American agreement, the Treaty of Paris, was signed on September 3, and on the same day the Treaty of Versailles concluded terms among the European powers. (See Map 7, page 149.) The independence of the United States was established, and Britain ceded East and West Florida back to Spain.

The British were not completely run out of North America as France had been a generation earlier, since Canada and the West Indies were firmly under their control. The British hoped to maintain trade and military relations with the Cherokee and other Indians while inhibiting the influence of the Americans and Spanish. The Spanish were anxious to open new trade and military relationships with the Cherokee and other southern tribes, who might prefer doing business with them rather than the hated Americans. The Spanish King even agreed to a request from the Cherokee to allow some of them to live in Pensacola and possibly to help them fight the Americans in the future.

The British Indian Superintendent Colonel Thomas Brown held a conference with various friendly northern and southern tribes at St. Augustine in January. The Six Nations and the Cherokee discussed forming a British alliance, and the Cherokee even talked about relocating their villages to places along the Tennessee and Ohio rivers. There were also suggestions of relocating some of the Indians in St. Augustine.

Major Arant De Peyster held similar meetings with the Cherokee, the Hurons, and several other tribes at Detroit over the next few months. The Indians came asking for supplies so they could maintain the war effort against the Americans. De Peyster was unable to accommodate the requests and asked that the Indians remain peaceful while the British concluded negotiations with the other warring parties.

Meanwhile, the Cherokee hunters, unaware that Britain was negotiating the return of Florida to Spain, continued to travel to St. Augustine with their peltry. The British were anxious to preserve their relations with the tribe but were unable to provide fair provisions in return for the furs, much less offer the traditional presents. Colonel Brown, without adequate support from Commander-in-Chief Guy Carleton, realized that he would no longer have credibility with the Cherokee. He ordered the evacuation of British officers, traders, and interpreters from Cherokee territory. Brown warned Carleton that the Cherokee were in a very exposed position and would likely have to yield even more hunting lands to the rebels.

By the end of the year the Treaty of Paris had been signed and the Indians were resigned to the fact that the British were leaving. There

Map 7

was no point in organizing a large British alliance of tribes, and even Joseph Brant of the Six Nations told the Cherokee that they intended to honor the peace. Little Turkey and some of the Overhills met with Thomas Brown in the fall and expressed regret that the British were leaving, but all of the tribes were nervous that the British may have ceded to the Americans rights to Indian lands.

The central government of the United States did not yet have a coordinated Indian policy; each state negotiated with the tribes independently. The Cherokee were poverty stricken and weakened by another outbreak of small pox. They could negotiate only from a position of vulnerability. Virginia's Governor Benjamin Harrison hoped to establish peaceful relations with the Cherokee and appointed Joseph Martin, John Donelson, and Isaac Shelby as commissioners. At a meeting at Chota in January, while many of the Cherokee were in St. Augustine, Old Tassel told Martin that the Cherokee were desperate for ammunition merely for hunting. In one of his last public acts before dying, Oconostota pled for price concessions from the traders, since the people were impoverished. Keneteta (Rising Fawn) thanked Martin for his help and dismissed symbolically the British by turning over British papers to Martin and scattering dust between Chota and the British position.

While Sevier was raiding the Chickamauga villages in 1782, Georgia's General Andrew Pickens led a force of four hundred troops into Cherokee territory to punish them for raiding settlements in the upper Broad River area. Picken's expedition was very successful and in essence the Cherokee were forced to buy peace by relinquishing more land. The Cherokee signed a treaty at Augusta on May 31 by which (under duress) they ceded a tract of land just northwest of the parcel sold 1773. (See Map 3 #10, page 26.) Later the Creeks also relinquished all claims to the same tract of land. After the British had abandoned the Cherokee territory, Georgian frontiersmen burned Cowee and began the process of settling the newly acquired lands.

The Cherokee were at the lowest point in their history. They had grown dependent on the white people for guns to hunt for food and for fur to trade. They found themselves starving and their best hunting grounds inhabited by white people. The venerable Cherokee leaders had died, and a new generation of leaders was emerging. The community had been divided by the foundation of the Chickamauga Confederacy, and Dragging Canoe, its leader, continued hostilities toward the Americans against all odds. The persistence of Chickamaugan acts of terrorism threatened the newly established relationships between the Cherokee and the victorious Americans.

Chapter Seven

1784–1788

The Aftermath of the Second Cherokee War

After the end of the Revolutionary War the United States was a loose confederation of states, each with its own political agenda. The Cherokee had been brutalized during the conflict. They had supported the losing side in the Anglo-American conflict and were left divided and impoverished. The aged leaders Oconostota and Attakullakulla had died and Old Tassel emerged as the Principal Chief. Old Tassel's influence was mostly limited to the Overhills, however, as Attakullakulla's son, Dragging Canoe, organized the Chickamaugan Confederation of refugee Cherokees and allies. The Chickamaugans were essentially independent of Chota and were much more hostile toward white encroachment. Nonetheless the Americans often made no distinctions between the actions of the two groups.

Much as the Cherokee had once been caught between the interests of the British and the French and later between the British and the Americans, they soon found themselves between the Spanish and the Americans. Although Spanish influence was limited at first, their growing presence encouraged the Creeks, Cherokee, and even the western settlers to oppose the states to the east.

During the colonial days the governing elite in the coastal areas defended the rights of the Indians, but they were unable to control the actions of the westernmost settlers. After the war the situation was even worse. Not only did the settlers obey no treaty obligations; the western settlers in North Carolina even set up their own government, the abortive State of Franklin. While the central government of the United States struggled to bring unity to Indian policy, Franklin ignored it. The United States signed the Treaty of Hopewell with the Cherokee, by which they were permitted to remove encroachers, forcibly if needed. Franklin did not recognize the legitimacy of the Hopewell document and forced the Cherokee to sign treaties under duress.

The conditions of the treaties were irreconcilable and the weak federal government was unable to enforce the Treaty of Hopewell. There was an escalation of border violence, which climaxed with the brutal assassination of Old Tassel by a Franklin militiaman and the subsequent desertion of Chota. As 1788 came to a close the Cherokee chose Little Turkey as the next Principal Chief with Ustanali as his capital. The United States was about to choose a new President under its new Constitution.

1784

The Cherokee Rebuff Spanish Diplomacy

The Congress of the United States ratified the Treaty of Paris on January 14, 1784, officially ending the Revolutionary War. To the dismay of their erstwhile Indian allies, the British had been defeated and were abandoning the southern half of the continent. The Cherokee and their neighboring tribes had supported the losing side and were being left to the mercies of the Americans and the Spanish. The Spanish did not intend to be passive neighbors of the new republic. Rather they challenged the United States immediately for influence over the southern Indians and closed navigation of the lower Mississippi River. The Cherokee established a trade relationship with the Spanish and were invited to attend an Indian conference in Pensacola, but the Raven and Old Tassel were reluctant to risk offending the Americans. The Cherokee diplomatically told the Spanish Governor Esteban Miro that the distance was too far and that they did not want to travel through Creek territory. Actually, the Spanish felt that the Cherokee were located too far away to be of much concern to them anyway.

After the death of Oconostota, Old Tassel and the Raven had assumed power and they believed that the best option was to build on the friendly overtures from Virginia's Governor Benjamin Harrison. Virginia was strapped for cash and was happy to foster a new trade relationship with the Cherokee. Indeed after the harvest the Cherokee did sell corn to settlers in the Holston area.

Not all of the Cherokee were enthusiastic about the leadership in Chota. Relations with the other states were not as friendly for one thing, and the inhabitants of the Lower and Middle Towns had suffered much worse at the hands of the Carolinians and Georgians. Chilhowie remained a hotbed of anti-American sentiment, and the Chickamaugan influence continued to grow. Continued attacks against American settlers by Rattlesnake of Chilhowie and Bench of the Chickamaugans threatened to provoke fresh retaliatory expeditions from North Carolina. Despite Cherokee protests to the representatives of the southern states, encroachment (as before) continued unabated.

While Old Tassel and the Raven sought to avoid being suspended between the Spanish and the Americans, the strategy had not worked well during previous conflicts. North Carolina ceded its western lands to Congress in June, much as Virginia had done. When the settlers of the Nolichucky and Watauga areas (North Carolina's Washington, Sullivan, and Greene counties) learned of the cession, they felt themselves to be without effective representation in government. For the same reasons they had declared independence from Britain, John Sevier and his followers believed they should declare independence from North Carolina. At a meeting in Jonesborough on August 23, the new State of Franklin was created. By the time the Franklinites met to establish the form of their new government, they were unaware that the newly elected North Carolina legislature had voted to rescind the western cession. There would be no basis for the State of Franklin as the lands were officially part of North Carolina again.

1785

The Treaties of Dumplin Creek and Hopewell

During 1785 American settlers continued their westward push despite opposition from the native tribes and competition from the Spanish. There were reports of English and French attempts to organize a western alliance of Indians from Canada to Florida to oppose American expansion and encroachment. Although alliances were formed under Shawnee leadership, the Six Nations, Delaware, Cherokee, and other tribes remained friendly to the new nation. The Chippewa, Ottawa, Delaware, and Wyandots ceded a tract of land to the United States that included most of modern Ohio. The increased settlement of previously established western outposts such as Kentucky and the Cumberland Settlement increased the friction with the Spanish.

The western settlers depended on navigation of the Mississippi to get agricultural products to market. Spain had closed the lower Mississippi to the Americans and was reluctant to open it, despite Ambassador John Jay's negotiations. The Spanish had been offended by Georgia's creation of Bourbon County (most of Alabama and Mississippi), since Spain had already laid claim to the same area by virtue of the Treaty of Versailles. Furthermore, Governor Don Estevan Miro of Louisiana received reports of more than three hundred boats being built on the Cumberland and Cherokee rivers. This sighting seemed to confirm suspicions that the Cumberland residents were planning to attack Spanish territory, perhaps with the help of General George Rogers Clark.

The rivalry between Spain and the United States found the Cherokee and the other southern Indians in the middle. The Indians were concerned that Britain may have illegally ceded rights to their lands and wanted to be included in negotiations between the Americans and the Spanish. Although the Indians tended to favor dealing with the United States, they were frustrated by the lack of a unified national Indian policy and even the Cherokee saw the Spanish as a potential ally should the Americans get unreasonable.

Virginia's new governor, Patrick Henry, continued Harrison's policy of friendship with the Cherokee. Trade continue between the Overhills and the western Virginia settlements, and Old Tassel even sought Virginia's influence in the struggle against the Carolinians and Franklinites. Virginia feared that reckless actions by the rebellious Franklinites could so offend the Creeks and the Cherokee that war would be unavoidable. Henry feared that the Indians would be pushed into an alliance with the Spanish. The Chickamauga faction was raiding western settlements already.

The Franklinites were the wild cards in this drama. Governor Alexander Martin sent Franklin Governor John Sevier a letter asking about Franklin's intention now that North Carolina's Assembly had rescinded the western land cession. Martin warned that Franklin would be left on its own to deal with the Indians should it insist on independence. Franklin's General Assembly replied by affirming its plan to form a new government and to deal with the Indians on its own terms. And it did. Governor Sevier invited the Cherokee for talks to define the boundary between them. Old Tassel, reluctant to lend legitimacy to the breakaway province, sent the inexperienced Anco of Chota with a delegation of lesser dignitaries to meet with Sevier at Henry's Station on Dumplin Creek, at the French Broad River. The Treaty of Dumplin Creek, which was signed on June 10, 1785, gave legitimacy to the settlements on the south bank of the French Broad River. The document gave Franklin the right to all lands south of the Holston and French Broad rivers, as far south as the ridge that divides the Little Tennessee from the Tennessee River. Although the Cherokee delegation received gifts, Old Tassel and the Council did not ratify the treaty. It is doubtful that Anco even knew what he was signing. Almost immediately a wave of Franklinite settlers moved onto the French Broad. Soon they would be building structures within two miles of Chota!

Meanwhile the United States Congress had recognized the need for a more unified Indian policy and had appointed commissioners to deal with the southern Indian tribes. The delegation, led by Benjamin Hawkins, included Daniel Carroll, William Perry, Lachlan McIntosh, Andrew Pickens, and Joseph Martin. The Commission organized a conference to be held at Hopewell, South Carolina, on the Keowee River. Old Tassel and Hanging Maw led a delegation of over nine hundred Cherokee at this, the first Indian conference sponsored by the federal government. The various states also sent representatives. William Blount, for example, represented North Carolina, but his main goal was to protect his own land investments in the Muscle Shoals area.

The conference at Hopewell began with an opening statement from a commissioner, stating that the Congress was now sovereign of the entire country and that it had no desire for Cherokee land. Old Tassel confirmed Cherokee friendship with the Americans and handed the commissioners a set of white beads. He went on to complain that the people of North Carolina had taken their lands without consideration and were making their fortunes from them. He especially complained about Richard Henderson, whom he called a liar. He said that Henderson had proposed buying a small tract of land in Kentucky at the Sycamore Shoals meeting, not the entire Kentucky and Cumberland territories. He said that if Attakullakulla had signed the deed, the Cherokee leadership was unaware of it and that any signature of Oconostota was a forgery. The Commission replied that the three men in question were all dead, and perhaps Old Tassel's memory was failing. An original copy of the document (signed by all three chiefs) was displayed. Thousands of Americans lived there and it would be impractical to move them. Old Tassel consented to the Commission's statement but implied that the Cherokee still had a claim.

Old Tassel went on to draw a map indicating the boundaries with which the Cherokee would be satisfied. He agreed to the highest ridge between the Tennessee and Cumberland rivers as a natural boundary (see Map 8 #10b, page 158) and then proceeded to complain about the illegal settlements between the Holston and French Broad rivers. The Commission agreed that the Treaty of Dumplin Creek was void, but did not promise at first to remove the Franklinites. In the final document, signed November 28, 1785, the southern half of the so-called State of Franklin was ceded back to the Cherokee! (See Map 3 #10a, page 26.) Cherokee boundaries with the Creek and Chickasaw also were defined. Before the signatures were applied, Old Tassel asked the Commission to allow Nancy Ward, the *ghigau*, to speak. She offered the peace pipe and spoke eloquently for the perpetual friendship between the Cherokee and the Americans.

The Treaty of Hopewell had a final clause that stated that any settler who had not removed himself from Cherokee lands within six months would be outside the protection of the United States and at the mercy of the Cherokee. Naturally this treaty was not popular with

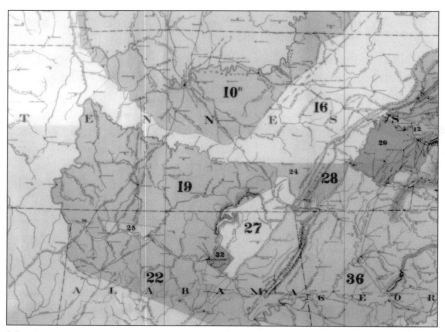

Map 8

North Carolina, Franklin, or the Cumberland settlements—it invited the Indians to attack. The question remained: Would the United States be able to enforce its new treaty?

1786

Problems with Franklin

The Treaty of Coyatee

In 1786 the Spanish hoped to dominate the Mississippi Valley and to secure claims to the lands north of Florida, although the Americans could easily overrun Florida and Louisiana if so provoked. The Spanish hoped that by blocking navigation of the Mississippi and access to the port at New Orleans, they could inhibit the growth of the American's westward settlement. Despite Spain's position of relative weakness, John

Jay, the American diplomat, did not succeed in lifting the blockade and even accepted a twenty-five-year extension of it. The eastern states accepted the terms of Jay's treaty since they had little to gain from opening the Mississippi, but in the end the opposition of the western states prevented its ratification.

The Spanish hoped that the southern Indians, especially the Creeks, would be useful in keeping the Americans out of the disputed territory. The Creeks held the best claim to land around Muscle Shoals that was within the area claimed by Spain. Alexander McGillivray, the mixed-blood chief of the Creeks, complained to the Spanish that the American claims had been based on illegal cession treaties. Unable to remove the American settlers from Muscle Shoals by peaceful means, McGillivray was determined to go to war. He requested help from the Spanish and personally visited the Cherokee to ask for their assistance. Requests also were sent out to the Chickasaw and Choctaw. As Georgia prepared a force of fifteen hundred men under Brigadier General Twiggs and Colonel Clark, it became clear that Franklin would probably support them. The Spanish King, however, offered little more than shelter to Creek refugees in the event of war. McGillivray feared that if the Cumberland settlements joined the force from Georgia, the Creeks could be destroyed much as the Cherokee had been before.

The Cherokee had their own problems in 1786. The Treaty of Hopewell had given encouragement to the Chickamauga and other hostile groups to attack white settlers along the French Broad and other parts of the Cherokee land. A large body of warriors, led by the mixed-blood chief John Watts, attacked the closest group of settlements. John Sevier retaliated by invading the Valley Towns and destroying three of them. A group of Cherokee warriors then brought back fifteen white scalps in retaliation for the murder of four Cherokee. The Cherokee declared that they wanted peace, but if Franklin wanted war, they were ready for a fight. Dragging Canoe was already preparing an invasion of the Cumberland area anyway. The Franklinites were incensed, for among the dead was Colonel John Donelson and Colonel William Christian.

In August General William Cocke and Colonel Alexander Outlaw marched two hundred fifty men into Chota and demanded satisfaction. Old Tassel and Hanging Maw protested that they had not murdered Donelson and Christian and that Chota should not be punished. The

Franklinites moved into Coyatee, about twenty miles away, where they caught two of the braves involved in the murders. The Cherokee chiefs were rounded up and under duress forced to sign the Treaty of Coyatee, by which the Treaty of Dumplin Creek was upheld and the Treaty of Hopewell denied. The Franklinites claimed that North Carolina had granted them all of the land north of the Tennessee River all the way to Cumberland Mountain. Even though the language of the document included references to peace and brotherly love, the Cherokee were told in no uncertain terms that Franklin would make good its claims by force if needed. Old Tassel asserted that the United States commissioners had not mentioned any such cession and in this passive way refused to recognize this bald-faced attempt to steal Cherokee land. The motivation for the Franklinites was more than just blood revenge. Governor Sevier and others were investors in land speculation around Muscle Shoals, which was included in the cession. The operation also put Franklin in a better position to help Georgia in its attempt to rid the area of the Creeks.

1787

Chickamaugans Continue Guerrilla Warfare as
Virginia and Franklin Allow Encroachment

The year 1787 was critical for the United States. The Articles of Confederation had proven unsatisfactory, so a Constitutional Convention was convened in Philadelphia. Over the course of the year the Constitution was drafted and on December 7, 1787, Delaware became the first state to ratify it. Although Indians did attend the conference (Sconetoyah is reported to have represented the Cherokee), the document says very little about them, other than that Congress was granted powers to regulate trade with them.

During 1787 Spain continued to be an irritant on the southern frontier. The blockade of American navigation of the Mississippi angered the western settlers, some of whom were even considering seceding from the United States in order to negotiate directly with Spain. Governor Arturo O'Neill of Spanish West Florida developed a friendly relationship with Chief Alexander McGillivray of the Creeks and lent support to the Creek attacks upon illegal American settlements at Muscle Shoals. He discouraged attacks on the Cumberland settlements, however, for fear of retaliation, but the Creeks and Chickamauga waged war there anyway. As Georgia prepared over three thousand troops to attack the Creeks, the United States asked Spain to stay out of the conflict.

Continuing violence marred Cherokee hopes for peace in 1787. Early in the year the Council met at Chota and decided to move some of the towns further south, as the Franklinites were encroaching even on the cornfields of Chota! Old Tassel observed that the Americans moved onto Cherokee land faster after a treaty than before. The circumstances were very confused and tense. Cherokee retaliations against encroachment had become numerous, as the Treaty of Hopewell sanctioned them. The State of Franklin ignored the treaty and further inflamed the situation by opening a land office to sell deeds to the land in question.

Colonel Benjamin Logan organized an expedition to punish the Chickamaugans for attacks on American settlements. His group killed some Cherokee near Cumberland Mountain, one of whom was a chief from Chota. Logan tried to lie about the situation but eventually admitted to Virginia Governor Edmund Randolph that they had mistaken the innocent Cherokee for some Chickamaugans. This was just one of many aggressive actions that spoiled relations between the Cherokee and the Americans. Governor Randolph apologized to the Cherokee and promised to prosecute the guilty party. He went on to warn the Cherokee, however, that it was up to them to keep the peace.

Old Tassel was offended by Governor Randolph's tone and suggested that the Virginian should get his facts straight before blaming the Cherokee. He blamed the Creeks and the Shawnee for many of the attacks. Old Tassel pointed out that he had once been part of the Chickamauga, but that now he was devoted to peace and that he had thwarted many Indian plans for violence. He went on to complain about how the Americans had taken so much of the Cherokee lands illegally and quipped that if the Cherokee had less land, they would have fewer enemies! Old Tassel ended by noting that if Virginia could not help the Cherokee cause, then perhaps Spain could. The Cherokee continued a guerrilla campaign against the Franklin settlements along the French Broad, and despite assurances of friendship from Abram of Chilhowie

(Halfbeer) and Allekieskee (another Chickamauga chief), attacks on the Cumberland continued as well.

1788

Escalation of Fighting with Franklin

The Murders of Old Tassel and Old Abram

The year 1788 was tumultuous for the Cherokee, and it was a pivotal year in the history of the United States. The individual states pursued their own Indian policies while the United States government struggled to create a unified approach. The situation was worse than before, however, since the most aggressive and hostile settlers were now organized into the rebellious State of Franklin.

On July 2, Cyrus Griffin, President of Congress, announced that nine states had ratified the Constitution and that it was officially adopted as the nation's charter. The individual states had agreed to forfeit certain rights for the welfare of the nation as a whole. Congress elected Joseph Martin Agent for the Cherokee, at the urging of Governor Edmund Randolph of Virginia. Secretary of War Henry Knox asked Martin to apprise Congress, through him, of any grievances the Cherokee may hold. On September 1 Congress issued a proclamation defining the borders of the southern Indians, including the Cherokee. The proclamation declared that Americans living on land promised to the Indians through the Treaty of Hopewell should move. The document also directed Secretary Knox to provide troops to protect the Cherokee, as had been requested by Virginia and South Carolina. Within a month Cherokee representatives petitioned Congress for protection against Franklin and Kentucky. Despite the intentions of Congress, the body adjourned on November 1. This was the last Congress under the Articles of Confederation, and the first Congress under the new Constitution would not meet until April. There would be no federal government for several months.

The Spanish felt insecure in their positions in Louisiana and Florida, which they believed Britain wanted back. They were also nervous about the possibility of an invasion by militias from Kentucky, the Cumberland settlement, and Franklin, since all of these territories were affected by Spain's blockade of the Mississippi River. Also, North Carolina, Franklin, and Georgia all asserted claims to Muscle Shoals (which the Spanish considered part of Florida), and were perhaps willing to take it by force. The western Americans, on the other hand, feared that Spain was encouraging the Creeks to wage war against Georgia and South Carolina. The truth was that the Spanish had no desire to be drawn into a war with the United States on behalf of the Creeks. Florida Governor Arturo O'Neill did not trust Alexander McGillivray since he was simultaneously negotiating an end to war against the Cumberland settlements while asking for help against Georgia. While encouraging McGillivray to seek a peaceful solution with Georgia, O'Neill recommended to Governor Miro that the Spanish limit the amount of ammunition sold to the Creeks. The Spanish even offered to allow settlement of expatriate Americans and Indians in Florida and Louisiana. But for McGillivray the issue was not negotiable. The Treaty of Hopewell (between the United States and the Creek Nation) had forced the Creeks to cede land that McGillivray thought was vital to the Creek national interest. Again the Spanish felt that the Creeks had not been sufficiently provoked to warrant a new war.

Interestingly, the western settlers believed the Spanish declarations of peaceful intentions and abandoned any plans for hostile intervention. Indeed, many of the settlers were disappointed with their own governments. They felt that neither the individual states nor the central government was capable or willing to provide military protection against the Indians or to protect their trade interests. Individual settlers had expressed a willingness to pledge loyalty to Spain in exchange for military protection and trade privileges. As the government of the irregular State of Franklin began to unravel, Governor John Sevier even made serious overtures toward the Spanish. The new governor of North Carolina, Samuel Johnston, had called for the arrest of John Sevier, for treasonous acts against the state. In letters he wrote to Diego de Gardoqui, the Spanish representative in the United States, Sevier expressed a desire for an alliance with Spain and asked for immediate material aid. He had just defeated the Cherokee in a new set of raids and he wanted Spain to restrain the other southern Indians from helping them. Time was of the essence, since North Carolina had not yet ratified the Constitution and was not technically part of the United States, so it was argued. By the time Governor Miro learned of this intrigue, John Sevier had been arrested and taken to North Carolina for trial, and the State of Franklin was essentially defunct. Sevier reconciled with North Carolina and was not punished. Ironically, he was appointed United States Representative in 1789 for the congressional district in the western part of the state, now known as the "Mero District."

For the Cherokee in 1788 the most important "foreign" relationship was with the State of Franklin. Despite peaceful intentions of the leadership at Chota, the influence of Old Tassel and Hanging Maw was waning. Cherokee continued to abandon the Overhills to join ranks with the Chickamauga. The national festivals were no longer even held in Chota. The Chickamaugans and the Creeks continued to attack the Cumberland settlements and were probably responsible for most attacks against the Franklin settlements south of the French Broad. Casualties were significant. Even James Robertson lost a son to Indian raids in the Cumberland. The most significant Cherokee act of violence, however, was Slim Tom's murder of the Kirk family in May. The Kirk family flouted the Cherokee by daring to settle within nine miles of Chota on the Little Tennessee River. John Kirk Jr. was away at the time of the massacre and came home to find the bodies of his mother, father, and siblings.

This heinous act prompted Governor Sevier to organize a retaliatory expedition against the Cherokee. The Overhills blamed the Chickamauga, and General Joseph Martin tried to persuade Sevier not to fight, but the Franklinite was not subject to the laws of other states. Governor Sevier and Major James Hubbard led one hundred fifty men in a two-pronged attack against Chota and the towns on the Hiwassee. Sevier destroyed the town of Hiwassee, then turned his men toward Chota to meet up with Hubbard. Chota, which had flown a white peace flag for three years, had been abandoned and so avoided destruction. While passing through Chota on the way to Chilhowie, Hubbard issued an invitation for the chiefs to meet with him. Old Tassel, Old Abram, and several others gathered to meet with the Franklinites in the council house in Chilhowie. Once all were seated, the Cherokee chiefs were forcibly restrained while John Kirk Jr. was allowed to personally slaughtered them with a tomahawk.

The brutal assassination of the Cherokee chiefs led to a fresh outbreak of violence against the settlers, and led North Carolina to seek the arrest of John Sevier. Joseph Martin was forced to lead a war party against the Chickamaugans later that summer to try to quell the hostilities. The Chickamaugans were ready for the expedition, however, and had abandoned their towns. Martin's advance scouts drew heavy fire from Indians lying in ambush, so he called for a hasty retreat. The Chickamaugans followed up in October with an attack on Gillespie's Station (on the Holston River, near the Little Tennessee). In a letter addressed to John Sevier and Joseph Martin and signed by Bloody Fellow, Categiskey, John Watts, and Glass, the Indians apologized for killing the women and children. The letter also reminded them of the cruel assassination of Old Tassel and Old Abram and suggested that peace would return when the white people left Cherokee land. The letter threatened to attack with a force of five thousand men unless the area were cleared within thirty days. Naturally the Gillespie massacre inspired Sevier to raise another militia and to sweep into Cherokee territory all the way to the Coosa settlements. By year's end the Cherokee representatives were asking for protection, and Congress was promising relief.

Little Turkey assumed power as the new Principal Chief, even though he was not from Chota. In fact, Chota was abandoned, as it was too close to Franklin for comfort. Many more of the Cherokee moved southward to join the Chickamauga or to settle in South Carolina and Georgia. Ustanali, on the headwaters of the Coosawatie River, became the new capital. Richard Winn, Indian Superintendent for the Southern Department, recognized the new regime and met with Little Turkey, Hanging Maw, Dragging Canoe, Watts, and others at Ustanali in November. Once again a time of great promise had become a time of cataclysm.

Chapter Eight

1789–1794

The Early Federal Period

The establishment of the new government of the United States under the Constitution sparked a rebirth of interest in centralization of Indian policy. War with the Indians was raging in the Northwest Territory so it was necessary to maintain peace in the South. Eventually a program would be introduced to "civilize" the Indians by teaching them English, converting them to Christianity, and establishing new agricultural economies. These goals were delayed while the United States and Spain competed for influence over the southern tribes. The Cherokee and the others were once again used as pawns between two white powers.

American governmental policy and the actions of Americans were not necessarily the same. Although federal laws mandated that only Congress could declare war, the inhabitants of Georgia and the Southwest Territory thought that they always had the right to defend themselves. While an offensive measure might actually be defensive in that it prevented future attacks, the leaders of the states and territories understood that the federal government would not tolerate such actions. William Blount and James Robertson were two leaders who mastered the art of "getting the job done" while maintaining an appearance of propriety.

The Cherokee themselves remained divided and at war. The nation had been fractured since the outset of the American Revolution and had been subject to destructive raids ever since. After the assassination of

Old Tassel in 1788, Little Turkey, the new Principal Chief, established a new capital at Ustanli, a hundred miles to the southwest of Chota. During the next few years the Cherokee were gradually subdued by the Americans and abandoned by the Spanish. At the end of the period the tribe was at peace for the first time in nearly twenty years, but the tribe had been transformed almost beyond recognition!

1789

The Cherokee Look for Allies

President Washington Proposes a "Civilization" Program

This was a year for new beginnings. After the murder of Old Tassel and the abandonment of Chota, the new Cherokee Principal Chief Little Turkey established his capital at Ustanali. The new Constitution of the United States went into full effect with the opening of the first Congress and the inauguration of George Washington as president. While the new republic quickly took measures to establish a stronger federal authority, the new Cherokee regime presided over a more deeply divided people. The distinction between the Cherokee and the Chickamauga was becoming more blurred as the Cherokee government became more of a loose association of villages. Conditions were so bad that many Cherokee even migrated westward to settle near St. Louis and along the Arkansas River under the protection of the Spanish.

Although border incidents continued in 1789, the intensity of the warfare was much less than it had been the year before. The Cherokee had been severely chastised and were unable to prosecute much of war effort without significant outside assistance. The Creeks were natural allies in the struggle against encroachment, but they were likewise stymied by the lack of support from Spain. Although the Spanish had been willing to provide refuge to both Indian and white refugees, they were involved in a diplomatic dispute with Britain over claims to Nootka Sound, and were reluctant to offend the United States. In 1788 John Sevier had made overtures to Spain that Franklin was interested in detaching from the United States in order to join the Spanish Empire. Similarly, after the murder of James Robertson's son, the Cumberland leader also suggested that the Spanish might be better able to protect settlers from Indian attacks. Although the Spanish governor did offer some minor navigation concessions, Miro realized that the westerners were more interested in independence from North Carolina rather than any real alliance with Spain. He also did not think that it was worth the risk of provoking the United States. Finally Spain offered no help for the western settlers in achieving independence, although he said that Spain would be friendly if they did separate from the United States.

With Spain remaining neutral, the Creeks and the Cherokee looked for other potential allies. At a meeting in Creek territory the two tribes petitioned their old friend King George III of Great Britain for help in a letter signed by Little Turkey, Hanging Maw, Dragging Canoe, and others. The letter wound up in the hands of William A. Bowles, whether he was at the meeting or not. Although it would eventually make its way to Europe, it had no immediate effect on the Indians' condition. The Cherokee and the Creeks also met with the Shawnee and the Iroquois at Buffalo Creek in September. The Cherokee pled for assistance and chastised the other Indians for lack of support and for disunity among the northern tribes.

With a lack of allies and their own state of disarray, the Cherokee were lucky that the frontier was relatively quiet in 1789. The western settlers were in a bit of disarray themselves. The State of Franklin collapsed in 1788, and John Sevier took an oath of loyalty to North Carolina in 1789. The Cumberland settlers were in a weakened condition and posed no immediate threat. Political maneuvering led North Carolina to ratify the Constitution in November, and the next month its legislature ceded its western lands (including all of the former Franklin and the Mero District) to Congress (again). It seems that the westerners were too preoccupied with their own problems to launch any new initiatives against the Cherokee.

Not that the United States failed to seek diplomatic opportunities with the Cherokee. Early in the year arrangements had been made for the Chickamauga and the Cherokee to meet with Joseph Martin in May. When the Cherokee failed to show up at the designated spot, Martin and his commissioners waited twelve days before moving on into Creek territory. Meanwhile the Cherokee were staging frontier raids and had met with British representatives (Bowles?). Martin learned of the new attacks and tactfully declined a new Cherokee offer to meet in council.

The United States had not forgotten about earlier commitments to the Cherokee. Secretary of War Henry Knox worried about a possible alliance of the Cherokee, Creeks, and Spanish. He urged President Washington to order a review of the Treaty of Hopewell and to commit to enforcing it. He went on to propose a new program of "civilizing" the Cherokee and other Indians. Knox envisioned a program by which the Cherokee would be given sheep and taught the principles of cultivation and animal husbandry. Missionaries would be sent into Indian territories to convert the native peoples to Christianity.

1790

Creeks and Cherokee Appeal for Help from Britain through William A. Bowles

The year 1790 was a quiet one of rebuilding for the Cherokee. There were hostilities committed against white settlers, but no large-scale wars were fought. The new national government was becoming organized and was beginning to assert its federal powers. Thomas Jefferson arrived from France and assumed his role as Secretary of State on March 22. A couple of weeks later Secretary of War Henry Knox sent a stern warning to General Anthony Wayne that Georgia could not negotiate a separate treaty with the Indians; that power was reserved for the federal government.

Now that North Carolina had formally ceded its western lands to Congress, the strip of land including Franklin and the Mero District was organized as the Territory of the United States South of the River Ohio. Since Kentucky was part of Virginia, the land known as "The Southwest Territory" really just included what is now Tennessee. President Washington appointed William Blount (who had represented North Carolina at the Constitutional Convention) as both Governor and Indian Superintendent for the Southern District. Jefferson confirmed to Knox that the Treaty of Hopewell was still in effect and that North Carolina no longer had any right to obtain lands directly from the Cherokee: the states had to ask the United States to negotiate for them. Knox instructed Blount to begin negotiations with the Cherokee, offering a one thousand dollar annuity for all lands occupied by settlers. The Cherokee were initially cool to the proposal.

The United States had a more serious problem with the outbreak of war with the Indians in the Northwest Territory and thus was motivated to keep the peace with the Creeks as well. Knox met with Alexander McGillivray in Federal Hall in New York that summer. A treaty was signed by which the Creeks recognized American sovereignty over their lands. McGillivray was rewarded with a commission as a Brigadier General. The era of peace between the United States and the Creeks was short-lived as the Spanish quickly reasserted their influence over the tribe and began to arouse hostile sentiments, inducing the Creeks to resume attacks on the southern frontiers.

The Creeks were easy to arouse because of the attempts of the Yazoo Company to settle westernmost Georgia and the efforts of others to settle Muscle Shoals. The Creeks were obviously opposed to any encroachment on their lands since Congress had defined all of their boundaries and there was no more new land to compensate them. James O'Fallon of the Yazoo Company assured Governor Miro that the settlers would consider themselves subjects of the King of Spain, but Miro feared that he would have a new Franklin or Kentucky on his own doorsteps and rejected the proposals. Florida Governor Arturo O'Neill did not trust McGillivray, and he was afraid that the Creeks would help Great Britain take back St. Augustine. But overall, the Creeks and the Spanish found that they had more to gain from mutual assistance.

One of the stranger events of 1790 was reminiscent of Alexander Cuming's adventure sixty years earlier. William Augustus Bowles, who had no more legitimacy as a diplomat than Cuming had had, carried letters from the Creeks and the Cherokee to take to the King. He went to Canada with several Indians and met with Secretary of State Lord Dorchester. Bowles announced his desire to accompany the Indians to London to present their letters directly to King George III. Dorchester advised against such a plan and offered to send the letters by post, but Bowles insisted that the Indians were authorized by their leaders only to deliver the notes personally. Bowles went on to explain that he had information that the Americans were planning to attack the northern outposts (still occupied by the British in defiance of the Treaty of Paris) and that the southern Indians were planning on taking St. Augustine back for the British. Dorchester relented and even agreed to provide money for the trip to England. Even though Lord Grenville approved of Dorchester's actions, the King finally refused to grant Bowles an audience or to accept the letters from the Indians!

1791

The Treaty of Holston

In January 1791 William A. Bowles continued his efforts in London to obtain an audience with King George III. He insisted to Lord Grenville that the Cherokee wanted the right to trade with the British West Indies (which was denied to the United States) and that they were willing to take over Spanish ports to access the sea, if needed. When repulsed by the British minister, Bowles then addressed a letter to the Spanish King asking for an alliance with the Creeks and Cherokee. The Spanish recognized Bowles as a "huckster" and suspected his retinue of Indians of being masqueraders. Upon learning that Bowles had returned to North America and was possibly in Florida, Spain issued a warrant for his arrest. Meanwhile Bowles met with the Creek Indians and informed them that the British had granted them the right to return to the lands taken from them during and after the American Revolution. Wisely, the Creek leaders decided that they would not try to stake that claim unless the British arrived with military support. When Jefferson asked the new British Ambassador about Bowles' assertion, George Hammond disavowed any knowledge of Bowles and stated that the British had no such policy regarding Creek lands!

It turns out that the British were fostering a growing relation with the Cherokee, or at least the Chickamauga Confederation. Dragging Canoe had made overtures to the British in Canada for material and military assistance. Alexander McKee sent Dragging Canoe some presents and a letter promising further support. British influence was waxing as the Spanish influence was beginning to crumble. Britain had won concessions from Spain in the Nootka Sound negotiations. The Spanish felt threatened by the British, the Americans, and the Indians. They feared that the British might forcibly take back Florida, and the Bowles affair reinforced this concern. Meanwhile the persistent pressures of the Yazoo Company and other American land companies added concerns over encroachment into Spanish territory and the establishment of more American states close to New Orleans. The western settlers still needed access to the Mississippi River, and even though James O'Fallon, James Wilkinson, and other westerners still maintained an interest in becoming Spanish subjects, the Spanish governors did not believe they were sincere. Hector, Baron de Carondelet, the new Governor of Louisiana, hoped that the Cherokee and other Indians might serve as a buffer between Spain and the United States. There was still mutual distrust between Spain and the Indians, however. The Chickasaw and the Choctaw opposed the building of Fort Nogales in their territory, but Spain feared that without it the Americans would soon be encroaching there too.

The Cherokee were generally at peace in 1791 although Bloody Fellow, John Watts, and Glass were involved in hostilities at Muscle Shoals and in the Cumberland. Nonetheless, the peace process was not to be derailed. William Blount confided to Joseph Martin that he had instructions to meet with the Cherokee in June and that if the Cherokee did not appear to negotiate, another punitive military expedition would be launched. Governor Blount opened the meeting on June 26 at White's Fort on the banks of the Holston River at the mouth of the French Broad. Dragging Canoe, Bloody Fellow, Doublehead, John Watts, Lying Fawn, and others represented the Chickamaugans. The conservative faction included Little Turkey, Hanging Maw, and several others. Blount began by offering a treaty similar to one accepted by the Creeks in 1790. The Cherokee were reluctant to give up lands that they loved, but did accept the treaty.

The Treaty of Holston was signed on July 2, 1791. (See Map 3 #11, page 26.) The treaty confirmed Cherokee cessions of the Cumberland area and most of the settled areas of the eastern part of the Southwest Territory. The United States was given exclusive rights to regulate trade with the Cherokee, and the Cherokee were prohibited from engaging in negotiations with any other political entity or individuals. Americans were prohibited from hunting on Cherokee lands or from trespassing without a passport, although they were allowed to build a road connecting the eastern counties with the Cumberland. It was agreed that Cherokees committing crimes against citizens of the United States would be punished according to American law, while American citizens committing crimes against Cherokees would be punished according to tribal law. The Cherokee also agreed to a proposal by the United States to establish a "civilization" program in their territory. Alexander McGillivray, who was present at the negotiations as an observer, told the Spanish that he supported the treaty too because the Americans promised not to establish posts on the Cherokee (Tennessee) River nor at the mouth of the Ohio.

Once again the Cherokee had given up land as the price for peace, but this time there seemed to be a better sense that the terms were fair and that future relations with the United States would be better under the new government. Still, many of the Cherokee were unhappy with the terms of the new treaty and a delegation led by Bloody Fellow was sent to Philadelphia to reopen negotiations.

1792

Cherokee Leaders Refine Relations with the United States

The Five Lower Towns Declare War

The year 1792 witnessed a flurry of diplomatic activity as tensions between the United States and Spain increased and the importance of the southern tribes was heightened. Carondelet, the new governor of Louisiana, was more aggressive about using the Indians to help protect Spanish interest than was his predecessor, Miro. He envisioned the formation of a defensive alliance of southern tribes that could repel American aggression through unified action. Carondelet was certain that the United States would eventually try to push all of the Indians west of the Mississippi and that they would do it by gaining the confidence of the tribes one at a time. The achievement of statehood for Kentucky underscored the risk of allowing any new settlements near the Spanish possessions. As the Americans aggressively tried to build new settlements at Muscle Shoals, Tombigbee, and Natchez, Spain could only hope that the Indians who held title to these lands would refuse to cede them. Carondelet believed that the time was ripe for the southern Indians to attack the United States, since the American army was preoccupied in the Northwest Territory and would not be able to defend Kentucky and the Mero District. For all of the governor's encouragement of the southern alliance, the policy of the Spanish King was to support the Indians only if attacked by the United States. Spain could not risk supporting them in a war of aggression.

During 1792 the Cherokee became even more deeply divided. Opposition to the Treaty of Holston, especially in the five Lower Towns (on the south bank of the Cherokee River), spurred the Cherokee to send a delegation to Philadelphia to protest. Bloody Fellow, Kingfisher, the Northward, the Disturber, and the Prince met with President Washington on January 4, and over the next weeks meetings were held with Secretary of War Henry Knox too. The Americans agreed to increase the annuity granted in return for the lands in eastern Southwest Territory and promised to oppose encroachment. Furthermore, the United States agreed to oppose the settlement of Muscle Shoals. Leonard Shaw was appointed as an agent to live among the Cherokee. Bloody Fellow was re-named "Iskagua" or "Clear Sky" and was given the title of Brigadier General. He was given an American flag, and a peace medal was struck in his honor. Knox also responded to letters brought from other tribes. He reassured the southern Indians that the military build-up was directed toward the Kickapoos and their allies and that the United States did not covet any Chickasaw or Choctaw land. He also reassured them that William Bowles was a fraud and had no backing from Spain or Britain.

While Bloody Fellow was away, differences between the Chickamauga and peace factions approached the breaking point. Dragging Canoe died suddenly on March 1 during a dance ceremony. John Watts picked up the mantle of leadership of the Five Lower Towns and encouraged closer cooperation with the Creeks and Shawnee, who were on the verge of declaring war on the United States. Little Turkey, the leader of the peace faction, disassociated the Cherokee from the action of the Lower Towns and at one point even suggested to the Americans that he would not object to efforts to chastise the Lower Towns.

On April 22 at Knoxville Hanging Maw welcomed Bloody Fellow and the rest of the delegation returning from Philadelphia. Leonard Shaw, the new agent, briefed Governor William Blount about the amendments to the Treaty of Holston. Blount may have been offended at being left out of the new negotiations, since he was also Indian Commissioner for the southern tribes, but he did not show it. The Cherokee decided to meet at Coyatee, and Blount joined them there to discuss the new terms. The Cherokee chiefs attending the May 20 conference at Coyatee included Bloody Fellow, John Watts, Nontuacka, Hanging Maw, and several others. At the conference Governor Blount invited the Cherokee to send representatives to a meeting to be held in Nashville to address issues affecting the Chickasaw and Choctaw.

Apparently the meeting at Coyatee did not go very well. The next month at the Grand Council at Ustanali Little Turkey lamented that they had granted free navigation of the Cherokee River and that nothing had been done to thwart the settlement at Muscle Shoals. John Watts and Bloody Fellow skipped the Grand Council to travel to Pensacola and New Orleans. Perhaps under the influence of John McDonald, the veteran trader from Chickamauga, the Lower Town chiefs decided to see if Spain had more to offer them than the United States. By July the Lower Towns had seceded from the other Cherokee, and their warriors were attacking the Cumberlands and trying to intercept boats carrying treaty goods. A militia was formed at Nashville with intentions to punish the Lower Towns. Despite having been wounded during a raid, James Robertson enforced the policy of the United States and prevented the militia from acting, except as a defensive force.

Meanwhile Blount's meeting was held at Nashville on August 7. Over five hundred Chickasaw attended, as did one hundred seventy Choctaw and a small group of Cherokee. The Spanish and the Creeks put pressure on the financially destitute Choctaw not to attend; otherwise their delegation would have been much bigger. Blount asked for help in opposing Shawnee aggression. The Chickasaw complained about possible Cherokee designs on their territory. Blount asked the tribes to mark off their boundaries but did not pressure any of them for land cessions. He agreed to Chickasaw requests for farm implements, much as the Cherokee had already received.

In September the Five Lower Towns declared war on the United States and immediately organized a joint attack on the Cumberlands with the Creeks and the Shawnee. Two hundred Cherokee warriors under John Watts joined five hundred fifty Creeks and about thirty Shawnee in an expedition aimed at destroying Nashville. The Cherokee insisted that they should attack Buchanan's Station before moving on Nashville, despite objections from the Creeks. Robertson was prepared with his defensive militia and the Indians were routed. Two Creek leaders were killed and John Watts was seriously wounded. The warriors had no choice but to retreat and abandon the attack on Nashville.

Meanwhile, Bloody Fellow met with Governor Carondelet in New Orleans and asked the Spanish to occupy the old French forts at Tombigbee and Muscle Shoals. Much to Bloody Fellow's chagrin, the Spanish insisted that the Cherokee end the war against the United States. Carondelet suggested that Spain would negotiate with the Americans on behalf of the Cherokee. At the same time Spain was making overtures toward the peace faction. The Cherokee were evidently concerned that John Sevier and his new militia were not likely to distinguish between the Five Lower Towns and the rest of the tribe. The Cherokee failed to show for a meeting in October to demarcate the boundary, but amidst this confusion Hanging Maw arrived in Knoxville on Christmas Day to deliver peace talks from John Watts.

1793

Escalation of War Between the Cherokee and Southwest Territory

On the global stage the first three months of 1793 were tumultuous. The execution of King Louis XVI of France and his Queen, Marie Antoinette, was followed by a declaration of war by the revolutionary government of France against Britain, Spain, and the Netherlands. In the United States George Washington was inaugurated for his second term as President, and he continued to face the challenges of forging a federal government out of a collection of states while avoiding unnecessary warfare.

Although a general Indian conference was held at Miami Rapids (which Cherokee representatives did attend), Indian policy was dominated by the prosecution of war in the Northwest Territory against the Kickapoos and their allies and the avoidance of war against the southern Indians. For the Cherokee, their concerns in 1793 were entirely local. Except for a plea from Little Turkey for assistance from the British in Canada, Cherokee diplomacy was limited to dealing with the United States and Spain. Spain continued to see the southern Indians as a necessary buffer between the United States and Louisiana. Governor Carondelet accused the United States of planning the eradication of the Cherokee after the Kickapoo war was over. He feared that the Americans would win over the tribes one at a time and eventually move them all west of the Mississippi. The Spanish possessions would then be at the mercy of the United States.

Carondelet's strategy was to organize the four southern tribes into a defensive alliance. Each tribe would be equally represented, and no tribe could declare war or negotiate peace without the consent of the others. Contrary to reports in the western newspapers, Carondelet did not encourage the Indians to attack the United States, and it was clear that Spain would not directly aid them unless they were themselves attacked. Spain hoped that this alliance of Indians would allow them to maintain forts along the Mississippi, giving them control of both banks all the way to the mouth of the Ohio. The United States would be contained to its current territory.

Plans to organize a conference of the four southern tribes were quickly complicated by a series of events. War broke out between the Creeks and the Chickasaw in February, with the Cherokee maintaining neutrality. Alexander McGillivray, the Creek chief and Spanish ally, died a few days later. Undoubtedly Spanish influence over the Creeks suffered, and the tribe as a whole was splintered into factions. Carondelet immediately suspected that Governor Blount of the Southwest Territory had trumped up this war to distract the Creeks from their constant raiding of the Cumberlands. Carondelet further suspected that the Americans would use the situation to gain access to fortresses at Muscle Shoals and at the old French fort at Chickasaw Bluffs. He was furious to learn that James Robertson's son arrived at Nashville not just with corn for the Chickasaw, but also with small cannons! Fortunately the Creeks and the Chickasaw seem to have worked out their differences by the middle of the summer and Carondelet could get on with his conference.

The meeting was to be held at Nogales in the fall after the Green Corn Festival. The Choctaw were initially reluctant to meet with the Creeks and the Cherokee because they were notorious for stealing horses. In the long run the Choctaw agreed to attend and even ceded a tract of land for the Spanish build a defensive fort. The newly reconciled Chickasaw and Creeks sent representatives to the meeting at Nogales, and on October 28 a treaty was signed. An invitation had been sent to Bloody Fellow, but no Cherokee chiefs attended. The Creeks claimed to represent the interests of the Cherokee. Spain promised the Cherokee in their absence an annuity plus military protection.

A Cherokee delegation arrived in Nogales a couple of weeks later. Little Turkey explained that Bloody Fellow had been detained by war and that the travel distance was great, considering the circumstances. The Cherokee ratified the treaty and were glad to attain the help of the Spanish since they were in the midst of a war with local American militias. There were no substantial gifts for the Cherokee at Nogales or Natchez, so they were directed to proceed on to New Orleans. Carondelet was satisfied that so long as the Cumberland settlements were preoccupied with defending themselves against Indian attacks, they could be no threat to Louisiana.

In 1793 the Cherokee were a destitute people still divided into a peace faction, led by Little Turkey and Hanging Maw, and the Chickamaugans (closely identified with the Creeks), led by John Watts and Bloody Fellow. As usual the peaceful Indians suffered from indiscriminate retaliations for deeds perpetrated by the others. At the beginning of the year the Creeks and Chickamaugans were raiding the Cumberland settlements with such intensity that people could hardly leave their fortifications for fear of being killed. Some prominent citizens such as Evan Shelby and Isaac Bledsoe met their deaths during these raids. Doublehead and his followers were responsible for one particularly brutal act in which Captain William Overall and his companion were killed and cannibalized.

Meanwhile Governor Blount faced a difficult situation. The citizens of his territory needed relief from the Indian attacks and were organizing themselves into militia, but without a federal declaration of war, they could not be allowed to go on offensive expeditions. Although President Washington had appointed Blount, he eventually had to answer to his people—and protect his land investments. Under orders from Philadelphia Blount held a meeting at Henry's Station with Hanging Maw, John Watts, and Doublehead. Blount explained to them how peaceful Cherokee could protect themselves from being misidentified as warring Creeks. Blount was going to Philadelphia in April to ask

Washington to declare war on the Creeks and invited the Cherokee to meet him there. Perhaps under the influence of Agent Leonard Shaw, who warned the Cherokee not to trust Blount, the Indians decided not to go to Philadelphia. Rains and flooding had caused a lull in the fighting, but the weather cleared up and the raids resumed. John Watts met with Blount again at the mouth of the Holston and received direction to meet at Chota the next month. Although Blount would not be there, his representatives would be.

Governor Blount left Knoxville on June 7, leaving Secretary Daniel Smith in charge of the Southwest Territory. Blount was going to ask the President to declare war on the Creeks whether the Cherokee joined him or not. Before he left, the Governor dispatched Major Hugh Beard to defend the Mero District against Creek attacks. Blount had not been gone a week before Beard defied orders and committed an aggressive act. The Cherokee leaders were assembled at Chota as had been directed by the President. Beard's men burst into the home of Hanging Maw and killed several, including his wife. Hanging Maw was wounded, as was the daughter of Nancy Ward, the *ghigau*. In further defiance of Secretary Smith, Major Beard proceeded to march against the Hiwasee villages and kill more Cherokee.

The violent betrayal of Hanging Maw triggered a new wave of hostilities, led by John Watts and Doublehead. An assembly of a thousand warriors marched toward Knoxville where the public stores were kept. Disorganization among the warriors lead to some strategic mistakes, and the attack on Knoxville never took place. They did attack a small station nearby and (under the direction of Doublehead) committed atrocities against innocent women and children. Secreatary Smith was under extreme pressure to exert military force against the avenging Cherokee, but he could not lawfully promote the vigilante militia. He therefore directed General John Sevier to lead an expedition against the Creeks, Cherokee, and Chickamauga. Sevier led seven hundred men to Ustanali. The town was deserted but it was full of provisions left behind. The Cherokee tried to dislodge Sevier through nighttime attacks but were unsuccessful. After a few days the soldiers burned the town and went on to Etowah, a town occupied by Creeks and Cherokee. Despite their fortifications, the Indians were routed and the town was destroyed. Having lost but three men, Sevier headed back home.

While Sevier was in Georgia, other Cherokee and Creeks attacked settlements further north, taking advantage of his absence. Little Turkey went to Nogales to seek Spanish aid. Once the news of Sevier's success came, however, Indian attacks came to an end for the rest of the year. Meanwhile Governor Blount had arrived in Knoxville in October with instructions that Major Beard was to be court-martialed. Eventually he would come to trial but, as could be expected, he was acquitted by a jury of his peers. More importantly, Blount arrived with no declaration of war from the President. He learned that only the Congress can declare war.

1794

Chickamaugan Terrorism against the Cumberland Settlements Triggers the Nickajack Expedition

During 1794 the United States gained the upper hand in the battle with Spain for influence over the southern tribes. Spain had been drained by the war with France and had little money to spare on supplies for the Cherokee and their neighbors. Despite creating an alliance with the southern tribes at Nogales in 1793, Spain refused to help the Cherokee and the Creek in their undeclared war with the United States. Governor Carondelet explained that Spain could not help them fight a war of aggression. The Indians appreciated that the Spanish wanted their allegiance but would give nothing in return. By the end of the year, only the most aggressive Creeks and Lower Town Cherokee were considered allies of Spain.

The British were also at war with France. British violations of American neutrality were on the verge of provoking a new war in North America. The British could possibly win over the allegiance of the Cherokee and other southern tribes, but Canada was geographically too distant. The British would have little influence unless they could demonstrate successful intervention on behalf of the Kickapoos and other Ohio Indians. On August 20, American General Anthony Wayne's victory at the Battle of Fallen Timbers, however, essentially won the war against the Indians in the Northwest Territory. The northwestern frontier was secure; more attention could be given to the problems in the Southwest Territory.

In the Southwest Territory Governor Blount was facing discontent among the citizens who resented the federal government's refusal to declare war on the hostile Creek and Chickamauga Indians. Unless the territory achieved statehood, its citizens would have no representation in the Congress, which had the exclusive power to declare war. Even after Sevier's punitive expedition in the fall, vicious attacks continued in the Mero District and along the French Broad. Governor Blount envisioned leading the territory into statehood, giving him an opportunity to become a United States Senator and certainly enhancing the value of his land investments. In order to start the process of achieving statehood Blount called for an organizational meeting of the House of Representatives for February 24. Blount adjourned the group after a week, but not before the group had passed a resolution calling for the United States to declare war on the Creeks and Cherokee and to erect forts in the Southwest Territory.

The Cherokee remained deeply divided as they had been for almost twenty years. Little Turkey and Hanging Maw led the peace faction and dealt exclusively with the United States. Bloody Fellow, John Watts, and Doublehead represented the more aggressive Cherokee, and they negotiated with both the United States and Spain. The Lower Towns were not completely controlled by any leader, however, as Volate and Breath led their own missions to New Orleans and Pensacola. While Spain's influence waned from lack of credibility, the Americans used both the carrot and the stick to gain more support from the Cherokee.

An olive branch was extended by the Washington administration in June when they invited both the Cherokee and the Chickamaugans to Philadelphia for talks. Little Turkey represented the peace faction, and Doublehead led the others. The talks resulted in a revision of the Treaty of Holston on June 26, and the Cherokee's annuity was increased from fifteen hundred dollars to five thousand dollars. The Cherokee agreed to make reparations for stolen horses. The results of this treaty were apparently minimal as Doublehead distributed the goods (mostly for his own benefit) at Oconee without the Overhills even being invited. Not only were the two faction more deeply divided, the Chickamaugans did not even stop their attacks on the settlements.

Bench, a particularly aggressive Chickamaugan warrior, had been killed during a raid in Kentucky. John Watts, although he later professed only friendly intentions toward the United States, vowed to avenge the death of Bench. Hanging Maw claimed that Watts was going to use the incident as an excuse to escalate the war and to blame it on the Overhills. Anyway, the attacks raged against the Mero District.

Meanwhile Governor William Blount and General James Robertson conspired to take matters into their own hands. They both knew that the federal government would not condone an offensive expedition against the Cherokee and Creeks, and yet that was the only way they thought they could end the attacks. Robertson quietly assembled a militia of over five hundred men at Nashville under Colonels William Whitley and John Montgomery. Blount sent a force from Knoxville to join them and their leader, Major James Ore, assumed command even though the colonels outranked him. Blount and Robertson had decided to launch a punitive campaign against the hostile Indians even though it would be seen as illegal. Blount sent Robertson a letter condemning his actions, and Robertson sent a letter taking full responsibility and offering his resignation. Of course Blount had planned the whole thing.

Ore's expedition left Buchanan's Station on September 7 and arrived at the Tennessee River on September 12. The group had not encountered any aggressive Indians that might have justified crossing the river, but they did it nonetheless. Ore's men surprised the town of Nickajack and destroyed it. Even though they no longer had the advantage of surprise, the force went on to attack the town of Running-water, destroying it as well. Legal or not, the Nickajack expedition was successful in its execution and had the desired results of stopping Cherokee raids. Governor Blount held a meeting at Tellico Blockhouse in November with Hanging Maw, John Watts, Tickagiskee, and John Davidson. Watts claimed that the Chickamaugans had already decided to move away from the Spanish influence and to make peace with the United States, even before Nickajack. Whether true or not, the Cherokee raids stopped. Although the Creeks continued to fight, for the Cherokee this new treaty represented the end of twenty years of warfare with the United States. They had been with the losing side in the Revolutionary War and had suffered continual death and destruction at the hands of Americans ever since. Not only did the villages suffer physically, the whole culture of the Cherokee was altered as the religious ceremonies and festivals had been disrupted and the economy based on fur trading had been ruined by the loss of hunting grounds.

Chapter Nine

1795–1808

Land Traded for Peace

*Civilization Brings Agriculture, Missionaries, and
Written Laws*

In 1795 the Cherokee enjoyed the beginning of their first prolonged period of peace with the white men since the 1750s. A steady
stream of defeats had left even the Chickamaugans without the will to
fight. Furthermore, the United States had gained adjacent territory so
that the tribe had become an American enclave. The Spanish quickly
lost interest in the Cherokee since they shared no common border, and
in fact the Spanish withdrew from eastern North America in stages.
The Treaty of San Lorenzo (1795) ceded all lands east of the Mississippi River, north of the thirty-first parallel to the United States, and five
years later the secret Treaty of Ildefonso ceded all of Louisiana to the
French. The French quickly lost interest in the prospect of administering the American territory and sold it to the Americans in 1803. With
the Louisiana Purchase completed, never again could the Cherokee be
used as pawns between two "European" powers.

The Cherokee were now free to concentrate on domestic issues.
They remained divided into the moderate Upper Towns (older estab-
lishments) and the more conservative Lower Towns (Chickamaugans).
The Upper Town leaders were mostly mixed-blood Cherokee who em-

braced the federal government's "Civilization" program. They promoted the development of agriculture and even allowed the Moravians and Presbyterians to establish missions after the turn of the century. Among the Upper Towns were capitalists and even slave owners.

The Lower Towns were dominated by more pure-blooded Cherokee who distrusted the white men and their customs. Many of them were willing to relocate to Spanish Louisiana onto good hunting land far away from their homeland and the white men in order to preserve the old culture based on hunting. They suffered from poor leadership during this period: The somewhat erratic Doublehead was the main spokesman for the Lower Towns, and unfortunately he succumbed to the bribes of the American agent, Return Jonathan Meigs.

The Americans had more or less resolved the conflict between federal policy and local demands by negotiating from the Indians what the locals wanted. In 1798 the First Treaty of Tellico secured for the Americans almost all of the land that they had settled illegally in the past. Further revisions were negotiated over the next few years. Under the direction of Secretary of War Henry Dearborn, Agent Meigs secured treaties by signing secret side agreements with the chiefs willing to agree to them. The Upper Towns were already resentful that the Lower Towns received an unfair amount of the annual payments and presents. When it became known that Doublehead had ceded cherished Cherokee hunting grounds in return for valuable pieces of real estate, the rift between the two factions widened almost to the breaking point. Leaders from the Upper Towns assassinated Doublehead in 1807 and asked the United States to recognize the two factions as separate tribes. The Lower Towns were without effective leadership at that point, and the American proposal to reconcile the two factions was accepted. In 1808 the Cherokee Council adopted the first codification of Cherokee law, which modified the traditional rules of property ownership and blood revenge.

1795

Southern Tribes Meet with Governor Blount at Tellico Blockhouse

At the beginning of 1795 the southern Indians were generally at peace with the United States, except for the more aggressive Creek factions. William Blount, Governor of the Southwest Territory and Indian Agent, encouraged the Cherokee and the other friendly tribes to oppose the Creeks. The Cherokee didn't take the bait, but the Chickasaw were more than willing to reopen hostilities with this traditional enemy. Governor Carondelet of Louisiana immediately protested that the Americans were fomenting discontent between the tribes in order to gain permission from the Chickasaw to build forts at Muscle Shoals and Chickasaw Bluffs. Carondelet was further outraged that the Georgia legislature had illegally authorized the sale of thirty-five million acres of Indian lands to four land companies. Carondelet complained to the American ambassadors and encouraged the Indians to attack any settlements in the disputed territory.

Although the federal Indian policy of the United States did not allow the Southwest Territory to get involved in the Creek/Chickasaw conflict, General Robertson allowed Kaspar Mansker—a private citizen—to organize a militia to aid the Chickasaw. He furthermore shipped large supplies of corn from Nashville to the Chickasaw, knowing that the war effort was interfering with their planting season. If the end justifies the means, then all went well. By the end of the month the Creeks were petitioning Blount for peace talks. Timothy Pickering, who had recently replaced Henry Knox as Secretary of War, was angered that Blount and Robertson had conspired to create an alliance of Indians against the Creeks while it was not official policy of the United States.

He demanded that Blount follow the treaties and evict illegal settlers where necessary in order to keep the Cherokee happy. Blount was instructed to dismantle Fort Grainger and the Tellico Blockhouse, if needed, but in no way was the fort at Southwest Point to be disturbed. A few weeks later Robertson resigned as General for the Mero District (replaced by General James Winchester), although he remained Agent for the Chickasaw and Choctaw.

In response to Robertson's actions Carondelet ordered an invasion of Chickasaw Bluffs and the subsequent erection of Fort San Fernando de Barrancas. The Spanish apparently obtained rights to the land from the Chickasaw after the fact. The motivation of the Spanish action is unclear, although it was probably aimed toward improving their position in the ongoing negotiations with the United States over boundary locations. A few months later the two countries signed the Treaty of San Lorenzo, establishing the thirty-first parallel to the Mississippi River as the boundary. Spain agreed to open the lower Mississippi to navigation and allow the Americans to store cargo at New Orleans for three years. Spain also agreed to abandon Fort Barrancas (although it would be a couple of years before that actually happened).

With peace restored among the Indians and with Spanish influence at a low point, Blount felt secure in complying with Pickering's request to order the removal of some illegal settlers. He was further motivated to push the territory toward statehood, anticipating that representation in Congress would give the people a voice for federal protection against the Indians. Of course, Blount's election to the Senate would also put him in a better position to enhance the value of his land investments. He opened the territorial assembly on June 29. It called for a census to see if the population was large enough to qualify for statehood, and a referendum was held simultaneously to determine if a majority of the citizens favored statehood.

While the canvassing was taking place Blount organized a general meeting of the southern Indians at Tellico Blockhouse in October. John Watts, Bloody Fellow, Glass, Richard Justice, Doublehead, Tahlonteeskee, and Otter Litter were among the Cherokee representatives. There were general discussions of peace between the Creeks and the Chickasaw and between the Creeks and the United States. The positive climate of the meeting was carried over to informal meetings at which Little Turkey, Hanging Maw, and some others were entertained at Blount's personal residence. At the same time the Spanish were coming to terms with their inability to supply the Indians with adequate provisions. The very next day the Treaty of San Lorenzo was signed, and Spain essentially relinquished influence over the Cherokee and the other southern tribes.

In November the results of the census were certified. The population of the territory was 77,262, which exceeded the sixty thousand minimum required for statehood. Although the Mero District opposed statehood (perhaps hoping for their own state later), the majority of the voters in the Southwest Territory favored statehood. Governor Blount called for a constitutional convention to meet early the next year. Meanwhile, he called for more illegal settlers to move, and yet he petitioned the federal government to purchase more land north of the Clinch River. He argued that the new purchases would create a more natural border and minimize hostilities. For the Cherokee the question was, How would they get along with the creation of a new state in their back yard, with the first governor likely to be John Sevier, the veteran Indian fighter?

1796

The Cherokee Become an American Enclave

During the last full year of Washington's presidency the United States moved closer to war with France over the issue of the mercantile rights of neutral nations. Relations with Spanish Louisiana and Florida became less of a flash point as the Senate ratified the Treaty of San Lorenzo, which had defined the boundaries between the territories. Governor Carondelet tried to maintain some influence among the Cherokee and other southern tribes but to little avail. After the newly elected Georgia legislature invalidated their predecessors' illegal sale of Yazoo land tracts, the way was paved for peace with the Creeks. President Washington appointed Benjamin Hawkins to negotiate a treaty with the Creeks and a treaty was signed at Colerain, Georgia, on June 29, 1796, establishing peace between the Creeks and the United States. All of the southern tribes were at peace now, and the Cherokee were effectively an enclave within the jurisdiction of the United States.

The Cherokee had ended 1795 on good terms with Governor William Blount but when the district entered the union as Tennessee, John Sevier became its first governor. Cherokee concerns about the new administration were heightened when the state's first Congressman, Andrew Jackson, introduced a resolution in the House of Representatives proposing that Tennessee be reimbursed for the expenses of John Sevier's 1793 campaign against the Cherokee. The resolution failed and was in contrast to the Indian policy of President Washington, who favored peaceful relations with the native tribes and promoted the introduction of farming, Christianity, and other features of civilization.

Washington appointed Benjamin Hawkins Principal Temporary Agent for the Southern Indians and sent him to Cherokee territory to assess the conditions there. When he traveled across the Cherokee land in November and December, the towns appeared nearly deserted since most of the men were out hunting. Most towns had a white trader, usually married to a Cherokee, living in high style. Although the people showed the physical and mental scars of warfare, Hawkins was impressed by the productivity of the women and their enthusiasm for learning the skills of weaving as well as farming and animal husbandry. There was some resistance to growing excess corn to sell for profit since the profit was so minimal to begin with. Although the Cherokee leadership endorsed the need to convert from an economy based on hunting to one based on agriculture, there was resistance among the men to becoming farmers. In Cherokee mythology the first man, Kanati, was responsible for hunting and the first woman, Selu, was responsible for growing corn. To ask a man to become a farmer was to contradict his concept of gender roles.

Benjamin Hawkins sent a laudatory report about his journey to Secretary of War James McHenry. Although the report was generally positive, he was disturbed to find that the Chickamaugans had succeeded in siphoning away more than their fair share of farm implements and other goods provided by treaty. When confronted about this inequity committed against the mountain-dwelling Cherokee, Chiefs Doublehead, Will, and John Watts said that what was done was done and that it was too late to complain. Even as the Cherokee entered into the first truly peaceful period in almost thirty-five years, there were continuing divisions within the tribe.

1797

The Cherokee Receive Instructions on Agriculture and Animal Husbandry

Although Spain abandoned Fort San Fernando de Barrancas in 1797 and the King forbade further financial aid to the Indians, Governor Carondelet and his compatriots in Florida continued to seek friendship with the Cherokee and other southern Indians. Having heard of an incident in which some Tennesseans killed a Cherokee hunter, Carondelet expected trouble and promised Bloody Fellow personal protection as well as support for his followers. He even proposed paying off Bloody Fellow's debts to the financially ailing trading company Panton and Leslie. The Louisiana Governor had no direct need for the company but he wanted to maintain influence with the Indians; he still feared the possibility of an armed invasion by the American western settlers or the British. Bloody Fellow did not see eye to eye with the Spanish on all accounts. He asserted that since Spain had ceded all claims to Cherokee land to the United States, the Cherokee had no choice but to treat with the Americans and to keep faith with them. Nonetheless Bloody Fellow was angry because he thought the United States was reneging on a promise not to settle Muscle Shoals.

Carondelet also approved the resettlement of some Cherokee refugees along the St. Francis River, near New Madrid, Louisiana (now Missouri). Although the United States had not tried to settle the lands ceded by the Treaty of San Lorenzo, some Cherokee feared that they would eventually force the removal of the Indians. Although Carondelet approved the allocation of farmland to the Cherokee, he did not grant them larger tracts of hunting grounds.

In 1797 the new administration of President John Adams continued the foreign and Indian policies of the Washington administration. Tensions between the United States and France nearly reached the breaking point after the infamous XYZ Affair, when French agents demanded bribes from the American ambassadors. Earlier in the year William Blount, now a United States Senator, feared that Spain was going to sell New Orleans back to France. Such a move would be disastrous for the westerners in general and for his investments specifically, since France was not compelled by treaty to grant free navigation of the lower Mississippi River. Blount conspired with John Chisholm, a British resident of Knoxville, to organize an expedition of American citizens and Indians to attack the Spanish possessions in Louisiana and Florida on behalf of Britain. The British, who were at war with both Spain and France, would in return grant the organizers tracts of land, appoint Chisholm Indian superintendent, make New Orleans and Pensacola free ports, and guarantee free navigation of the Mississippi.

While Chisholm was away trying to sell the plan to the British ambassador (it was flatly rejected), Blount was called back to Philadelphia for a special session of Congress. Blount wrote a letter to James Carey, a federal translator and co-conspirator, stating that the invasion might take place in the fall. He warned Carey about Benjamin Hawkins and asked that he try to damage his reputation. If the Cherokee were angry toward Blount over the latest treaty negotiations the blame was to be put on the shoulders of former President Washington. Unfortunately for Senator Blount, Carey apparently got drunk and inadvertently allowed Blount's incriminating letter to fall into the wrong hands. This turn of events led to Blount's impeachment and eventual expulsion from the Senate.

Meanwhile President Adams replaced Thomas Lewis by appointing Silas Dinsmoor as Agent for the Cherokee and stationed him at Tellico Blockhouse. He was given the charge of instructing the Cherokee on animal husbandry, the use of the plow, weaving, and other mechanical skills. While the Cherokee remained at peace (with only rare violent incidents reported), Governor Sevier was not pleased with the current status. There were a large number of Tennesseans who lived within the Cherokee boundary, according to the most recent treaty. Sevier addressed this anomaly in a speech to the state legislature on September 22, saying that this was actually an extension of the Indian boundary and that great harm would come to individuals and the public if these people were compelled to abandoned their possessions and improved land. Sevier called for a memorial to Congress requesting satisfaction on this issue. The conflict between local needs and federal Indian policy continued. (See Map 9, page 192.)

1798

The First Treaty of Tellico

The year 1798 witnessed further erosion of Spanish influence among the southern Indians, especially the Cherokee. The Cherokee had been divided by some misunderstandings about how the annual gifts were distributed. Reconciliation was achieved, however, and it was determined that the trouble had been stirred up by a mischievous translator. Division existed within the Spanish ranks as to how the Indians should be treated. The military was assuming control of Indian affairs until the United States could exert full authority as per the Treaty of San Lorenzo. The political leaders still felt it was wise to distribute presents to the Indians to keep them happy until the transition was complete. Agent Juan Morales sent five hundred pesos to the Cherokee but declared that it would be their last payment. Now that the Spanish had no contiguous border with the Cherokee it did not make sense to continue supporting them. Signs of further tension between Spain and the Cherokee surfaced as Moses Price (a Cherokee horse trader) was arrested entering West Florida and then taken as a prisoner to New Orleans. The Cherokee living near New Madrid received a letter late in the year

Map 9

threatening their eviction by the Spanish authorities, but the authenticity of this note was uncertain.

Spain and the United States continued to cooperate in implementing the Treaty of San Lorenzo and made plans to survey the boundary at the thirty-first parallel. Although the United States accused Spain of inciting the Indians against the boundary marking, it appears that the four southern tribes met independently of Spain in August at Tuckabatchee and agreed to oppose it. Meanwhile the United States organized the Territory of Mississippi in the land stretching from Georgia to the Mississippi River north of the thirty-first parallel to thirty-two and a half degrees north. Georgia claimed the strip of land between the Mississippi Territory and Tennessee. Once the Spanish withdrew from Natchez it became the capital of the territory.

In 1797 the survey of the boundaries of Tennessee with the Cherokee found that a large number of whites were illegally settled on Cherokee land, including the prominent Judge David Campbell. Governor John Sevier had asked the state legislature to send a memorial to Congress requesting negotiations for new boundaries, and new commissioners were appointed to address the issue. The commissioners suggested that the meeting be held at Chota, but the Cherokee now insisted that Ustanli was the new capital. A compromise site near Tellico Blockhouse was chosen, but when the conference opened in July it was immediately stymied by the Cherokee's refusal to cede any more land or to allow the return of ejected settlers.

Negotiations continued all summer and on October 2 an agreement was signed, to be known later as the First Treaty of Tellico. (See Map 3 #12, 13, page 26, Map 5 #14, page 95.) Since trade with the Spanish had dropped considerably and they could no longer depend on them for assistance, the Cherokee had little choice but to treat with the Americans. The Cherokee ceded three tracts of land: an area south of the Hawkins line to the Tennessee and Little Tennessee rivers extending west to Chilhowie Mountain; an area northwest of the Clinch River extending to the eastern edge of Cumberland Mountain; and a triangle of land in North Carolina on the heads of the French Broad and Pigeon rivers, including Mount Pisgah.

Nearly all of the ejected settlers could return to their homes. The Cherokee further agreed to allow the construction of the Cumberland Road stretching from east Tennessee to Nashville across Cherokee hunting grounds. For consideration of all these cessions the United States promised five thousand dollars in goods and increased their annuity by another thousand dollars. A trade post would be maintained, and the boundaries would be respected for eternity.

Meanwhile Agent Silas Dinsmoor reported back to Philadelphia that the Cherokee were continuing to make progress in weaving, crafts, and literacy. He did note, however, that the Cherokee practice of indulging their children was a problem. In fact it became apparent that the key to "civilizing" the Cherokee was the education of the children, since they had not been old enough to fight against the white people and maybe would not be as biased against American ways. Furthermore, a growing number of them were of mixed heritage.

Although there had been attempts to convert the Cherokee to Christianity over the preceding sixty years, none had been successful. There was greater motivation at the turn of the century as the civilization policy of the United States officially encouraged it. The Cherokee might even be more susceptible to the process now that they were struggling to build a new social and economic structure. An article in a Knoxville newspaper mentioned that the Cherokee would welcome missionaries. This report prompted the deacons of the Society of the United Brethren for the Propagation of the Gospel among the Heathen to send representatives to the Cherokee. Abraham Steiner and Frederic de Schweinitz arrived at the federal agency in October, but it was a month after the Cherokee Council had met and most of the men had gone hunting for the winter. Although Major Thomas Lewis (agent at Southwest Point) told the two that they would likely have to wait until the next fall to discuss their mission at the next Council, Steiner and Schweinitz decided to tour the Cherokee territory. They met with Chief Arcowee of Chota and Chief Kulsatahee of Hiwassee Town. The chiefs provided the missionaries with important insights into the Cherokee belief system. Meeting with ordinary Cherokee citizens gave the men understanding of the deep distrust they held for the white men.

1799

Moravian Missionaries Petition the Cherokee

Spanish influence over the southern tribes continued to diminish in 1799. Spain had difficulty supplying Panton, Leslie and Company with goods to sell to the Creeks and the others. Furthermore Spain could not prevent Panton from becoming the target of a group of bandits led by Mankiller. The erratic William A. Bowles surfaced again, declaring that the United States, by purchasing Indian lands, was in violation of the Treaty of Fort Stanwix. He once again tried to arouse the Indians to oppose the Spanish in support of the British. Spain voiced objections to the United States that it should not allow him to operate against Spain from American territory. Spain had relatively little to do with the Cherokee in 1799, although the migration was allowed to continue to the New Madrid area. Most of the migrant Indians were Chickamaugans who were the most vehemently anti-American in sentiment. A more peaceful majority was left in the east.

The Moravian missionaries, Steiner and de Schweinitz, continued their exploration of the Cherokee in 1799. Chief Kulsatahee of Hiwassee asked whether the Moravians believed that the Indians, like the Negroes, were inherently inferior and thus incapable of becoming good Christians and citizens. He was pleased to learn that the Moravians denied that the Cherokee were innately inferior because of their race. Kulsatahee supported their application to found a permanent school, and promised to talk to the younger chiefs when they returned from the hunt. The chiefs of the Lower Towns, however, were more powerful and more suspicious of the white men. While Little Turkey was supportive of the school, Doublehead, Glass, Richard Justice, Bloody Fellow, and Tahlonteeskee were more reluctant. Although Doublehead was a full-blooded Cherokee and could neither read nor speak English, he had learned to manipulate the economic system to his advantage and had even begun to acquire Negro slaves. He was perhaps the most reluctant of the chiefs to allow the missionaries to establish a school. The issue was to be presented to the Council in the fall of 1800.

1800

The Upper Towns Allow the Moravians to Build a School

The years 1800 was quiet, but events of this final year of the century had major repercussions. The Spanish still worried about the antics of William Bowles and continued to subsidize the traders in Florida so as to keep the favor of the Indians and minimize the risk of invasion. Nonetheless, in October Spain secretly ceded all of Louisiana to France by the Treaty of Ildefonso.

The United States continued to grow, and in 1800 Washington, D.C., was established as its new capital. President Adams ran for re-election against Thomas Jefferson in December, but the votes would not be counted until early 1801.

The major issue for the Cherokee was whether or not to allow missionaries into the territory. The Moravians had sent representatives to the Cherokee the previous year, but they were too late to present their proposals before the National Council. They contacted Colonel David Henley early in 1800 and discussed their wish to bring knowledge of Christianity to the Cherokee. Henley explained to them that their approach would not work with the Cherokee. They needed to stress the basics of education and farming before preaching about Christianity. When Henley met with Little Turkey, Doublehead, Bloody Fellow, and others in May his explanation indicated that he thought he had convinced the Moravians to alter their strategy. The chiefs accepted Henley's proposal and allowed the Moravians to send representatives to the National Council in October.

The Cherokee were deeply divided over the missionary issue. The Upper Town leaders were generally favorable and many of them actually had white fathers: Charles Hicks, James Vann, Will Shorey, and Richard Fields. Many traders had mixed-blood children who were already being sent to nearby towns to be educated. Certainly it would be desirable to have a school established nearby. The Lower Towns were more geographically isolated from the white towns, and there were not as many inter-marriages. The Lower Town chiefs did not see much practical value in setting up a new school and were suspicious of any attempt by white people to settle on Cherokee land. The Moravians, Abraham

Steiner and Frederic de Schweinitz, met informally with the Lower Town chiefs (Little Turkey, Bloody Fellow, Doublehead, the Boot, and the Glass) to discuss their mission. The chiefs told them that they would consider allowing them to build a school, but did not approve of efforts to convert the Cherokee to Christianity. They were insulted by the Moravian's plan to charge the students for room and board, and that issue nearly derailed the whole project.

The National Council met at Tellico in October and the Moravian mission was discussed. The Upper Town leaders were so strongly in favor of the establishment of a school that they told the Lower Town chiefs that they were willing to grant permission despite their objections. Charles Hicks and James Vann were the strongest promoters of the mission. Neither one of them had much need for Christianity, but both of the men were successful businessmen and slave owners. These mixed-blood sons of traders saw that education of the Cherokee would only increase commerce between them and the nearby white settlers. Certainly they would benefit financially. The Council gave final approval for the experimental establishment of a school for the purpose of instruction only. The teaching of Christianity was not approved directly, and the Council reserved the right to cancel the mission depending on its performance. After the meeting the missionaries visited four spots for the possible establishment of their school. James Vann wanted them to locate the school on land he owned with a bold spring. It was close to Vann's own home and also near a major road. The missionaries left the decision up the Lord (by drawing lots) and coincidentally chose Vann's place. Vann arranged for the Cherokee to purchase the farm buildings and other improvements from Robert Brown, who had worked for Vann and who had made the improvements. No title was granted since all Cherokee land belonged to the nation and it was therefore unlawful to sell land to white men.

1801

The Moravians Establish a School at Springplace

In 1801 the French acquisition of Louisiana was revealed to the rest of the world, and they began plans for its exploitation. Meanwhile the Spanish continued to worry about William Bowles and the behavior of the southern Indians near Florida. The Presidential election of 1800 had resulted in a tie between Vice President Thomas Jefferson and Aaron Burr, but the House of Representatives elected Jefferson. After Jefferson was inaugurated he chose Henry Dearborn to be Secretary of War.

The Moravians chose Abraham Steiner and Gottlieb Byhan to be the first missionaries to the Cherokee. They were sent from Salem, North Carolina, and arrived at Vann's property in April. They renamed Brown's farm Springplace and began building a new cabin and plowing the farmland. Steiner became ill and had to return to Salem in the fall. Jacob Wohlfahrt and his wife were assigned to replace Steiner, and a marriage was arranged for Byhan. The four of them returned to Springplace in November to continue work on new buildings and to clear more land.

1802

Moravians Begin Teaching and Conducting Church Services

In 1802 the Treaty of Amiens ended the European war. Even as the French were evaluating the costs of maintaining friendly Indian relations in Louisiana, the Spanish were bribing the Osages. They were upset that the Cherokee and other tribes were settling in their territory along the Arkansas River. The Spanish reneged on a promise made in the Treaty of San Lorenzo when they refused to allow Americans to continue storing cargo at New Orleans. Even before that President Jefferson had authorized Ambassador Robert Livingston to negotiate for the purchase of land at the mouth of the Mississippi River and for free navigation of the river.

The Moravian missionaries were busy building their farmhouses and school, but the work was meticulous and slow. They reluctantly agreed to hire some of James Vann's slaves even though they would have to work on the Sabbath. While the missionaries were busy with the construction they were pressured to begin teaching as well. They accepted Vann's children and some others as day students, but refused boarders and spent very little time actually teaching.

The Moravians began holding church services on Sundays and even though German was their primary language, the Council had authorized them to preach only in English. They did not have an interpreter, and few of the Cherokee who lived nearby understood the language. A few Cherokee attended services at first out of curiosity, but interest quickly waned. Many of Vann's slaves understood English and showed interest in the church services, but the Moravians did not accept that the Negroes were capable of being baptized.

1803

The Cherokees Distrust the Moravians but Welcome the Presbyterians

In 1803 the Spanish finally succeeded in capturing William Bowles as he tried to attend a conference of southern Indians hosted by the Seminoles. As the Spanish prepared to turn Louisiana over to the French, they restored the rights of American traders at New Orleans. Meanwhile, war loomed between France and England, and Napoleon was anxious not to get overextended in North America. Toussaint L'Ouverture's successful slave rebellion in Haiti further convinced the French to abandon their imperial plans for North America. American Ambassadors Robert Livingston and James Monroe negotiated for the mouth of the Mississippi River but wound up purchasing its entire basin. Less than three weeks after Spain formally ceded Louisiana to France, the United States took possession on December 20.

The Louisiana Purchase doubled the size of the United States, but interest in Indian lands in the east continued. Ohio entered the union as the seventeenth state, and negotiations with various tribes yielded more tracts of land along the Wabash River. There was continued interest in Cherokee land as usual but there were no cessions this year. Agent Return J. Meigs reported, however, that there was an error in the 1791 Treaty of the Holston. The Cherokee denied that they had ceded the Long Island and now were demanding compensation for it.

Meanwhile the Cherokee were losing confidence in the Moravian mission. The missionaries had never learned to speak Tsa-La-Gi, had never converted a single person, and had scarcely taught anyone. The sturdiness of the structures they had built suggested that they were planning to establish a permanent presence and might someday want more land. Charles Vann had been negotiating with the federal government for years about a road being built through his property. The United States wanted to build a road from Georgia to Tennessee through Cherokee territory. The Lower Towns did not want the road for they thought it would bring more white people into the area and result only in greater pressures to cede more land and in more opportunities for conflict and violence. The Upper Town leaders felt that the road would be beneficial in that they could obtain franchises for inns, stables, ferries, and so on. Vann especially thought that if the road were run through his property he could obtain several franchises, including that for the mail delivery. Doublehead and the Lower Cherokee who distrusted Vann assumed that the Moravians were in sympathy with him.

Even the Upper Cherokee were fed up with the Moravians. The Upper Town chiefs met at Ustanali in June and decided that the mission had failed to deliver. Instructions were given to Assistant Agent Major William Lovely to inform the Moravians that they were to make good their promises within six months or leave. Jacob Wohlfahrt traveled to Salem for consultations and when he returned in August he met with some chiefs and offered to take four students as boarders. He refused a request to accept twice as many students, but the chiefs consented to a one-year extension of the mission. Doublehead and some of the other chiefs were upset that the school had not opened as late as October, but no further sanctions were proposed. The Cherokee basically lost interest as a new missionary appeared on the scene.

A Presbyterian missionary, Gideon Blackburn, arrived in the fall of 1803 with a different style of mission. He offered to bring four teachers to take on thirty students each. They were to teach the basics of learning and not emphasize conversion to Christianity. Despite reservations among the conservative Lower Town leadership, the Council approved Blackburn's proposal and instructed him to establish his first school on the Hiwassee River in Tennessee. Blackburn had no interest in creating a model Christian community or establishing farms. He set up rules that would encourage discipline among the students and allow supervision by the Council.

1804

Second Treaty of Tellico

In 1804 Napoleon's self-coronation was the opening act for a new European war. North America was quiet as France was no longer a factor there. The Cherokee and the other southern Indians traveled to Pensacola to ask the Spanish (in disbelief) about the Louisiana Purchase and about its boundaries. The Spanish told them to mind their own business. Meanwhile Meriwether Lewis and William Clark left St. Louis to explore Louisiana for the United States. The Americans continued to have interest in eastern Indian lands, and purchases were arranged in Indiana as well as from the Cherokee.

Little Turkey died in 1804 and was succeeded as Principal Chief by the full-blooded Black Fox (Inali). The United States had been pressuring the Cherokee to part with more land ever since the last "permanent" treaty of 1798. The Cherokee sent a delegation of chiefs to Washington to protest against any further land sales, but they eventually succumbed and signed the Second Treaty of Tellico (Wafford's Purchase) on October 24, 1804. (See Map 3 #15, page 26.) A settlement had been established in northwestern Georgia by a Colonel Wafford after the Revolutionary War. It was found later that the territory lay outside the boundaries of the Treaty of Hopewell of 1785. The Cherokee agreed in 1804 to cede this rectangular tract of land for five thousand dollars plus an annuity of one thousand dollars. Negotiations continued for more land.

Meanwhile Gideon Blackburn's school opened in February with Jonathan Blacke and his wife in charge. Months before the Moravians admitted any children to their school, the Presbyterian School's enrollment exceeded twenty students. They established separate dormitories for boys and girls, and Agent Return J. Meigs provided blankets and other assistance. With the Blackes well established, Blackburn was free to return to his church work. He returned to the school twice a year to conduct public exercises to display the progress of the children and to award prizes.

1805

The Third and Fourth Treaties of Tellico

In 1805 the outbreak of war in Europe made it difficult for the Spanish to protect traders in Florida, but otherwise the war did not directly affect the southern Indians. Thomas Jefferson began his second term as President, and the United States continued to explore the western lands and pressure the Indians for more land cessions.

Secretary of War Henry Dearborn directed Agent Return J. Meigs to negotiate new land cessions and encouraged him to use secret deals with willing chiefs if needed. The Third and Fourth Treaties of Tellico were signed on October 25 and 27, respectively. The treaties ceded a large tract of the best hunting land, including territory north of the Duck River and extending east to include the Cumberland Plateau. The newly acquired land connected eastern Tennessee with the Cumberland settlements, and the Cherokee no longer claimed land in Kentucky. The United States also acquired Southwest Point, with the understanding that it would become the new state capital. In addition the Cherokee ceded First Island of the Tennessee, at the mouth of the Clinch River. Permission was granted to build two mail roads through Cherokee territory into Alabama and Georgia. In compensation, the Cherokee received over fifteen thousand dollars in goods and cash as well as a three thousand dollar annuity.

Agent Return J. Meigs secured the Third and Fourth Treaties of Tellico by bribing Chief Doublehead and his brother-in-law Tahlonteeskee. In separate treaties (not included with the official copies) Doublehead was awarded two square-mile tracts of land at the mouths of the

Clinch and Hiwassee rivers, and Tahlonteeskee was given a similar tract at the mouth of the Duck River. (See Map 8 #16, 17, 18, page 158.) The secret provisions would not remain secret for long, and Doublehead would pay another price. Negotiations continued for further cessions.

1806

Dearborn's Treaty

In 1806 the United States was concerned with British violations of the rights of American mariners. The United States remained neutral in the European war, but was being brought closer to war with Britain. At home President Jefferson disclosed the discovery that former Vice President Aaron Burr was involved in a conspiracy to lead the American Southwest into seceding from the union.

The Cherokee chiefs had agreed to the cession of a large tract of land in Tennessee in 1805, but the Americans were not completely satisfied. The negotiations continued into 1806, but were shifted to Washington, D.C., because the Cherokee were becoming suspicious of their own chiefs. On January 7, 1806, Dearborn's Treaty was signed. The Cherokee ceded seven thousand square miles of land between the bend of the Tennessee River and the Duck River—essentially the last of the really good hunting grounds. (See Map 8 #19, page 158.) They also ceded the once-sacred Long Island of the Holston, the ownership of which had been disputed after an earlier treaty. (See Map 5 #20, page 95.) The United States was to pay them ten thousand dollars in five installments plus a life annuity of one hundred dollars for the aging Principal Chief Black Fox. The Cherokee also were to receive a gristmill, a cotton gin, and other items. There were some uncertainties about the exact boundaries, which would have to be ironed out later.

The effects of the treaty on domestic life was evident in the bonanza reaped by Doublehead, Tahlonteeskee, and James Vann, all of whom profited personally from secret clauses. Doublehead was the most obvious in his abuse. Even though Black Fox was the Principal Chief, Colonel Meigs preferred to deal with Doublehead, who was a stronger and more charismatic leader. Doublehead led the faction of Cherokee that were most resentful of the white men, and yet he began to amass a fortune by leasing land to them—land that he obtained illegally by secret additions to the recent treaties. His behavior did not go unnoticed by his political enemies.

Meanwhile, the Presbyterian missionaries opened a second school in March. As the first school was located among the Upper Towns, this one was among the Lower Towns on Sale Creek. Gideon Blackburn appointed Robert Denham to be the schoolmaster, but he was later replaced by Daniel Bayles. They could not afford to build a dormitory at this time so arrangements were made to board the students at the home of Richard Fields, a white man married to a Cherokee.

1807

The Assassination of Doublehead

In 1807 the *Leopold* and *Chesapeake* incident brought the United States and Britain closer to war and inspired the American Embargo Act, by which maritime trade with foreign countries was prohibited. Aaron Burr was captured and even though he was brought to trial and acquitted, he fled to Europe and would never threaten the United States again.

The Upper Town chiefs were disgusted with the selfish actions of Doublehead in 1805 and were determined to punish him. The Ridge, Charles Hicks, and James Vann decided that he had violated the Cherokee law forbidding the sale of tribal land. Punishment would have to be death. It was decided that Ridge, Vann, and Alexander Saunders (a half-blooded relative of Vann's) would execute the punishment. Ridge hated Doublehead, as did Vann. Recently Doublehead had murdered his own wife—who happened to be the sister of Vann's wife. He was promised the first strike against the guilty party.

The trio decided that the assassination should take place before the Council meeting in August, when the tribe would receive annuities from the United States. When Ridge and Saunders arrived at Vann's house to gather for their mission, they found him in a drunken stupor.

When Vann became sick en route, Ridge and Saunders abandoned him along the road! They traveled to Hiwassee and waited for Doublehead at McIntosh Tavern. Doublehead had spent the day at a ball game, and when he arrived in the evening he was drunk. Ridge approached Doublehead, who was sitting at a table by himself unafraid. Ridge shot him in the head and then fled with his accomplice.

Ridge and Saunders learned that the shot had not been fatal. They trailed the wounded chief to the loft in a home owned by one of the Presbyterians. Although the Presbyterians were officially neutral in the rivalry between the Upper and Lower Towns, there was no doubt that Blackburn favored Doublehead. When the two had Doublehead cornered in the loft, he charged them with a knife but missed. He survived a bullet wound in the hip and succumbed only after Saunders planted a hatchet in his head.

Probably the only person beside Gideon Blackburn who seemed to be upset by Doublehead's murder was Agent Return J. Meigs. He had been able to exploit the chief's greed in order to obtain valuable land for the United States. He predicted that the Cherokee government would become less centralized and more difficult to manage. The people respected Ridge as a hero, and his political influence continued to rise as that of Black Fox declined. The Cherokee signed another treaty on September 11 at the Chickasaw Old Fields, which clarified the boundaries defined in Dearborn's Treaty. The Chickasaw also claimed some of the land, so the United States had to negotiate a separate treaty with that tribe. The Cherokee were compensated with two thousand dollars, although Colonel R. J. Meigs secretly promised each chief who signed the treaty one thousand dollars and some rifles. Among those signing the treaty (and receiving bribes) was the illiterate and incompetent aging Chief Black Fox. His lapse of judgment did not remain secret, and he was deposed as Principal Chief the next year.

Incidentally the State of Tennessee moved its capital to Southwest Point to fulfill a requirement of the 1805 treaty. The legislature met on September 21, 1807, and adopted a resolution to move the capital back to Knoxville! Technically Tennessee had kept its promise to the Cherokee.

1808

Upper and Lower Towns Reunited

Introduction of Written Laws

During Thomas Jefferson's last year as President the rivalry between the Upper Cherokee and the Lower (Chickamauga) Cherokee reached a climax. A delegation of Upper Town chiefs journeyed to Washington to complain that the Lower Town chiefs had a majority in the Council and that they were keeping all of the annuities and tools of civilization for themselves. They proposed that the nation be formally divided, with the Upper Town Cherokee becoming citizens of the United States. Jefferson did not agree to this proposal, citing likely troubles in defining the boundary, but he did suggest that the Upper Cherokee could trade their current lands for territory west of the Mississippi River.

The meeting ended with no resolution of the problem. Agent R.J. Meigs saw an opportunity to expand on Jefferson's proposal to relocate the Upper Cherokee. He met with Black Fox, Tahlonteeskee, John Jolly, and the Glass prior to the autumn meeting of the Council and influenced (bribed) them to propose the removal of the entire tribe. At the Council meeting Principal Chief Black Fox did indeed introduce such a resolution. After Black Fox offered to cede the entire territory of the nation for a "good price," the Council was silent. The first to speak was none other than the Ridge. (See Figure 3, page 207.) He gave his respects to Chief Black Fox but pointed out that Black Fox had no right to minimize the importance of the Cherokee homeland and certainly no right to sell it without the consent of the Council.

Meigs' efforts had failed. The Council gave Ridge an ovation, and the others were disgraced. Black Fox was temporarily deposed as Principal Chief and was replaced by Pathkiller. Tahlonteeskee, fearing assassination, made arrangements with Agent Meigs to take more than a thousand of his Chickamaugan followers to settle west of the Mississippi. After their migration to Arkansas, Tahlonteeskee's group called themselves the "Cherokee West" or the "Old Settlers." They engaged in wars with the Osage Indians (who claimed the land) and never achieved the advances in cultural organization that the Cherokee established in their traditional homeland.

The Council also considered a revision of the national laws of the Cherokee and on September 11, 1808, they enacted their first written law. The law was based on codes established by Benjamin Hawkins in 1797. The Council was established as both the legislative and judicial body. The code also established the Lighthorse Guards—a group of men to protect the Cherokee citizens from criminal action. The guards were empowered to apprehend criminals, judge them, and punish them. Ridge was selected to be their leader. The blood revenge rules of clan membership were suppressed and the ways of civilization were embraced.

MAJOR RIDGE.

A CHEROKEE CHIEF

Figure 3 — Major Ridge

The Council appointed six leaders (three each from the Upper and Lower Towns) to travel to Washington to ask for a meeting with President Jefferson before his retirement. Ridge, the youngest member of the delegation, personally asked Meigs to join the delegation. The group traveled to Salem, North Carolina, and visited the Moravians first. They moved on and met with the President on December 21, 1808. The Upper Town chiefs hoped for assistance in furthering the civilized economy of the nation and asked for help in establishing improved political institutions. The Lower Towns were not united with them and inquired about the possibility of being transported to lands further west. Jefferson offered assistance to both groups and all were pleased. Migration or not, Ridge would not see a division of his nation. As the group headed back home he was determined to keep the Cherokee a united nation under one central civilized government.

Chapter Ten

1809–1819

Tribal Reform, The Creek War, and Removal Crises

During the second decade of the nineteenth century the Cherokee remained divided into two factions. The mixed-blood leaders of the Upper Cherokee encouraged cooperation with the "civilization" program of the United States and the development of an agricultural and trade economy. The full-blooded leadership of the Lower Towns rejected the new culture and embraced emigration from the homeland as an alternative to assimilation with the white men. The administrations of Thomas Jefferson, James Madison, and James Monroe encouraged removal of the Cherokee and used coercive and underhanded means to keep the tribe divided and to weaken opposition to removal.

The outbreak of hostilities between the United States and Great Britain opened up opportunities for the Americans to acquire land from various Indian tribes by forceful means. Before the War of 1812 erupted, the Shawnee Chief Tecumseh started organizing various tribes into an anti-American alliance. Tecumseh preached a revival of traditional Indian religion and rejected acceptance of the European/Christian culture. Tecumseh allied his warriors with the British in hopes of containing the expansion of the United States. The visionary leader was killed in battle, however, and the victory of the United States over the northern tribes paved the way for their removal from the Great Lakes region and the establishment of the new states of Indiana and Illinois.

The War of 1812 coincided with the outbreak of the Creek Civil

War. The hostile Upper Creeks, led by mixed-blood Chief Red Eagle (William Weatherford), attacked the pro-American Lower Creeks. After Red Eagle's men obtained arms from Spanish Florida, a militia from Mississippi attacked them in a surprise move. Although the Americans had drawn first blood, the Creeks escalated the conflict into a full-scale war by slaughtering the Americans at Fort Mims. The Americans, under General Andrew Jackson and with the help of friendly Upper Cherokee, routed the Creeks. Even though Cherokee assistance was vital for the American victory, Jackson did not acknowledge their help and even forced the Creeks to cede land claimed by the Cherokee.

Throughout this period, missionaries from the American Board of Commissioners of Foreign Missions established schools among the Cherokee. The ABCFM supported the civilization process and hoped that it would lead to conversions to Christianity. The Cherokee Council, which was by this time dominated by the Upper Town chiefs, supported the efforts of the missionaries. The chiefs were grateful for their help in suppressing the fundamentalist religious revival aroused by the preaching of Tecumseh and the severe earthquakes that rocked the country in 1811 and 1812. During the removal crisis of 1819 the ABCFM helped negotiate the treaty by which the Cherokee ceded a third of their land to compensate for the emigration of the third of the tribe that had moved to Arkansas. The treaty also established an endowment for new schools, and it appeared that the Cherokee Nation was no longer in danger of being evicted against its will. President Monroe visited the mission at Brainerd—the Era of Good Feelings was extended to the Cherokee. The Cherokee Council knew that the governmental structure of the tribe placed them at risk of future exploitation and began exploring new reforms. The Arkansas Cherokee found that their emigration was rewarded with further contempt and abuse.

1809

The Upper Towns Seek Governmental Reorganization

The Lower Towns Consider Removal

In the waning days of Jefferson's presidency Congress passed the Enforcement Act to prevent smuggling in violation of the Embargo Act. The law pitted New England against the rest of the country and provoked a diplomatic crisis for President Madison's administration.

The Cherokee had sent a delegation to meet with the outgoing President late in 1808, and they met with Jefferson the first week of January 1809. Tewchale (Flute) was the principal representative of the Lower Towns. He asked the President for boats, guns, and other materials that would help them migrate to Arkansas. The next day a delegation from the Upper Towns, led by Ridge, told Jefferson that they did not know that the Lower Towns were planning to move. They insisted that they had no intention of leaving the homeland and requested further help in establishing an agricultural society with a republican government. Although Jefferson would have preferred that all of the Cherokee relocate, he promised to help both groups meet their goals. The Cherokee, however, would have to delineate the boundary between the Upper and Lower Towns.

Ridge was against any division of the Cherokee nation and decided that he and his allies, Charles Hicks and James Vann, must lead the way. Hicks, who had been personal secretary to Agent Return Jonathan Meigs, resigned his position, charging Meigs with a pattern of corruption. Hicks' loss of influence might be seen as a setback, but Vann's behavior was becoming more of a liability. Vann was known for his excess drinking and cruelty. He was known to beat his wife savagely and had spent a night torturing and then killing a slave girl whom he had accused of stealing. James Vann was murdered as he sat in a tavern, probably by his brother-in-law.

At the autumn Council a new National Committee was appointed, with Ridge retaining his position as commander of one of the Lighthorse Guards. The Committee was charged with the preparation of a new constitution to be modeled on that of the United States. Ridge and Hicks persuaded the Council not to adopt a boundary between the Upper and Lower Towns, and in fact the western migration movement was quieted. Only Talunteeskee and his followers eventually headed for Arkansas.

Figure 4 — Tecumseh

The northern Indians continued to cede more territory to the United States in Indiana, but some among their ranks were organizing to defy the Americans. A delegation of northern Indians led by Shawnee Chief Payhamaskaku visited the Cherokee at Hiwassee in March. Chief Black Fox expressed the Cherokee desire for peace among all of the tribes and the United States. A few weeks later Tewchale met with representatives of the northern Indians in Washington and advised them to stay out of the white man's quarrels. He explained that the Cherokee were now civilized farmers and that they even made their own clothes. He may have been planning to migrate, but he did not see the wisdom in provoking a war with the Americans. Later that summer, the Shawnee Chief Tecumseh and his brother, The Prophet, began a campaign to unite all of the eastern Indians against the Americans. (See Figure 4.) With religious intensity, they began to visit other tribes to cement a new pan-Indian alliance. Perhaps the British in Canada would help.

1810

A More Centralized Government

In 1810 the United States crept closer to war with the Europeans. American settlers in West Florida claimed that their territory was actually part of Louisiana and rose up against the Spanish. President Madison responded by announcing the annexation of West Florida and ordered a military occupation of the land. Meanwhile Congress passed the Macon Act, which extended the Non-Intercourse Act. This limitation of trade with nations that violated American maritime sovereignty angered both France and Spain. Later, Madison mistakenly believed that France had promised to respect American naval neutrality, and so he lifted the sanctions against it. Britain was outraged even further.

The year 1810 was climactic in the evolution of the Cherokee government. After the departure of Tahlonteeskee and his followers, the tone of the Lower Towns was less aggressive, and they had no strong leaders. The death of the controversial James Vann probably helped Ridge and his associates take over control of the Cherokee National Council. The Patriot Faction (as Agent Meigs called Ridge's group) was committed to an agriculture-based market economy. They welcomed skilled white laborers who could help strengthen the nation's financial security. They developed a more centralized government in which the chiefs of all of the towns were members of the Council. Their unanimous approval was necessary for new legislation—thus making it impossible for one clique to dominate the others. The Council passed major legislation including the abolition of blood revenge for murders and manslaughter. It became illegal for clan members to seek revenge outside of the established judicial system. Soon a patrilineal inheritance system would be established as well.

The great accomplishments of this period represented a political movement rather than a spiritual one. Again the Patriot group welcomed the whites and embraced many of their customs. The missionaries, however, were falling out of favor. Blackburn closed down his schools after he was implicated in the sale of whiskey (which was confiscated by the Creeks). Whether or not he was guilty was less important than the fact that the Cherokee thought he was guilty. Many had felt all along that the missionaries had ulterior motives for living among them.

1811

Tecumseh, Earthquakes, and the Old-Time Religion

In 1811 the reinstatement of the Non-Intercourse Act against Britain, based on misleading information from France, further propelled the country toward war. British impressment of an American sailor likewise intensified the tone of the confrontation.

Americans were becoming more resentful of British aid to Tecumseh's Indian alliance (through Canada), and they were developing more aggressive feelings against the Spanish in Florida.

In February three Cherokee reported that they had encountered a ghost who berated them for becoming farmers and abandoning the traditional ways. They were implored to cast undesirable whites out of their lands and to disband the Lighthorse Guards since they were unfair and brutal. Ridge suspected that the whole story was a lie that was inspired by Tecumseh. When the Council met at Ustanali in May, the story was retold, and the man who had seen the vision swore that if anyone denied his message that they would be struck dead. Amidst the commotion, Ridge stood up to deny that the story was from the Great Spirit and to point out that the man's plan would lead to war with the United States. He declared that the storytellers were imposters and dared for death to come and take him if he was wrong. Although he was mobbed and attacked on the spot, he survived the ordeal and thus proved his point valid.

Tecumseh tried to inflame anti-American feelings amongst the various Indian tribes by visiting their councils and using religious revivalist language. He brought his mission south, meeting with the Choctaw, Chickasaw, and Creeks. When he visited the Creek Council meeting at Tuckabatchee in October, Tecumseh called for them to join the grand Indian alliance. Ridge had been appointed as the Cherokee representative at the Creek Council and had heard Tecumseh's words. Ridge told the visionary that if he dared to visit the Cherokee Council, he would personally kill Tecumseh. He decided not to visit the Cherokee and headed back home.

While Tecumseh was gone the settlers at Vincennes decided to strike the Shawnee villages along the Tippecanoe River preemptively. General William Henry Harrison fought to a draw, but the Canadians decided to abandon their Indian allies and the frontiersmen developed a deepening hostility toward the British.

The Indian religious revival had not made too much headway among the Cherokee so far, but the movement was far from over. On December 11, 1811, the huge New Madrid earthquake shook the southeast and triggered a series of tremors over the following months. For many Cherokee it was clear that the Great Spirit was indeed unhappy.

1812

Cherokee Neutrality as the Creek Civil War and the War of 1812 Erupt

As the newly reorganized Cherokee government struggled to establish a new order, the world around them began to fall apart. President Madison's failed diplomacy led to the declaration of war against Britain by Congress on June 18, 1812. The establishment of the State of Louisiana out of the Territory of New Orleans assisted American aggression in West Florida, but in the northwest the Americans suffered immediate losses as General William Hull abandoned Detroit to the British. The peace with the northwestern Indians that followed the Battle of Tippecanoe was broken in the spring when raids were resumed against the frontier settlements. After Madison's formal request for a declaration of war, Governor General Sir George Prevost invited the charismatic Shawnee leader Tecumseh to Ontario. Despite the shortcomings of Madison's foreign policy and the immediate military reverses, the declaration of war pleased many western voters, who saw an opportunity to push the frontier further west and south, at the expense of the Indians and the Spanish. James Madison was re-elected President in December.

For many Indian nations the war represented an opportunity to settle the score with the United States as well. Tecumseh had inspired many followers with speeches spiced with Native American religious revivalist rhetoric. Although Ridge had warned Tecumseh not to come to the Cherokee Council, his influence was felt in the Creek nation and indirectly among the Cherokee. The religious revivalist movement influenced the Upper Creeks the most, and under the leadership of Weatherford they became more and more hostile toward the United States and white men in general. The war-mongering Upper Creeks became known as the Red Sticks for the vermilion war clubs and red religious staffs they adopted. Ridge attended a Creek Council meeting early in the year and foresaw that a civil war was brewing between the Red Sticks and the Lower Creeks, who were still friendly to the United States and hopeful of a Cherokee alliance. Fratricidal war erupted that summer as the Upper Creeks attacked and destroyed some of the Lower Creek villages.

The Cherokee struggled to keep the external chaos from affecting their progress in creating a new economy consistent with the civilization policy of the United States. A revival of the old-time religion was fueled by continuing earthquakes—a warning, perhaps, that the Great Spirit was planning to punish the Cherokee for adopting the ways of the white men. Indian Agent Colonel Return J. Meigs reported a revival of Cherokee religious dancing and related the story of a Cherokee who died suddenly after publicly denouncing some fundamentalist religious prophecies. Even Ridge wondered about the meaning of the earthquakes and consulted the Moravians. They suggested that God was angry with the white men, not the Cherokee, but that his punishment would spare no one. John Gambold, the Moravian missionary, accepted Ridge's invitation to visit the Council that spring.

At the Council meeting at Ustanali, The Reverend Gambold explained the Moravian interpretation of the earthquakes and reassured the Cherokee that God still approved of their adoption of modern civilization. Chief Sour Mush listened to Gambold's words and began an angry tirade in Tsa-La-Gi. He wasn't angry with Gambold; rather he was rebuking those Cherokee who touted belief in the old ways but who acted with shame by stealing horses and committing other offenses. Although the Cherokee leadership was forced to dampen their enthusiasm for the civilization process during the height of the religious revival, a series of unfulfilled prophecies began to undermine the credibility of the movement.

The Cherokee leaders tried to reassure Meigs that the Cherokee were not interested in joining forces with Tecumseh. Ridge, John Walker, and John Lowrey even offered Cherokee assistance in the upcoming war with the British, although the sentiment of the majority was to remain neutral, both in the Anglo-American war and in the Creek civil war.

1813

Cherokee Warriors Join American Forces Against the Upper Creeks

In January 1813 President Madison appointed John Armstrong to be the new Secretary of War, after a series of setbacks in the War of 1812. Within weeks there were American victories north and south. On April 15 General James Wilkinson captured and occupied Mobile, which had been used by the British, even though it was in Spanish territory. Two weeks later the Americans under General Henry Dearborn captured Fort York and went on to burn the Canadian capital buildings. Later Admiral Oliver Hazard Perry led the United States Navy to victory at the Battle of Lake Erie, and in October General William Henry Harrison overtook the retreating British and Indians at the Battle of the Thames. The Shawnee patriot Tecumseh was killed and the British/Indian alliance was sundered.

The Spanish feared American forays into Florida, but not enough to discourage them from offering arms to the Red Stick Creeks. On July 27 at the Battle of Burnt Corn, a small Mississippi militia ambushed a party of Red Sticks returning from Pensacola with supplies. Although the Americans made off with the bulk of the arms, the Creeks ran them off the battlefield. This was the opening act of the Creek War—the southern phase of the War of 1812. The Red Sticks were encouraged by their limited success and were ready for more action.

On August 30, 1813, Chief Red Eagle (William Weatherford) led a surprise attack against Fort Mims, a stockade forty miles north of Mobile. (See Map 10.) The fort housed three hundred men, women, and children, including one hundred twenty militiamen. The commanding officer, Major Daniel Beasley, ignored warnings of a possible attack so when the assault came, the Creeks overwhelmed the defenders. Only a handful of Americans survived to tell the story of Fort Mims. Exaggerated accounts of Creek savagery spread alarm across the southwest, but also inspired interest among the southerners in prosecuting a war against them. Tennessee alone provided twenty-five hundred volunteers, half of whom were placed under the command of General Andrew Jackson. (See Figure 5, page 219.) They built Fort Strother on the Coosa River as a staging ground for future attacks.

The volunteer spirit was not limited to the Tennesseans. The Cherokee leader Ridge attended a Lower Creek meeting at Coweta in September where he received an invitation to join in opposing the Red Sticks and the British. The Cherokee Council was cool to the invitation, and no formal declaration of war was issued against the Creeks. The sentiment of the people had changed, however, since the year before and Ridge was able to recruit a few hundred volunteers to join the battle.

In a defensive move, Jackson successfully dispatched one thousand men (including four hundred Cherokees) under Colonel Gideon Morgan and Chief John Lowrey to aid Pathkiller, whose men were in danger of being cut off at Turkey Town. On

Map 10

November 3, 1813, a group of volunteers under General John Coffee and a group of Creek and Cherokees led by Captain Richard Brown attacked Tallushatchee. Coffee's men formed a semi-circle around the town to induce the Creeks to come out to attack. He closed the ends of the line around the Red Sticks, inducing severe losses while suffering minimal casualties himself. A few days later Jackson learned that the Red Sticks had surrounded friendly Indians at the town of Talladega. He led twenty-five hundred men in an attempt to encircle them much as Coffee had done at Tallushatchee. The Red Sticks were able to break the line, but once again they suffered great casualties while the Americans suffered minimally.

General Jackson was forced to head back to Fort Strother because of dwindling supplies and the threat of desertion among his own men. He was open to peace offerings from the residents of Hillabee Town and sent messengers back asking the town to discuss terms. Meanwhile, General James White (who was not under Jackson's command) led one thousand men, in-cluding four hun-

Figure 5 — Andrew Jackson

dred Cherokee under Colonel Morgan and Chief Lowery, toward Hillabee. While they surrounded the town, its inhabitants were unpre-pared for battle since they were under negotiations for peace. White's men destroyed the town and with it any hope that the Creeks would ne-gotiate another peace.

1814

*Cherokee Soldiers Turn the Tide at the Battle
of Horseshoe Bend*

During 1814 the American armed forces experienced ups and
downs. On one hand the British were able to torch the White House
and otherwise wreak havoc along the Middle Atlantic coast, and the
Americans were forced to abandon plans to invade Canada. On the
other hand, the Americans forced the Shawnee, Delaware, Wyandot,
Seneca, and Miami to sign the Treaty of Grenville, by which the Indians promised to make peace with the United States and to declare war
on the British.

The most impressive military gains for the United States occurred
in the Creek War phase of the larger conflict. General Andrew Jackson
had commanded his troops to impressive victories in 1813, but he had
to take his men back to Fort Strother for supplies, reorganization, and
reinforcements. He commissioned the Cherokee leader Ridge as a major and also recognized the leadership of John Ross and Charles Hicks.
The newly reinforced troops headed off toward the Creek stronghold
at Horseshoe Bend (Tohopeka) on the Tallapoosa River. (See Map 11.)

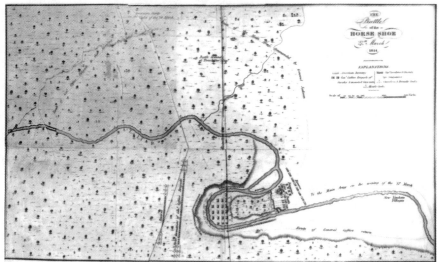

Map 11

While they were encamped at Emuckfaw Creek on the northern side of the Tallapoosa, an aggressive party of Creek warriors surprised the soldiers. The arrival of friendly Indians to the rear allowed Jackson's men to disengage and head back toward Fort Strother. After a furious battle at Enotochopco Creek on January 24, the American forces made it back to the fort. Although the Creeks had taken more casualties, they had forced a larger and better-armed force to retreat. At the same time General John Floyd advanced again from Georgia with a force of thirteen hundred Americans and about four hundred friendly Indians. They were surprised by a party of Creeks on Caleebee Creek on January 17 and had to retreat.

Over the next month Jackson's forces were joined by motivated volunteers, and discipline was restored after a mutinous soldier was convicted by a court-martial and executed. By the middle of March Jackson had over four thousand men under his command and was ready for another assault on the Creeks. He left a garrison at Fort Strother then descended the Coosa River to the mouth of Cedar Creek, where his men erected Fort Williams. He left his stores under protection there and then proceeded toward the Horseshoe Bend of the Tallapoosa River, where the Creek forces were known to be amassed. The Creeks had built breastworks across the narrows of the bend, enclosing about one hundred acres of land. The isthmus was the home to about a thousand warriors and over three hundred women and children.

General Jackson commanded Colonel John Coffee with his mounted men and virtually all of the Indian forces to cross the river and surround the bank opposite the bend, so as to preclude escape. Some men were likewise positioned on an island just downstream to intercept any escapees swimming that way. Jackson's men placed cannon on a small rise about eighty yards from the breastworks. The cannon sent volleys toward the fortification for hours while the soldiers kept up a rain of bullets. While the situation seemed to be a stalemate at the breastworks, the Cherokee, led by Major Ridge, became impatient with the waiting game. They began swimming over to the Creek side of the River and stealing their canoes. They used the Creek's own boats to ferry warriors across for an attack from the rear. The Cherokee warriors set buildings on fire and advanced toward the Creek side of the breastworks. This distraction allowed Jackson to send his troops over the fortification in a frontal assault. At the end of the day several hundred Creek warriors lay dead on the ground, and more than two hundred had been killed as they tried to cross the river. About three hundred women and children were taken as prisoners. There were almost no men taken prisoner and perhaps only a couple of dozen who successfully escaped. Jackson and his Indian allies lost no more than fifty men killed. Among the Cherokees who served with distinction were Colonel John Lowrey, Major Ridge, Major John Walker, Captain Richard Taylor, Adjutant John Ross, Kunnessee, and Junaluska.

The Battle of Horseshoe Bend was the turning point of the Creek War. William Weatherford surrendered two weeks later, remarking that he had no army left with which to fight. Clearly the brave rear assault of the Cherokee warriors had been the deciding element of the battle. Ironically, while the battle was raging a group of soldiers from eastern Tennessee (who were not under Jackson's command) raided and destroyed a number of Cherokee farms and towns. When Agent Colonel Return J. Meigs reported this abuse, General Jackson was enraged. He was enraged not because of the terrible injustice done to his brave allies; he was enraged because the Cherokee complained about it, and he denied that the incident had even occurred. In his official reports of the battle he downplayed the significance of the Cherokee participation.

General Jackson met with representatives from the Creeks and on August 9, 1814, signed the Treaty of Fort Jackson. Even though only the Upper (Red Stick) Creeks had fought against the United States, Jackson forced all of the tribal leaders to sign the document, and thus cede over twenty million acres of land in southern Georgia and eastern Mississippi—over half of the Creek territory. It did not matter to Jackson that much of the land that the Creeks had been forced to cede was claimed by the Cherokee. The "Articles of Agreement and Capitulation" did state, however, that property taken from friendly Creeks, Cherokee, Choctaw, and Chickasaw would be returned.

General Jackson spent no time resting on his laurels. In defiance of orders from Secretary of War James Monroe, he invaded and captured Pensacola. From there he went on to New Orleans where he anticipated his first major battle with the British. Meanwhile, the War of 1812 was not being decided on the battlefield. President James Madison asked Congress to repeal the Embargo and Non-Importation Acts, which he felt hurt the United States more than they had helped. Even though the overthrow of Napoleon had given the British a free hand to concentrate on the American phase of the conflict and despite the fact that the British forces had forced the evacuation of the American capital, the time for peace had come. On Christmas Eve, 1814, the United States and Britain signed the Treaty of Ghent, thus ending the war. Although some clarifications were made of the border between the United States and Canada, there was no conclusion reached on the issue of impressment of American sailors or of the other issues that had precipitated the war in the first place.

The War of 1812 fizzled out, in a sense, but not before the Cherokee had demonstrated that they could be loyal and effective allies of the United States. Their rewards did not seem to match their contributions.

1815

General Jackson Betrays the Cherokee

On January 8, 1815, British Commander Sir Edward Pakenham attacked the entrenched American forces of General Andrew Jackson at New Orleans. The battle was meaningless in that the Treaty of Ghent, ending the war, had already been signed in Europe. The lopsided victory for the Americans, however, greatly boosted American morale and propelled Jackson toward a political career.

In the aftermath of the War of 1812 the United States negotiated the Treaty of Portage-des-Sioux, ending hostilities in the old Northwest Territory and opening up the area south of Lake Michigan for settlement. The Cherokee were involved in negotiations centered on clarifications of the Treaty of Fort Jackson. General Jackson had forced the Creeks to cede over twenty million acres of land, some of which was claimed by the Cherokee. Furthermore, the Cherokee were incensed that American soldiers had destroyed some of their homes while they were in Alabama fighting with Andrew Jackson. Jackson denied that the pillaging ever took place or that the Cherokee warriors had been of much help.

Meanwhile the Christian missionaries were experiencing difficulties. The disruptions caused by the Cherokee religious revival in 1811–1812 and the war with the Creeks lessened Cherokee interest or availability for participation in the mission. Samuel Worcester (writing from Salem, Massachusetts) instructed the missionary Jeremiah Evarts not to worry about teaching the Bible. He explained that it would be best just to teach the Indians English first and that the religious work would follow. Ironically, the Cherokee had been making the same argument for over a decade! A new era in Christian missionary activity was beginning among the Cherokee as the American Board of Commissioners for Foreign Missions took an interest in the Cherokee.

1816

The Treaty of Fort Jackson Revised

During the last year of James Madison's presidency, the nation was preoccupied with the financial aftermath of the War of 1812 and with the naval war against the Dey of Algiers. Peace with the northwestern Indians allowed Indiana to be admitted to the union, but Florida presented a special problem. Runaway slaves from Georgia, abetted by Seminoles, Creeks, and perhaps even Cherokee, took over the abandoned Fort Apalachicola at the Flint and Chattahoochee rivers. General Andrew Jackson issued warnings to the Spanish that the United States would not stand for the fort to continue as an enticement for slave rebellion. The Spanish were powerless to prevent the actions of the slaves and their Indian allies so on July 29 the United States sent in an expeditionary force and destroyed it.

The Cherokee had grievances with the United States stemming from the conduct of the Tennessee militia during the Creek War and the terms of the Treaty of Fort Jackson. The Cherokee Council appointed a delegation of chiefs (including Colonel John Lowrey, Major Ridge, Captain John Walker, Captain Richard Taylor, Cheucunsenee, and Adjutant John Ross) to meet with President Madison in Washington. Agent Colonel Return J. Meigs served as negotiator and was successful in concluding two treaties, both of which were signed on March 22, 1816.

By the terms of the first treaty the Cherokee ceded their remaining land in South Carolina (the extreme northwest corner bordered by the Chatuga River) for five thousand dollars. (See Map 3 #21, page 26.)

The second treaty awarded the Cherokee compensation for damages to their property incurred during the Creek War. The treaty stipulated that there would be free use of roads cutting through the Cherokee territory and free navigation of the rivers. The Cherokee gained the right to establish various commercial enterprises along the routes. The most controversial clause of the agreement was the definition of the boundary between the Cherokee and the Creeks. The line was drawn between the Tennessee and Coosa rivers. (See Map 8 #22, page 158.) The United States effectively returned land that had been ceded by the Creeks by the Treaty of Fort Jackson, but claimed by the Cherokee. The Chickasaw also claimed this land, and Andrew Jackson was furious since he had already attained this region once. (See Map 12.)

Jackson was determined to get the land back and immediately went about opening negotiations. He was able to attain the desired cession by bribing about a dozen Cherokee chiefs, mostly from the Lower Towns. Among them were Pathkiller, Glass, Boat, Sour Mush, Chulioa, Dick Justice, Richard Brown, and Chickasantchee. Fearing reprisals

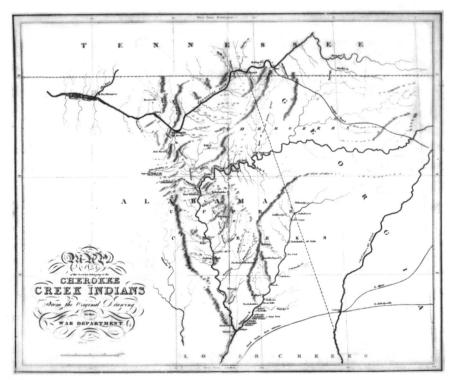

Map 12

for selling land illegally (remembering the execution of Doublehead), the group stipulated that the treaty was valid only if it were ratified by the Cherokee Council. The group took the treaty from the Chickasaw Council where it was signed and brought it to Turkey Town where the Cherokee Council accepted it. The Cherokee were granted over sixty thousand dollars and other compensations.

Meanwhile the American Board of Commissioners for Foreign Missions selected Cyrus Kingsbury to head its first mission among the Cherokee. He met with Creek and Cherokee representatives at Turkey Town early in the autumn and, with help from Agent Meigs and Andrew Jackson, secured permission to start a new mission.

Glass promised to help him select a location for a new school, to be opened early the next year. The Moravian missionary John Gambold welcomed him as a colleague.

1817

An Illegal Cession Treaty Prompts More Governmental Reform

ABCFM Establishes Brainerd School

During James Monroe's first year as President the Era of Good Feelings did not extend to the Indians. The War Department authorized General Andrew Jackson to negotiate with the Cherokee to induce them to trade all lands reserved for them by the January 1806 convention in return for land west of the Mississippi. The new administration was able to obtain four million acres of land from Indians in Ohio and by the end of the year had appointed Jackson to be the commander of an expeditionary force charged with the responsibility of ending the Seminole War. The Seminoles were committing atrocities in Georgia in retaliation for the destruction of Fort Apalachicola.

Jackson gladly took on the responsibility of negotiating the removal of the Cherokee and chose as his deputies Tennessee Governor Joseph McMinn and General David Merriweather. A group of fifteen Cherokee from Arkansas were en route to Washington anyway and were available to negotiate at the Cherokee Agency in Tennessee. None of the eastern chiefs would join at first, although bribery and intimidation induced many of the Upper Town leaders to enter into the negotiations. Among those who opposed the talks were Pathkiller, Major Ridge, Charles Hicks, George Lowrey, and John Ross. Charles Hicks' wife had been murdered in an attempt to intimidate him into favoring removal. Among the Upper Town chiefs who participated in the talks, Tuckasee, Glass, and Utsala are suspected of having taken bribes, but perhaps all of them did.

A treaty concluded on July 8, 1817, had the signatures or marks of fifteen Arkansas chiefs and thirty-one eastern chiefs. A tract in Georgia east of the Chattahoochee River extending west to Wafford's Purchase and a tract in Tennessee including the southern half of the Sequatchee Valley (see Map 3 #23, page 26.) was traded for the rights to land in Arkansas already occupied by Cherokee. The United States argued that the value of these lands defrayed the cost of protecting the Cherokee settlers in Arkansas, who were at risk of war with the Osage (who claimed that land). The Cherokee also ceded two small pieces of land in Alabama. (See Map 8 #24-26, page 158.) One was the northern shore of the Tennessee River at Muscle Shoals. The other was also on the northern bank where Colbert's Ferry crossed the river at the Natchez Trace. These tracts were to pay for lands in Arkansas to be occupied by the Cherokee in the future. No money was exchanged officially, but over four thousand dollars was paid out in bribes. The United States couldn't wait for the Cherokee Council to ratify the new agreement and immediately began preparing for the removal of those Cherokee willing to leave.

The Cherokee Council swiftly reacted against the treaty. The diffuse nature of the Cherokee political structure had made them vulnerable to independent negotiations by local factions willing to trade land for bribes. Major Ridge and Charles Hicks secured the demotion of Chief Tewchale and engineered the election of Pathkiller as the Principal Chief, with Charles Hicks being appointed his second. An act created the Standing Committee, to be appointed by the Chiefs and Warriors in National Council Assembled. The Committee was to consist of thirteen men serving two-year terms and was to function as an executive, legislative, and judicial body of government. The Committee was forbidden from taking action that would affect common property of the tribe. Actions involving land cessions would require the unanimous consent of the Chiefs of Council.

One of the next actions of the Council was to appoint a delegation to go to Washington to meet with President Monroe and protest the treaty negotiated by Jackson. Going Snake and John McIntosh were among those appointed for this task. If the United States thought that it was important for the Cherokee to become civilized and assume the white man's ways, why was it necessary now for the Cherokee to be moved to Arkansas to reassume the old ways? Most of the Upper Cherokee, many of who were half-blooded Indians, were anxious to maintain their progress and continue building the new economy based on agriculture and trade.

The American Board of Commissioners for Foreign Missions was anxious to continue its work with the Cherokee. The Reverend Cyrus Kingsbury bought land from George McDonald early in the year and established Brainerd School in March. Kingsbury was well received by the Cherokee and by the Moravian missionaries. Later in the year the Board sent Elias Cornelius to prepare for the establishment of more missions among the Chickasaw, Choctaw, and Creeks. Certainly Kingsbury opposed the removal of the Cherokee. The Board considered the Cherokee and other natives as human beings worthy of respect and capable of becoming Christians.

1818

The Cherokee Council Rejects Removal

In 1818 the United States made significant progress expanding at the expense of the Indians and Spanish. Andrew Jackson played a central role in much of the action. He had been appointed head of an expeditionary force charged with ending hostilities with the Seminoles in Florida. The Seminoles were raiding southern Georgia and were accused of abetting runaway slaves. General Jackson sent a letter to President James Monroe in January asking for permission to invade Florida. When a reply did not come forth promptly, Jackson interpreted the silence as an approval of his plan. Jackson's men (over a thousand troops from Georgia and Tennessee, plus friendly Indians) captured Fort Marks, south of modern Tallahassee. An international incident occurred when Jackson executed two British traders accused of aiding the Indians, but the execution of a couple of Creek chiefs did not cause much alarm. The expeditionary force moved ahead and, after destroying a Seminole village, captured Pensacola and established a military occupation government. The war was essentially over. Although Monroe had not sanctioned Jackson's actions, Secretary of State John Quincy Adams defended his actions as defensive and suggested that if Spain could not control its colony then it should be ceded to the United States.

While Jackson was occupied with the Seminoles, Governor Joseph McMinn of Tennessee was left in charge of negotiating with the Cherokee. The Monroe administration wanted to try one more time to persuade the Cherokee to trade their homeland for safe removal to Arkansas. A party of Cherokee leaders already living in Arkansas had urged the eastern Cherokee to accept the terms offered in 1817 and then moved on to Washington in early 1818 to discuss border issues and other problems. Uncertainties about land ownership were the basis for ongoing conflicts with the Osage. The pressures to move were so strong that many of the Cherokee who felt removal was inevitable didn't even bother to plant crops in the spring.

A series of Council meetings were held to address the removal issue. A meeting of twenty-two Chiefs in Council at Brounstown convened in May and sent Agent Return J. Meigs a letter protesting the measures being used to affect the removal. Forty-nine members of the Council at Ustanali met in June and sent a message protesting the American negotiating tactics (bribes, coercion) that had been in use since 1805. At the Ustanali meeting the Cherokee women rose to speak, eloquently protesting against removal. At the end of the session at Turkey Town Principal Chief Pathkiller gave a message to Meigs formally rejecting the removal offer.

Governor McMinn was not finished with his negotiations and decided to attend a Council meeting personally. Citing Cherokee threats against his life, McMinn brought soldiers with him, violating the tradition of not bringing arms to the Council. Clearly it was an attempt at intimidation since the last time such a violation had occurred the Principal Chief was murdered. McMinn explained to the chiefs that removal was their best option. With the rapid increase in settlements in the area, the United States could no longer guarantee the safety of the Cherokee within their own boundaries. McMinn offered one hundred thousand dollars for the entire Cherokee territory in return for land in Arkansas and safe passage. The offer was rejected and then doubled. Again the Council would not accept money for their homeland.

Meanwhile the missionary work among the Cherokee continued. Secretary of War John C. Calhoun roundly criticized The Reverend Elijah Cornelias of the American Board of Commissioners for Foreign Missions for having sided with the Cherokee against the United States in 1817. The Reverend Samuel Worcester of the ABCFM defended the missionary as being neutral, although in truth the sentiments of the mission were with the Indians. The Reverend Cyrus Kingsbury was reassigned to start new missions among the other southern tribes and was replaced at Brainerd by The Reverend Ard Hoyt.

Toward the end of the year the United States celebrated its expansion with the admission of the State of Illinois into the union. After his successes in Florida, Jackson had been paired with former Kentucky governor Isaac Shelby to negotiate the purchase of western Kentucky and Tennessee from the Chickasaw. The Chickasaw had already ceded claims to lands in Middle Tennessee previously ceded by the Cherokee. The United States was not satisfied with McMinn's failure to affect the removal of the Cherokee. At the insistence of Colonel Meigs, the Council appointed a delegation to accompany him to Washington for further discussions.

1819

Calhoun's Treaty and a Presidential Visit

In 1819 the United States became embroiled in the worst financial panic since the Revolution. The effects of inflation, land speculation, and overextended investment were compounded by unwise policies of the Second National Bank. On the diplomatic front, however, the Seminole War led to the signing of the Adams-Onis Treaty in Washington in February. Spain ceded Eastern Florida and renounced all claims to Western Florida, which the United States already occupied. The United

States gave up claims to Texas and agreed to pay five million dollars for debts owed Spain by private citizens. The border was set between the United States and Mexico. The cession of Florida paved the way for the admission of Alabama into the union in December.

As the year began the Cherokee were in the midst of a crisis. Although Tennessee Governor Joseph McMinn had been unsuccessful in negotiating the removal of the Cherokee to Arkansas, he continued to pressure on the tribe by intimidation and by allowing the sale of Indian lands in violation of the Treaty if 1817. Although over two thousand Cherokee had moved to Arkansas the year before, the vast majority of the remaining thirteen thousand did not wish to leave. Once again they didn't know if it were worthwhile to plant crops that the white people would harvest later.

The Cherokee Council sent a delegation to Washington to seek a resolution to the conflict. Second Chief Charles Hicks led the group that included John and Lewis Ross, John Martin, George Lowrey, James Brown, Gideon Morgan Jr., Cabbin Smith, Sleeping Rabbit, Small Wood, John Walker, and Currahee Dick. John Ross made a point of visiting The Reverend Ard Hoyt, to assure him that they would look after the interests of the mission and even try to negotiate an endowment for the schools. In return, Hoyt promised the assistance of the American Board of Commissioners for Foreign Missions in conducting the negotiations.

The Cherokee delegation arrived in Washington at the end of January. Secretary of War John C. Calhoun did not trust Joseph McMinn, who had proved to be a poor replacement for Agent Return J. Meigs, and so did not invite him. Meigs did provide census data that suggested that five thousand Cherokee lived in Arkansas and probably no more than ten thousand in the East. These numbers were disputed by the Cherokee, who insisted that no more than twenty-five hundred Cherokee had left the homeland, and thirteen thousand remained. Although the Council had granted Hicks the authority to negotiate the sale of the entire national territory, Calhoun found that it was their intention to part with as little as possible. A treaty was drafted and presented to the Cherokee delegation on February 22. It met the approval of The Reverend Samuel Worcester of the American Board, who had arrived a few days earlier. In the end the Cherokee accepted Meigs' assertion about the number of Cherokee who had emigrated from the East.

Calhoun's Treaty was signed on February 27, 1819. The Cherokee ceded nine tracts of land totaling about four million acres (see Map 8 #27-35, page 158), the largest of which included the northeast corner of the nation. (See Map 3 #29, page 26.) The cession accounted for roughly a third of their territory and compensated for the land in Arkansas granted to roughly a third of the Cherokee. The cession was to cover the costs of all past and future emigration. The delegation agreed that the Arkansas branch would receive a third of the annual stipend. One of the tracts near Muscle Shoals was earmarked for the provision of a fifteen thousand dollar annuity for the development and maintenance of the ABCFM schools. This treaty resolved all disputes arising from the 1817 treaty. One clause granted three hundred forty-two tracts of six hundred forty acres apiece to Cherokees who wanted to stay in the east but who agreed to become citizens of the United States. After the treaty the Cherokee Nation was limited to the northwest corner of Georgia (where most of them lived), the southeast corner of Tennessee, the extreme western tip of North Carolina, and northeast Alabama.

Principal Chief Pathkiller was relieved that the removal crisis was over and praised Charles Hicks and the Ross brothers as saviors of the nation. John Ross was pleased that The Reverend Worcester was able to use his influence in Washington, and Worcester was glad that the Board received the endowment for the schools. Calhoun was perhaps less pleased and instructed Governor McMinn to cease all further efforts at removal and to finish up his (illegal) business. It was noted by the Board that since Florida had been ceded to the United States, it could no longer be argued that the removal of the southern Indians was necessary in order to protect the southern flank of the nation from foreign attacks.

With the removal crisis resolved, the American Board could concentrate on its mission. It decided to build more schools but to send the good students to the original school at Brainerd. The best students, however, would be sent to the Board's school in Cornwall, Connecticut. By the end of the year Elias Boudinot, Leonard Hicks, John Ridge, John Vann, and several other Cherokee scholars had arrived at Cornwall. As the Board planned new schools they did not ignore Arkansas. Although Glass opposed the construction of a school in the Arkansas territory, a party of missionaries was sent there at the end of the year to explore the possibility of a new mission. The highlight of the year undoubtedly was the visit of President James Monroe. The Reverend Worcester knew that the President was planning a trip to the area and invited him to come visit the mission his administration had just saved. The President's entourage visited on May 27, 1819. Perhaps the Era of Good Feelings did extend to the Cherokee.

Chapter Eleven

1820–1827

Civilization, Constitutional Government, and
Resistance to Removal

The organizational changes in Cherokee government that took place in the 1820s reflected the cultural evolution of the tribe. An elite ruling class emerged who were educated, Christian, capitalist, and mostly half-blooded. The degree of progress that had been made since the inception of the "civilization" program of the United States was illustrated by a census of the Cherokee that was completed in 1824. In fifteen years the population increased by almost a third and the number of slaves held by Cherokees more than doubled. Other measures of agricultural productivity, industrial growth, and commercial improvements were even more dramatic. The Cherokee also could brag that they had developed their own alphabet and were on the verge of operating their own printing press.

The missionaries, especially those of the American Board of Commissioners for Foreign Missions, pushed many of the changes in the Cherokee society for Foreign Missions of New England. During this time there were converts, although many clung to ancient ways that were not entirely consistent with the new religion. The ruling elite, who were the most likely to convert to Christianity, were also the most likely to benefit from governmental reform. The traditional Cherokee had little to benefit from more laws patterned after the white man's ways.

The capitalists, however, had gains to be protected and preserved. They pushed for a consolidation of power under a strong National Committee and a representational Council, at the expense of the individual chiefs. The local leaders would no longer have the ability to derail policies beneficial to the nation as a whole, and more importantly, would be less capable of cutting their own land cession deals.

Inevitably the conservative Cherokees rebelled against the reform movement and against the missionaries as well. Many Cherokee were offended when the ABCFM closed Cornwall School after two Cherokee Christians married white women. White Path and his followers heckled the Christians and argued about inconsistencies in their doctrine. White Path also established an alternate Council, although it never had the power that the official one had. The rebel movement was given new steam until the venerable Principal Chief Pathkiller died before elections for the Constitutional Convention. Pathkiller had been acceptable to all factions, but his death allowed the elite to dominate the Council.

President James Monroe had held on to George Washington's policy of promoting civilization of the Indians. John Quincy Adams seems to have concluded that removal of the eastern Indians was the only reasonable approach. When Adams sent a delegate to the Cherokee to negotiate for a removal treaty, it was on the eve of the Constitutional Convention. The American agent's actions pushed the Cherokee factions to compromise with each other, uniting in their opposition to removal. The result of the Convention was a new Constitution, signed July 26, 1827. The Cherokee boasted constitutional government led by Christians, a sound economy, well-organized schools, and the development of their own press. Certainly the United States would respect such a highly organized political entity, and removal should no longer be considered.

1820

Cherokees Establish Representational Government

During 1820 the United States dealt with growing sectionalism between the slave-holding southern states and the North. The Missouri Compromise allowed Missouri to enter the Union as a slave state, to counter the admission of Maine as a free state, and also limited slavery to the most southern part of the Louisiana Purchase. For a while the Union appeared to be intact. The economy had nearly collapsed during the Panic of 1819, but the Monroe administration had been taking steps to bring it around. The Public Land Act lowered the price of western land but forbade selling it on credit. The intention of the act was to lower the debt of the western settlers, but in the end only the land speculators benefited. Despite the trouble of the previous year, James Monroe was re-elected President, winning the electoral vote of every state.

The civilization process gained new steam among the Cherokee after the resolution of the removal crisis in 1819. The Reverend Samuel Worcester of the American Board of Commissioners for Foreign Missions reassured Secretary of War John C. Calhoun that they were in complete agreement about the civilization policy. The ABCFM faced competition from missionaries associated with other denominations, such as the Baptists, but it retained its dominant position among the tribe. Alfred Finney and Cephas Washburn left Brainerd and established a new mission in Arkansas. Meanwhile the ABCFM schools were becoming more popular among the Cherokee, with both John Ross and Pathkiller asking for new schools to be built near their homes. The missionaries began to meet with some success not only as educators, but also as evangelists. The baptism of David Brown and his subsequent enrollment at Cornwall School in Connecticut symbolized a growing acceptance of Christianity among the Cherokee.

The most dramatic manifestation of the success of the civilization movement was the governmental reform established at the autumn meeting of the Council. The fifty-four villages would no longer send representatives to the Council. Rather, the nation was divided into eight geographical districts, each with its own Council House to serve as a judiciary. Each district would have a judge and a marshal appointed by the National Council. The citizens of each district were to elect four representatives to the National Council. The Council was thus reduced from over one hundred members to only thirty-two. The National Committee (thirteen members) acted as an upper house and had veto power over the actions of the Council. The National Council had veto power over the Committee, but it empowered the Committee to act at times when the Council was not in session. The Cherokee National Council met at

Figure 6 — John Ross

the new capital, New Town, located at the junction of the Conasauga and Coosawatee rivers. John Ross was elected President of the National Council and was assisted by two other officers. (See Figure 6.)

The new form of representational government reduced the power of the individual chiefs since they were no longer all members of the Council. The tradition of rule by consensus was abandoned as the tribe assumed a system of majority rule based on the American system. A new Lighthorse system was organized with a ranger appointed for each district. They were responsible for enforcing was the abolishment of blood revenge—the seven clans would no longer maintain this tradition. Another new law made the sale of land to non-Cherokees an act of treason punishable by execution.

1821

Sequoyah Introduces a Tsa-La-Gi Syllabary

During the last weeks of James Monroe's first term as President New Spain granted Moses Austin the right to bring three hundred settlers to Texas. Within a few weeks Mexico declared its independence from Spain and Moses Austin was dead. Monroe did not hasten to recognize the new nation to the south since Spain had not yet relinquished control of Florida. On July 1, however, Andrew Jackson, the newly appointed military governor, took possession of Florida from Spain.

The ABCFM missions in Arkansas and at Brainerd met with difficulties and successes in 1821. Cephas Washburn and Alfred Finney reported a general lack of enthusiasm among the Cherokee for their mission, despite a visit from Chief John Jolly. Their efforts also were hampered by the outbreak of warfare between the Arkansas Cherokee and the Osage Indians. At Brainerd flooding by the Tennessee River destroyed stock and grain and added to the poverty. They suffered from a lack of manpower and skilled workers as well as a growing lack of confidence in the leadership. Competition from other missions was evident as the Moravians established a second school at Oochgeelogy, near Brainerd. Meanwhile John Ridge (see Figure 7) and Elias Boudinot (see Figure 8) set off a scandal at Cornwall by proposing marriage to two white

Figure 7 — John Ridge

Figure 8 —Elias Boudinot

Figure 9 — Sequoyah

girls. They were sent back home along with some other students. The Reverend Samuel Worcester came to visit Brainerd in the spring, but as fate would have it, he contracted an illness and died at the mission. On a positive note, The Reverend Ard Hoyt reported that he started leading services using Tsa-La-Gi, the Cherokee language.

The year 1821 was a red-letter date in the history of the Cherokee for another reason. Sequoyah (George Gist), son of Nathaniel Gist (George Washington's ambassador to the Cherokee during the Revolutionary War), revealed to the nation that he had invented a Tsa-La-Gi syllabary, which enabled the Cherokee to write in their native tongue. (See Figure 9.) He immediately demonstrated its use by recording speeches he heard in the Council. He also used it to record notes that helped him discuss boundary issues with representatives from Georgia.

The success of the new writing system was swift, as it stirred up great interest among the Cherokee.

1822

The Cherokee National Superior Court Convenes at New Town

At the Congress of Vienna in 1822, France, Prussia, and Russia promised to support Spain's efforts to recover its lost colonies in South America. Notably Great Britain did not support the Spanish and of course the United States responded by recognizing the independence of Mexico. The United States experienced a period of economic expansion and witnessed the opening of the Erie Canal. The South was threatened, however, by an aborted slave rebellion in Charleston—increasing the fears of slaveholders and inspiring stricter slave regulations.

The relationship between the United States and the Indians continued to change as the government relinquished its monopoly on trade. The Indian trade was no longer controlled in government-owned trade houses, but rather was carried on by private companies. On May 6, 1822, an "Act for Regulating the Indian Trade" was enacted as an amendment to the 1802 law. The new law revised the licensing rules for traders, placed restrictions on liquor sales, set regulations for the distributions of annuities, and created a special superintendent of Indian affairs to reside in St. Louis.

In the northwest the United States was successful in negotiating a treaty with the Fox and Sauk tribes that limited them to territory in Wisconsin Territory and Illinois. Georgia meanwhile was pressuring the federal government to remove the Creeks and the Cherokee. By the Compact of 1802 Georgia had agreed to give up its western lands to the United States. In return, Georgia was to have received titles to all Indian lands within the boundaries of the state. Disagreement over the interpretation of the Compact became a dispute between those who supported the supremacy of state rights and those who favored federal rights.

In January Charles Hicks sent a letter to the governor of Georgia stating that the Cherokee would sell no more land. In response to pressure from Georgia, Secretary of War Calhoun sent Commissioners D.G. Campbell and J. Merriweather to speak before the Cherokee National Council. Representatives of all eight districts agreed unanimously that when the commissioners arrived there would no negotiations for land cessions but that they would be treated respectfully as friends.

While the Cherokee National Council was meeting at New Town, the first session of the National Superior Court (later Supreme Court) was held. The court was to hear appellate cases from the eight district courts. With the creation of this court the Cherokee arguably had a more advance judicial system than the state of Georgia. Undoubtedly the advancement of civilization of the Indians was a threat to those who favored their removal.

Although the Christian missionaries among the Cherokee continued to make progress in both educating and converting the natives, the condition of the mission at Brainerd was poor. There was increasing jealousy among the missionaries, and the lack of skilled farming techniques and poor fiscal management meant that they were chronically impoverished. The morale of the missionaries was weakened by the prevalence of such diseases as measles. There was a disagreement as well between The Reverend Ard Hoyt and Charles Hicks. Hoyt favored building up the facility at Brainerd but Hicks distrusted the concentration of so many white people in one location. He wanted the missionaries and teachers to be dispersed among the different sections of the nation.

The mission at Dwight, Arkansas, had its share of troubles as well. The Reverend Alfred Finney noted that there was very little interest in the school, since the Cherokee had moved there to avoid civilization in the first place. He was disgusted by the immorality of the Indians (playing ball games naked in front of women and drinking alcohol). He also noted that the white people living in the area did not support the mission and contributed to the delinquency of the Indians by selling them liquor. While the relations between the Cherokee in the east and their Indian neighbors were good (the boundary with the Creek was measured off in 1822), the relations between the Arkansas Cherokee and their neighbors were poor. The Kickapoo, Sauk, and Fox Indians supported the Osage in a war against the Cherokee, who were seen as intruders. The United States did finally intervene to stop the fighting in the fall, but the hostility was far from resolved.

1823

The National Council at New Town Rejects Removal Proposals

In 1823 the United States declined Britain's invitation to join forces against the Holy Alliance and its efforts to help Spain regain its lost colonies. Instead, the nation chose an independent foreign policy and warned Spain and Russia that the American continents were now off-limits for new European colonization—the Monroe Doctrine. Meanwhile Emperor Augustin de Iturbide of newly independent Mexico re-confirmed land grants in Mexico to Stephen Austin, whose late father, Moses, had received grants under the Spanish regime.

Austin wasn't the only one with eyes on Texas. The Arkansas Cherokee had not fared particularly well as the United States had not lived up to its promises. The group found itself impoverished and at war with the Osages. The local white inhabitants were not particularly friendly although they didn't mind selling the Indians alcohol. The ABCFM missionaries were struggling to make the mission at Dwight sustainable, but the Cherokee weren't very interested, and the promised federal funds were delayed. A group of chiefs traveled to Washington to complain, stopping at Brainerd along the way. Secretary of War John C. Calhoun did appoint Benjamin Shattuck to survey the Arkansas Cherokee boundary as promised by the treaties of 1817 and 1819. By then Chief Ta-kan-caugh had already led a group of emigrants into Texas.

Among the most significant domestic events affecting relations between the United States and the Indians was the Supreme Court decision in the case of *Johnson and Graham's Lessee v. William McIntosh.* (See Figure 10, page 243.) The Court decided that in the case of conflicting land claims, titles issued by the United States always are valid over those issued by the Indians. The argument was that the Indians were mere savages incapable of functioning in a civilized manner and that they were legally mere tenants on their land, not owners. European colonists had already claimed the land by the grace of their sovereigns.

The Supreme Court decision gave new strength to white Americans intent on the removal of the Indians. Commissioners from Georgia came into Cherokee territory and tried to bribe chiefs they thought might be willing to cede more land. Return J. Meigs was dead now and the new agents, Joseph McMinn and Colonel David Brearley, were not friendly to the Cherokee. The agents also resented the missionaries and felt that they were encouraging the Cherokee not to cooperate with the United States' efforts to relocate them.

Meanwhile the missionaries and the Cherokee continued to make great progress, despite the adversity. The mission at Brainerd suffered from mismanagement too, but the Cherokee remained interested in schools and Christianity. They continued to learn Sequoyah's new alphabet and English as well, and efforts were made to obtain a new printing press. Each major chief wanted a school near his home, and Second Chief Charles Hicks asked The Reverend Ard Hoyt to build a new national school at New Town, the new capital. The warm reception that Cherokee scholar David Brown received when he visited Yale College underscored the achievement of the missionaries and their charges.

The Cherokee also continued to fine-tune their new governmental structure. When the National Council met at New Town in October it was dominated by the wealthy elite. John Ross, who didn't even speak

Figure 10 — William McIntosh

Tsa-La-Gi very well, was President of the Council, Charles Hicks was Second Chief, and Alexander McCoy was the Clerk of the Council. Major Ridge continued to wield great influence as well. The Council granted the National Committee the right to review and approve all actions of the Council, thus giving each body a check on the other.

The dramatic climax of the autumn Council meeting had nothing to do with governmental reform. Commissioners and agents from the

United States and Georgia attended the meeting in an effort to convince the Cherokee to abandon their lands and accept removal. Instead of addressing the Council immediately, the commissioners met with chiefs individually in an attempt to divide and conquer. When the Council showed no intention of ceding lands in Georgia, the commissioners adopted a more menacing tact. Meanwhile, Creek Chief William McIntosh arrived at the meeting. The half-blooded leader (who was related to the prominent Troup family of Georgia) urged the Council to accept the American offers. He argued that in the future the offers might not be so attractive. McIntosh met privately with some of the Chiefs and offered up to twelve of them two thousand dollars in cash to support removal. When pressed, McIntosh admitted that the United States commissioners had sanctioned his offers. President Ross had a letter written by McIntosh read before the Council. The aging Chief Pathkiller, nearly crippled by arthritis, stood to denounce McIntosh. The Creek meddler left the meeting immediately after his censure. The commissioners continued harassing the Cherokee leadership but finally gave up and left the Council meeting without success. The Cherokee did not like being told that they were not owners but merely tenants of their own homeland.

1824

Cherokee Leaders Meet with President Monroe to Oppose Georgian Land Claims

There were no major foreign threats to the United States in 1824. A treaty was concluded with Russia that determined the Pacific Coast boundaries. The newly recognized independent Mexico adopted a new constitution that established Texas as one of its states. American domestic politics heated up as four candidates emerged to replace the retiring James Monroe as President: Senator Andrew Jackson, Secretary of the Treasury William Crawford, Secretary of State John Quincy Adams, and Representative Henry Clay. Virtually every legislative or executive action for the entire year was affected by this competition. Secretary of War John C. Calhoun took himself out of the competition by accepting the nomination for Vice President, but he remained very influential in the cabinet. He established the Bureau of Indian Affairs as a branch of the War Department and appointed Thomas L. McKenney as its commissioner.

Calhoun encouraged Monroe to support the removal of the eastern Indians while the President still favored Washington's civilization plan. Early in the year delegations from both the eastern and western Cherokee arrived in Washington to negotiate with the administration. The Arkansas Cherokee were upset that they had not received annuities that were promised them when they agreed to move west. The United States countered that it could not be determined what percentage of the annuity the western band would get since they had not completed a census. The Arkansas Cherokee further complained that the United States had failed to define the western boundary of their territory, thus allowing a festering conflict with the neighboring Osage tribe.

The delegation from the Old Nation included John Ross, George Lowrey, Elijah Hicks, and Major Ridge. The Cherokee asked Monroe to abrogate the Georgia Compact of 1802 and demanded that Joseph McMinn be removed as agent. They asked that the United States help them collect taxes from white men living in Cherokee territory. The Cherokee further complained that the United States had never paid them for the Wafford Settlement (a tract of land in northwest Georgia that was ceded in 1804). Monroe denied that such a treaty even existed until the Cherokee produced a copy of the treaty signed by President Jefferson. The Cherokee proposed that the United States give Georgia the Florida Territory in return for its claims to Cherokee lands. Monroe did not consider that option viable. The eastern delegation stayed in Washington until the spring to see if the administration would get any legislative proposals to Congress. In the end the meeting was fruitless. Georgia's Governor Troup was furious that Monroe did not succeed in getting the Cherokee out of his state, but the President pointed out that the Compact of 1802 did not have a provision for the forceful removal of the Cherokee.

The Arkansas delegation left Washington first, having realized that they were wasting their time. David Brown, the mixed-blood missionary who had been assisting the tribe in Washington, traveled back to Arkansas with the chiefs. There the tribe was continuing to make progress in its political organization. The National Committee included President

John Jolly, Vice President Ta-kan-caugh, Speaker Black Fox, Chairman Walter Webber, and Secretary David Brown. Since the United States had failed to settle the western boundary dispute, the Cherokee chose representatives for negotiations with the Osage tribe: David Brown, Long Knife, Tahneh, John Thornton, John Jolly, and Black Fox. The United States also enacted a new trade bill that established a monopolistic trade post system for the western tribes. A well-organized tribal government would be necessary to counter the effects of that legislation. The ABCFM missionaries were also getting better organized at Dwight. Their leader, The Reverend Cephas Washburn, wrote Jeremiah Evarts, Secretary of the Board, requesting a printing press and printer for the mission. John Arch (Atsi) had published the first translation of a Bible passage into Tsa-La-Gi, and there was interest in translating the entire New Testament. Certainly the power of publishing would enhance the political position of the tribe as well.

The missionaries were having popularity problems on the eastern side of the Mississippi. The ABCFM was having a hard time raising money in the southern states because the people there generally did not support the civilization of the Indians. Fund[raising in New England was severely pinched after John Ridge (son of Major Ridge) married a white girl named Sarah Northrup. Eventually Cornwall School was closed in protest after another Cherokee student, Elias Boudinot, also married a white woman. The Prudential Committee of the Board resolved that the missionaries needed to concentrate on religious matters and ordered them to stop providing secular services (such as a blacksmith shop) to the Cherokee. Perhaps the Board did not realize that they were already losing esteem among the Cherokee.

The Cherokee were upset about inconsistencies among the missionaries regarding the Ridge/Northrup marriage. On another level the local chiefs found that the missionaries were threatening their authority—an authority already weakened by the consolidation of the tribal government. The chiefs at Etowah (Hightower) were particularly offended that the converts were not allowed to attend the local Council and thus had to go to the National Council to air grievances. They also noted that newly converted Negro slaves began refusing to obey their Cherokee masters.

The backlash against the missionaries took two forms: violence and revivalism. Moody Hall, a particularly strict missionary, angered his charges by forbidding ball playing and drinking, and he found himself a victim of violence. The emergence of prophets of traditional ways began this year although their influence was not yet great. Among the reactionaries was White Path, who questioned the validity of Christianity and promoted the return to traditional ways. Major Ridge countered their influence by inviting The Reverend William Chamberlin to open the fall Council meeting with a prayer. John Ridge, who had just arrived with his controversial new bride, provided the translation. The Council did not meet the next day in observance of the Sabbath.

1825

New Laws Consolidate the Power of the Ruling Elite

American presidential politics was in a state of chaos in January after no candidate received a majority of the electoral votes. The House of Representatives chose the new President from among the three highest vote winners: Senator Andrew Jackson, Secretary of State John Q. Adams, and Representative Henry Clay. Clay threw his support to the New Englander, so Adams was elected on February 9 and inaugurated just four weeks later. Jackson cried foul after Clay was rewarded with a cabinet post. The legislature of Tennessee followed by nominating the General to run again in 1828. Adams was forced on the defensive before he completed his first year in office.

The United States had three major issues affecting the Indians: conflict with western settlers, intertribal warfare, and the desire to remove the eastern tribes across the Mississippi River. General Henry Atkinson was sent on a military expedition up the Missouri River early in the year to frighten the Indians into concluding peace treaties with the United States. Intertribal warfare, which had been a problem in the northwestern territories, arose from contradictory land claims. The Treaty of Prairie du Chien (August 19) defined territorial boundaries for the Sioux, Chippewa, Sauk and Fox, Winnebago, and other tribes. The issue of removal was more complex. President Monroe had favored George Washington's civilization policy over removal, but under the influence of Secretary of War John C. Calhoun, he gradually agreed that removal was perhaps the best policy. In 1824 Monroe had rejected Georgia's demand that the United States honor the Compact of April 24, 1802, by which the federal government promised to extinguish all Indian land titles within Georgia in exchange for the its claim to the Mississippi Territory. The Compact specified that the extinguishing of Indian claims was to be done when practical and in a peaceful manner. In one of his last addresses to Congress as President, Monroe explained his desire to accomplish the removal of the eastern tribes under peaceful and generous terms.

Meanwhile, the Monroe administration was pressuring the Creek Nation to abandon its claims to land in Georgia (which was most of its territory). Most of the Creeks opposed any such deal, and they had the support of the neighboring Cherokee people as well. Chief William McIntosh and some of the other Creek leaders felt that it was time to cut their best deal with the United States. The Creek Nation hired Major Ridge to help conduct negotiations with the United States since he was held in high esteem by the tribe and had had experience in Washington. Much of the negotiation was actually done by his assistants, John Ridge and David Vann. The Creeks were offended by Ridge's request for ten thousand dollars, but this amount didn't seem so large compared to the amounts the various Creek chiefs were to be given to distribute "as they wished" in return for the land cession. The reaction of the Creek Nation to the new treaty was swift. One morning in April, about two hundred Creeks surrounded the buildings at the McIntosh plantation and set fire to them all. While his family escaped from the burning home, the doomed General McIntosh approached the entrance to his home where he was stabbed and shot repeatedly.

The Arkansas Cherokee had not escaped the pressure for removal as they may have thought. New boundaries had been established between the Arkansas Territory, the Cherokee, and the Osages, and nobody was really pleased about them. The United States pressured them to accept land west of Arkansas, but the Western Cherokee Council responded by making unauthorized sale of public property a capital crime.

The Cherokee Nation in the east had conducted a census in 1824, which illustrated the progress that the tribe had made toward civilization. The population had increased from 12,395 in 1809 (Meig's census) to 16,060. The number of Negro slaves had more than doubled to

1277. The number of schools had jumped from five to eighteen. Likewise there had been dramatic increases in the measurements of economic advancement, such as the amount of livestock and agricultural machines and the building of mills and shops. The presence of the missionaries and the development of a capitalistic upper class of Cherokee catalyzed the changes in the Cherokee civilization. These changes were not accepted by all and became the basis for serious cultural and political conflicts.

The missionaries of the ABCFM were largely successful in their efforts to educate the Cherokee and to convert them to Christianity. Among their most significant achievements of 1825 was the translation of the New Testament by David Brown and others. The Reverend Daniel Butrick reported that Cherokee were quickly learning the new syllabary developed by Sequoyah and that they were learning it on their own! The Board was anxious now to establish a printing press in the Cherokee Nation and was sending Samuel A. Worcester (a newly ordained missionary whose late uncle and namesake had been a leader of the Board's Prudential Committee). Elias Boudinot was to be his assistant.

Elias Boudinot was the center of some controversy, however. Like John Ridge, Boudinot had fallen in love with a white woman while in school at Cornwall. Boudinot married Harriet Gould, the daughter of an American colonel, before returning to the Cherokee Nation. Although The Reverend Jeremiah Evarts (Secretary of the ABCFM Board) defended the marriage between the two Christians, the conservative Prudential Committee was offended and felt growing pressure to close the school. The Cherokee were in turn offended that the white Christians opposed such a union.

The missionaries were not in complete agreement about other issues. The conditions were primitive, and diseases like tuberculosis were prevalent. Most of the missionaries recognized that they could not expect the Cherokee to adopt all of the Christian customs, even after they had been baptized. They accepted that they would retain many of their old ways. The Reverend Moody Hall, on the other hand, would not tolerate such excesses such as ball playing and fornication. Hall's strict attitude had already made him the target of violence the year before.

The changes in Cherokee culture and economy were echoed by changes in the governmental structure. The trend toward centralization of authority at the expense of the individual chiefs and towns continued.

This concentration of power was designed to prevent aberrant chiefs from negotiating land cessions without national approval. It also helped protect the economic advances of the wealthy elite with positions on the Cherokee Council and Committee.

When the Cherokee National Council met in October and November, thirty-one new laws were enacted. Some of them formalized the Council's control over land and other public property, giving it exclusive right to sell all Cherokee lands and the right to all annuities. Individual chiefs were strictly forbidden from negotiating treaties or otherwise disposing of public property without the Council's endorsement. The Council also established its supremacy over acts of the judiciary. One law established funds to lend to Cherokee businessmen who were capable of paying them back, and another mandated that if a man died intestate, his property would be distributed among his children and widow. This law effectively destroyed the matrilineal tradition that the home and other properties belonged to the wife and her brothers (who were of the same clan).

Another controversial law required Committee members to take an oath of office that included references to the Christian God. This oath was not a problem for most of the ruling elite, since they had mostly converted to Christianity already. White Path (Nunnatsunega), a conservative full blood from the Coosawattee region, refused to take the oath and was expelled from the Committee. William Hicks, the brother of Charles Hicks, was elected in his place. The ruling elite thus further enhanced their power at the expense of the individual tradition-minded chiefs.

Another important action taken by the Council was the establishment of a new permanent capital at New Town (where the Coosawattee and Conasauga rivers converge to form the Ustanali), that was to be renamed New Echota. Plans were drawn up for the new National Council, a Supreme Court building, and other public places. A printing press was to be established at New Echota run by Worcester and Boudinot. The new capital was a symbol of the success of the civilization program and the remarkable adaptability of the Cherokee people.

1826

White Path's Rebellion and His Alternate Council

As the United States celebrated the fiftieth anniversary of the Declaration of Independence, two of its architects, John Adams and Thomas Jefferson, died on the Fourth of July. The still-young Republic continued to fine-tune its political system as pro-Jackson candidates took control of both houses of Congress in the fall elections. The Cherokee also continued to fine-tune their government. Fifty years after their shattering losses in the American Revolution, the Cherokee were on the verge of creating their own constitutional republic.

The United States concluded the Treaty of Washington with the Creeks on January 24, and obtained the rights to a tract of land in western Georgia, smaller than the one ceded by McIntosh earlier. The Creeks agreed to vacate the ceded lands within a year. There was very little diplomatic activity between the Cherokee and the United States in 1826 as there were more pressing problems in the western territories.

As if there were not enough room in the former Louisiana Purchase, American settlers began encroaching on Mexican territory within Texas. Hayden Edwards organized one group of Americans in Texas to rebel against the Mexican government. A group of Cherokee had migrated to the area looking for a place to preserve the old ways and avoid "civilization." Edwards enlisted their help, promising them deeds to the lands they already occupied. Edwards taunted the Mexican government by declaring the independent Republic of Fredonia, but after some of his men lost the Battle of Ayish Bayou on January 21, 1827, Edwards fled and the Fredonia Rebellion was over.

The missionaries at Dwight, Arkansas, were probably glad to be rid of the Cherokee malcontents who moved to Mexico, but in general things were not going too well for their mission. They converted fewer natives compared to their counterparts in the east. Cephas Washburn thought that Alfred Finney was not an effective leader and discussed his shortcomings with ABCFM Secretary Jeremiah Evarts.

The greatest achievement of the ABCFM in 1826 was overshadowed by racist reactions to the intermarriage of Cherokee men and white women. Elias Boudinot met with Jeremiah Evarts in Charleston in January to organize a committee that would govern the new printing press. The committee was to consist of two Cherokee, two missionaries, and the United States Indian Agent. Thus Boudinot had a major role in the development of the first Native American publishing operation. But Boudinot was also the center of controversy, as the New Englanders considered his marriage to a white woman offensive. It seems that even though he was now a Christian, he was not good enough to marry into the white race. The upshot of the reaction was that the Prudential Committee of the ABCFM closed Cornwall School in November. It was imprudent to allow the Cherokee scholars out of their own territory and into the decent society. Obviously the Cherokee were offended by this racist sleight.

The Cherokee community was divided during 1826 into two parties: the ruling elite who controlled the National Committee and a conservative group of full-blooded leaders who opposed the Committee's attempt to take authority away from the local chiefs. White Path, who had been impeached from his leadership position in the Council the previous year, organized an alternate Council that had representatives (though not all of them were chiefs) from seven of the eight districts. The group voiced opposition to the official government and was perhaps even more popular, but it did not have any real power to effect change. The alternate Council gave the missionaries concern, however, as the conservative leaders encouraged the Cherokee to interrupt sermons and ask embarrassing questions that pointed toward inconsistencies in Christian dogma.

The National Committee recognized that its government was flawed by inconsistencies among the laws. It chose to create a new constitution that would reconcile these differences and also ensure that the laws were compatible with those of the United States. The ruling elite courted the conservative faction by including a provision that ensured that the new constitution would in no way destroy the rights and liberties of free citizens of the Nation nor impair the fundamental principles and laws by which they were already governed. The Council adopted the resolution on October 13, 1826, and nominated ten men from each of the eight districts to run as candidates to be delegates to the Constitutional Convention. Each grown male would vote for three candidates, and the three men with the greatest number of votes would become delegates. The Cherokee were on the verge of being the first Native

American tribe with its own constitutional government, its own written language, and its own printing press.

1827

A New Constitution: the Cherokee Stand United against Removal

Just two weeks after the United States Supreme Court ruled that only the President could summons a state militia for national causes, Governor George Troup called up the Georgia militia to oppose federal troops who had been sent to prevent the premature surveying of lands ceded by the Creeks. By the end of the year the Creek Nation signed another treaty ceding the rest of their lands in western Georgia. The old conflict between the states and the federal government with regard to Indian policy threatened to blow apart the Union. Sectionalism over trade issues also inflamed the states' rights issue. Vice President John C. Calhoun cast a tie-breaking vote in the Senate to defeat a tariff bill that may have pushed the southern states closer to secession.

In 1827 the Arkansas Cherokee were fighting with the Osage again, and those who had gone to the Mexican State of Texas to assist with the Fredonia Rebellion found themselves without an ally as the rebellious Americans were defeated and run out of Texas. The Reverend Cephas Washburn reported that the mission at Dwight was poorly run and his brother-in-law The Reverend Alfred Finney had done almost nothing for the sake of the Indians. Jeremiah Evarts, Secretary of the American Board of Commissioners for Foreign Missions, procured a censure of Finney and relayed it to Washburn in the spring. Finney defended himself declaring that he had been ill and then depressed. Indeed, he was dead within days of receiving his censure from Washburn.

The missionaries in the east continued to have mixed results. More Cherokees converted to Christianity, but The Reverend Isaac Proctor criticized many of them for continuing to practice conjuring, playing ball naked in front of women, dancing all night, drinking, and gambling. Meanwhile the Tsa-La-Gi type that was manufactured in New England was ready for shipment by the end of the year. Samuel A. Worcester and Elias Boudinot sought permission to move from Brainerd to New Echota where the printing press was located. Once the type was ready they were planning on producing a bilingual newspaper, the *Cherokee Phoenix*. Jeremiah Evarts traveled to Washington on behalf of the Cherokee to meet with President John Q. Adams and Secretary of War James Barbour. Evarts complained that the fraudulent treaty with the Creeks had upset the Cherokee, but Barbour's attitude was that removal was inevitable.

The Adams administration thought that removal was inevitable and they actively pursued it. Adams appointed General John Cocke Agent to the Cherokee and sent him to New Echota to negotiate a final land cession. Cocke arrived before the Constitutional Convention, and his presence helped push the various Cherokee factions toward compromise with each other. Constitutional government was one further step of civilization that would certainly shield them from removal pressures.

The Cherokee had been divided into two major political parties. The ruling party included such wealthy elite as John Ross, Major Ridge, and Charles Hicks. The conservative opposition party, which was perhaps supported by a majority of the Cherokee, was led by White Path and included Kelechulah, Rising Fawn, Big Tiger, Big Cabin, Katchee, and Terrapin Head. Pathkiller, who had been Principal Chief for over a decade, was a unifying figure. He did not speak English and had military credentials and thus was liked by White Path's followers. He had been supportive of the legal changes that the Council had adopted during his tenure and was thus acceptable to the ruling faction. The aging Pathkiller died, however on January 6, 1827. Charles Hicks became Principal Chief upon the death of Pathkiller. Within two weeks, however, he had caught pneumonia and was dead. According to the rules of succession, John Ross, President of the National Committee, became Principal Chief *pro-tem* and Major Ridge (Speaker of the Council) became Second Chief *pro-tem*.

White Path was afraid that after the death of Pathkiller his faction would not be treated fairly at the upcoming Constitutional Convention and called for an extralegal council meeting to be held at Ellijay. The eight Districts (Chickamauga, Chattanooga, Coosawaytee, Amohee, Hickory Log, Hightower, Tahquohee, and Aquohee) each chose three delegates for the Convention. Only four of them were full bloods likely to support White Path. General Cocke's arrival at New Echota underscored the importance of Cherokee unity. The Council met on July 3, on the eve of the Convention, to declare an assurance that all delegates, even those loyal to White Path, would be allowed to participate.

The Constitutional Convention assembled on July 4, as had been authorized by the Council's resolution of 1826. The delegates worked on the new charter for the next three weeks, and the final document was signed by twenty-one of the delegates on July 26, 1827. The Constitution was modeled after that of the United States and established three branches of government: executive, judicial, and legislative. The document was written in English, but as a compromise with the traditional faction, there was no mention of God. In fact, there were specific limitations imposed on missionaries, and only Cherokee would be allowed to hold positions of power. The boundaries of the Cherokee Nation were defined, and it was declared that all land was communal property of the tribe.

As ordered by the resolution of October 13, 1826, the Council met in the fall under the auspices of the old regime. An election was held and William Hicks was appointed Interim Principal Chief. John Ross was demoted to Interim Second Chief, and Elijah Hicks was named President of the National Committee. The Cherokee Nation now boasted constitutional government led by Christians, a well-developed school system, a printing press, and thriving agriculture and industry. They were a civilized people.

Chapter Twelve

1828–1835

The Cherokee Nation Struggles Against Georgia and Jackson

In 1828 the new Cherokee Constitution went into full effect, and John Ross was officially elected Principal Chief at New Echota. The new government quickly acted to suppress opposition from White Path, a conservative chief who favored a return to traditional ways. The Cherokee Nation proudly boasted the only tribal newspaper published in its native language. In that same year, Cherokees who had already moved to Arkansas Territory agreed to leave their new lands for tracts even further west. These Cherokee had removed themselves from the east to escape the ways of the white men, whereas Ross and his supporters embraced a new Christian capitalist Cherokee society in harmony with its white neighbors.

The State of Georgia was offended by the notion of a savage people, pretending to be civilized, governing themselves within its boundaries. Georgia set off a constitutional crisis for the United States by declaring that all of the Cherokee would be subject to the laws of the state and that all of the missionaries would be required to pledge allegiance as well. The Cherokee petitioned the administration of President Andrew Jackson, arguing that the federal government had guaranteed all of the Cherokee treaties. Jackson naturally would have supported federal rights over those of the individual states, but the animosity toward the Cherokee was so strong that it might provoke a secession crisis if he did not support Georgia.

Jackson signaled his intentions when he pushed the Indian Removal Act through Congress in 1830, and Georgia followed by enforcing its new laws. Cherokee lands were distributed to Georgia citizens by lottery, and the state seized the newly discovered gold mines. The United States stepped up the pressure on the tribe by withholding its annuities and refusing to grant the impoverished nation loans. The Cherokee sent Chief John Ross and others on annual delegations to negotiate with the administration, but it was to no avail. Lawyers for the Cherokee decided to wage the battle in the courts by asking for an injunction against Georgia. They were dealt a stunning blow in March 1831, however, when the Supreme Court refused to hear *Cherokee v. Georgia*, saying that they were not a foreign country but rather a dependent domestic nation.

The missionaries were caught in the middle as they were forced to pledge allegiance to Georgia or go to jail. In support of the Cherokee, Samuel A. Worcester and Elizur Butler so refused and were imprisoned. Their case went to the Supreme Court as well and in a dramatic turn of events, Chief Justice John Marshall declared in *Worcester v. Georgia* that the state did not have jurisdiction over the Cherokee territory. Even though the Supreme Court had found in favor of Worcester, Georgia refused to obey the ruling, and Jackson did nothing to enforce it either. President Jackson had coerced all of the other southeastern tribes into signing removal treaties, but he still could not risk setting off a secession crisis.

It was becoming clear to many of the missionaries and some of the Cherokee that removal was inevitable and that the best course of action was to cut the best deal possible with the United States. Among the early supporters of removal were John Ridge and Elias Boudinot, editor of the *Cherokee Phoenix*. When Chief John Ross learned of such attitudes, he engineered the replacement of Boudinot as editor, so as to avoid publication of pieces favorable toward removal. Furthermore, since Georgia had declared that the Council could no longer meet in Georgia, Ross and his followers were appointed to their leadership positions in perpetuity (or until the crisis was over), instead of the customary yearly term.

Chief John Ross continued his annual pilgrimages to Washington for futile attempts at negotiating with the Jackson administration. In 1834, his own brother, Andrew Ross, met separately with the Secretary of War to open negotiations for removal. The Council had continued to meet anyway and when John Ridge introduced a resolution favoring removal that fall, he and his father (Major Ridge) as well as David Vann were all impeached. One of the treaty supporters, John Walker Jr., was even murdered immediately after the Council.

The Cherokee favoring removal were essentially disenfranchised and intimidated by violence into forming their own party. With the blessing (and financial support) of Andrew Jackson, a meeting was held at the home of John Ridge, and the Treaty Party was founded. Members of the party found themselves the beneficiaries of a conspiracy generated between John Ridge and the governor of Georgia. Georgia would not confiscate the property of these men and would offer them full protection. Furthermore, Georgia would use its powers to thwart Ross and his followers.

In the winter of 1835 Ross and Ridge headed rival delegations in Washington. Jackson was more than happy to negotiate with the Treaty Party but more or less ignored Ross. Ross blundered into a position of proposing that the Senate determine a fair price for the removal of the nation, assuming that it would agree to an amount Jackson would be unwilling to meet. The Senate's unexpected approval of a modest price gave Jackson more momentum to press for a removal treaty. The administration did agree to Ross' demand that any treaty meet with the approval of the entire Cherokee Nation in Council.

The author of the removal treaty proposal, Agent John Schermerhorn, lobbied in Council but to no avail. Even when Chief John Ross was arrested in Tennessee and taken to prison in Georgia, the Council still refused to consent to removal. John Ridge and his allies attended the fall Council and pretended to be against the proposed treaty. After John Ross (who had been released from prison without formal charges) left for Washington, Schermerhorn organized a rump Council at New Echota, making sure that those in attendance were in favor of removal. The Treaty of New Echota was signed by a handful of Treaty Party leaders, representing a small minority of Cherokee. Jackson had gotten what he wanted.

1828

*Principal Chief John Ross Elected to Lead the New
Constitutional Government*

'Cherokee Phoenix' Begins Publication

The publication of the first issue of the *Cherokee Phoenix* (see Figure 11) on February 28, 1828, and the establishment of republican government under the new Constitution of 1827 highlighted the successful transformation of the Cherokee from traditional tribal organization into a modern nation.

Georgia Governor John Forsyth was enraged when he read the Cherokee Constitution in the pages of the *Phoenix*, and protested to President John Quincy Adams that the tribe must be removed from Georgian soil. In response to Georgia's demands Adams sent Colonel Hugh Montgomery to New Echota to negotiate a removal treaty, but he found no interest among the Cherokee. The election of Cherokee archenemies Andrew Jackson as President and John C. Calhoun as Vice President, however, gave new life to the Georgian cause. Knowing that the new administration would be committed to removal, Georgia passed laws in December that extended the state's jurisdiction to areas occupied by Cherokee. The ter-

Figure 11 — Cherokee Phoenix

ritory was to be divided into counties and surveyed into lots for sale to whites. The Cherokee in the state would have virtually no civil rights. Even whites living among the Cherokee (mostly missionaries who were thought to oppose removal anyway) would be required to pledge allegiance to the state or face prison terms. All Cherokee laws would become null and void after June 1830.

The Western Cherokee, who had already been removed from the homeland, sent a delegation to Washington including George Gist (Sequoyah) and led by David Brown. On May 6 the Treaty of Washington was signed. Although the treaty was generally felt to be favorable both to the Cherokee and the missionaries among them, it required them to cede all of their lands in Arkansas and re-establish themselves to the west in what is now Oklahoma. The land in Arkansas was traded for seven million acres of land with an outlet to the western edge of the United States, to remain theirs forever. Fifty thousand dollars was to be given to them to defray the costs of moving and to compensate for the inferior quality of the land. Several thousand dollars was also promised to compensate for losses of livestock and injuries committed by the Osages. A thousand dollars was set aside for a printing press, and a five hundred dollar honorarium was provided for Sequoyah (who happened to have signed the treaty). The Cherokee were required to leave Arkansas within fourteen months, but most of the Christian ones left right away. Many of the traditional Cherokee abandoned the United States altogether and joined the group already established in Texas.

For the Old Cherokee in the east, 1828 was a landmark year. The *Cherokee Phoenix* became the first American Indian publication. The newspaper, edited by Elias Boudinot, had articles in English as well as in Tsa-La-Gi (using Sequoyah's script). Although the missionaries were concerned that they might be blamed for its contents, the paper did publish many religious pieces. The paper was also a vehicle for the dissemination of information about the new constitution and about the elections. White Path called for the rejection of the new government and called upon the Cherokee to return to traditional ways. Many of the ruling elite countered by publishing articles supporting the Constitution of 1827 and favoring one candidate or another. In the summer election a new Council was chosen including many delegates who supported White Path. White Path himself was elected as a representative from the Coosawattee District.

The Council met in the fall and on October 17, 1828, John Ross was elected Principal Chief and George Lowrey was elected Second Chief. Major Ridge became the Advisor to the Chief and Going Snake became Speaker of the Council. John Martin was elected Treasurer, although there was no Cherokee currency and no money in a treasury. Alexander McCoy was elected to the office of Clerk of the Council, but John Ridge replaced him after it was revealed that he had negotiated with Colonel Montgomery over possible removal terms.

Among the first laws passed under the new regime was one that protected the rights of missionaries and that made it a crime to interfere with the activities of the congregations. Another law that Chief John Ross signed quickly was one that outlawed activities directed against the new government. This act essentially put an end to White Path's Rebellion. The new regime was securely established, but within a month Andrew Jackson had been elected President and the legislature of Georgia had passed laws to undermine the security of the Cherokee.

1829

The Gold Rush and the Rush for Removal

If the Indian policy of John Quincy Adams had been somewhat ambiguous, that of Andrew Jackson was straightforward. Principal Chief John Ross and a delegation of Cherokee dignitaries wrote a letter of protest to the Secretary of War suggesting that Georgia was violating the sovereignty of the United States by extending jurisdiction over Cherokee territory. They argued that all of their treaties had been with the federal government and that the supremacy of federal Indian policy over state policies had already been established. Meanwhile ABCFM Secretary Jeremiah Evarts met with President-elect Jackson to lobby for the Cherokee cause. Evarts took a stance of moral outrage and came away with little respect for the old general when it became clear that he would support Georgia.

Days after Jackson's inauguration on March 4, 1829, he sent a warning to the Creeks to obey Alabama laws or move across the Mississippi River. He also sent agents to the Cherokee Nation specifically to enroll tribesmen willing to move to Arkansas. Secretary of War John Eaton replied to the Cherokee delegation that the President believed that removal was the Cherokee's best option. The ABCFM leadership realized that the missionaries had to be careful not to antagonize the Cherokee since they were already inflamed over Jackson's statements. On the other hand the Board encouraged the Cherokee leaders to exert themselves and not to depend on friends or on faith in justice from the government. Failing action in Congress, the Cherokee were encouraged to try the constitutionality of the executive action before the United States Supreme Court.

On October 31 Principal Chief John Ross signed a new law stripping citizenship from any Cherokee who enrolled or enlisted with the intention of moving to Arkansas. The Cherokee Nation would resist any attempt to force their removal. A month later President Jackson gave his first address before Congress. During the speech he addressed the Cherokee/Georgia conflict, arguing that the Cherokee had no right to create a state within the boundaries of another state. He concurred with the states' rights argument made by Georgia and concluded that removal was the only sensible policy for the Indians still living east of the Mississippi River.

Ordinarily the discovery of gold is considered a blessing. Certainly the Cherokee treasury (which was empty) could benefit from an influx of revenue from mining precious metals. But when the discovery of gold thirty miles east of New Echota became known in 1829, a rush of miners moved from North Carolina into Georgia, anxious to begin digging for personal fortunes. The greed for gold in Cherokee territory brought further pressure for removal from Georgia. After Jackson's speech before Congress, the Georgia legislature passed a law forbidding Indians from mining gold. The law forbade Indians as witnesses in a court of law and invalidated their contracts. It would be unlawful for any man (chief or otherwise) to interfere with any Indian who had decided to move to Arkansas. The new laws would become effective June 1, 1830—just six months later. The stage was set for a political showdown, and the Cherokee were the underdogs.

1830

The Indian Removal Act

Georgia asserts its Jurisdiction

At the beginning of 1830 the Cherokee/Georgia conflict was coming to a head. The Georgia legislature had put the Cherokee on notice that Georgia law would supercede all Cherokee laws effective June 1, 1830. In anticipation of the new law, and driven by greed for land and lust for gold, Georgian settlers and miners began swarming into the Cherokee Nation. The Cherokee resisted the intruders and retaliated by burning their homes, many of which had been built by Cherokee who had already moved west. Major Ridge led a party in January that burned the homes of whites settling in land ceded by the Creeks and recognized by the United States as Cherokee land four years earlier. Needless to say Georgia responded by further intrusions, and some Cherokee actually wound up in prison.

The missionaries were caught in the crossfire but were generally supportive of the Cherokee. The ABCFM advised the Cherokee to behave in a dignified manner and to avoid arousing further conflict. It would be dangerous for the missionaries if the Georgians perceived them as abetting Cherokee resistance. The Board moved to sanction Moody Hall, a missionary who had aroused the ire of the Cherokee in the past for his strict attitude toward "uncivilized" behavior. Adding to the woes of the missionaries was the burning of the buildings at Brainerd. Principal Chief John Ross wanted to see the place rebuilt, but there were financial needs elsewhere. The Board would wait to see what would come of the proposed Indian Removal Act pending in Congress.

President Jackson made it clear that he intended to break with the Indian civilization policy of George Washington. He believed that the best course was to remove all Indians to lands west of the Mississippi. He was particularly offended by the rise of an elite class of half-blooded Indians who were exploiting the full bloods for financial gain. He identified with middle-class Indians who often were indebted to those in power.

The Cherokee sent a delegation to Washington to argue against the Removal Act, including Lewis Ross, George Lowrey, William Hicks, Richard Taylor, David Vann, and William Coodey. Jeremiah Evarts, Secretary of the ABCFM, advised the delegation prior to their meeting with President Jackson. He also met with various congressional leaders to lobby against the bill. Among those opposed to the bill were New Jersey Senator Theodore Frelinghuysen and New Hampshire Senator Daniel Webster. Frelinghuysen spoke in the Senate and quoted Chief Justice John Marshall as saying that the Cherokee land claims were perfect. Attorney General John Berrien countered Evart's efforts by circulating descriptions of Cherokee ball playing and other "uncivilized" activities. Much to Evart's mortification, the Senate passed the bill. Prospects for passage in the House looked favorable for the President. Ross and Coodey met with Jackson but came away discouraged. The Indian Removal Act passed the House and was signed into law by President Jackson on May 28, 1830. Half a million dollars was set aside to effect the removal of all Indians living east of the Mississippi River.

The very next week Georgia declared Cherokee laws to be invalid within the boundaries of Georgia. It would proceed to section off the Cherokee territory into lots for sale to white inhabitants. Accordingly, President Jackson ordered the Indian Agent Hugh Montgomery to suspend annuity payments to the Cherokee Council. An offer to distribute the annuity to individual Cherokee (forty-two cents per person) was declined, and the money was kept in escrow in a bank in Tennessee. A month later Jackson stopped the flow of money earmarked for the civilization program.

The Cherokee Council met in violation of Georgia law after the arrival of the delegation from Washington. The Council passed a resolution asking Andrew Jackson to honor previous treaties and to resume paying the annuity. John Ross was authorized to obtain legal counsel as needed (Jeremiah Evarts had already enlisted former Attorney General William Wirt (see Figure 12, page 265), although it would be difficult to pay any fees until the annuities were resumed. The President had asked the Cherokee to meet with him at his home in Nashville in July to negotiate removal. The Council refused the offer.

Other tribes were not as resolute. On July 15 at Prairie du Chien the Sioux, Sauk, and Fox ceded most of what is now is Missouri, Iowa, and Minnesota. Later a minority of Choctaw signed the Treaty of Danc-

Figure 12 —Attorney General William Wirt

ing Rabbit Creek, trading their land in Mississippi for new lands to the west. The Choctaw treaty was criticized since it was not authorized by the established tribal organization. This method of procuring a treaty had worked for the United States in the past and would work again.

Meanwhile, the passage of the Removal Act gave Georgia new enthusiasm for pressing their rights. Secretary of War Eaton had sent troops into Georgia in July to prevent any further gold mining in Cherokee territory. In October Governor Gilmer asked Jackson to remove the federal forces from the Hightower Creek area so Georgia could take full possession. Accordingly, on November 8 Jackson ordered all federal troops out of the mining district.

The next week Jackson instructed Secretary of War John Eaton to suspend efforts to effect individual emigration from the Cherokee Nation. Enrolling agents had made some progress in signing up middle-class Cherokees. They were indebted to the likes of Vann and others and had little to lose by leaving. The United States would no longer offer individual reservations but would wait and evacuate the rest of the Cherokee as a unit.

William Wirt began to oppose Georgia's action immediately. He started by finding a case pending in Georgia courts that could be appealed in federal court. He brought to the Supreme Court the case of George Tassel, a Cherokee who had been convicted of murdering a white man. The Supreme Court cited Georgia to show why a writ of error should not be issued. In response, Georgia swiftly executed Tassel, making the case moot. There would be another opportunity for legal battle later.

1831

'The Cherokee Nation v. the State of Georgia'

Missionaries Arrested

The American political landscape of 1831 was jolted by the harsh break between President Andrew Jackson and Vice President John C. Calhoun. Jackson was disturbed by Calhoun's formulation of nullification as a constitutional method of negating protective tariffs. Furthermore, Jackson took offense at the way Mrs. Calhoun and other cabinet wives snubbed Peggy Eaton, wife of the Secretary of War. Jackson likewise took personal offense when he discovered that Calhoun had actually been his critic, not his defender, after his controversial invasion of Spanish Florida during the Seminole War. Jackson favored Secretary of State Martin Van Buren and appointed him ambassador to England. After the Senate rejected Van Buren's appointment (Calhoun cast the tie-breaking vote that decided his fate), Jackson announced that Van Buren would be his running mate in 1832.

Later in the year a third party was organized based on mistrust of masons. Former Attorney General William Wirt (legal counsel for the Cherokee Nation) was nominated since he was a former mason, although he was not strongly affiliated with the views of the party. The National Republicans (the old Adams/Clay faction) nominated Henry Clay as their candidate. The division of the opposition strengthened Jackson's re-election chances. Among the major issues facing the United States was Jackson's opposition to the National Bank and his removal policy. Black Hawk, the leader of the Sauk and Fox Indians, reluctantly agreed to move west, but the refusal of the Cherokee to sign a removal treaty continued to vex the President. The legal conflict between Georgia and the Cherokee Nation intensified the debate over states' rights. Calhoun had already laid the groundwork for the debate on nullification and perhaps secession over the tariff issue. The unsuccessful but dangerous slave uprising organized by Nat Turner underscored the vulnerability of the South to domestic violence. The presence of a destabilizing savage nation within the boundaries of Georgia could not be tolerated.

The Cherokee Nation struggled for unity under the leadership of Principal Chief John Ross, and a delegation was appointed to lobby in Washington. Richard Taylor, John Ridge, John Martin, and William Coodey (all resistant to removal) were sent to Washington. Jeremiah Evarts, Secretary of the ABCFM, had planned to assist them but was unable to travel due to illness, and indeed he died that summer. The Arkansas delegation visited their counterparts in the eastern Cherokee territory and then traveled on to Washington escorted by John Walker and James Starr. Ross did not trust the Arkansas Cherokee very much since he knew many of them favored removal. It seems that the Western Cherokee would receive larger annuities if more Cherokee emigrated.

The Cherokee Nation was plagued by a lack of hard cash. The United States was withholding the annuity money and was refusing to grant them a loan. Whatever money they might earn from mining gold was not available since the Georgia Guard had taken over control of the mining district. The financial plight undermined their ability to pay attorneys' fees. John Ross retained attorneys in Georgia (Thomas Harris and Judge William Underwood) for work in that state. After William Rogers (an emissary of Ross) had been arrested, Harris sent the Cherokee a dun for fifteen hundred dollars. Ross angrily assured him that the Cherokee would honor all debts. By contrast, William Wirt sent a bill for one thousand dollars, but suggested that he would continue to serve even if the Cherokee could not pay. In response to the financial crisis some of the affluent Cherokee gave their own money for the defense of their nation and the missionaries. In October the Council authorized Elias Boudinot to go on a fund-raising tour of the country on behalf of the *Cherokee Phoenix*.

Principal Chief John Ross brought the legal crisis to the United States Supreme Court, seeking an injunction against the State of Georgia. William Wirt argued that the Cherokee were essentially a foreign nation, whose relationships were with the federal, *not* state governments. Nonetheless Chief Justice John Marshall (see Figure 13, page 268) and a majority of the Court declared that the Cherokee were a domestic dependent nation, and as such had no right to sue in federal court. The Supreme Court declared on March 18, 1831, that they did not have jurisdiction over *The Cherokee Nation v. the State of Georgia*. President Jackson, whether he approved the limiting of federal power or not, knew that politically he must support Georgia. Accordingly, when Governor

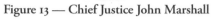

Figure 13 — Chief Justice John Marshall

George Gilmer insisted that the removal rolls be re-opened, Jackson appointed Benjamin F. Curry of McMinnville, Tennessee, as Superintendent of Removal for the Cherokee. Captain William L. McClintock was appointed Disbursing Agent for Cherokee Removal. After his arrival in Georgia in December, McClintock was authorized to give each Cherokee agreeing to enlist one rifle, one blanket for each family member, a kettle, and five pounds of tobacco. Only further Supreme Court challenges could derail removal now.

The next legal battle did not directly involve the Cherokee: On January 1, 1831, Georgia gave notice to the missionaries that they would pledge allegiance to the state or else move out of it. Ironically, on the same day the *Cherokee Phoenix* published a special edition in which the missionaries of all the denominations (organized by Samuel A. Worcester) declared in a manifesto their support for the Cherokee and opposition to removal. For the ABCFM the missions at Hightower, Haweis, Carmel, and New Echota all were within the boundaries of Georgia and were thus at risk. Worcester wrote the Prudential Committee of the ABCFM that the missionaries would not take the required oath because they did not believe that Georgia had jurisdiction over the Cherokee and that the federal government would come to their assistance. They did not want to inflict injury to the Cherokee, nor did they want to sacrifice their own work and property. Jeremiah Evarts agreed with Worcester and told him that the missionaries should be willing to go to jail if necessary.

On March 1, 1831, the deadline passed for the missionaries to pledge allegiance to Georgia. The oaths weren't recorded and within two weeks the Georgia Guard had arrested Worcester, some other missionaries, a printer, and some other whites living among the Cherokee. Judge Augustin Clayton heard the case and ordered the release of all of the missionaries, arguing that they were financed by grants from the United States government and thus were federal agents. Furthermore, as postmaster, Worcester was a federal employee. A new wave of arrests followed the declaration that the missionaries were no longer federal agents and after Worcester had been relieved of his position as postmaster. Among those arrested was The Reverend Elizur Butler, who had resolutely refused to pledge allegiance to Georgia. In all, eleven missionaries were arrested and forced to march up to sixty miles to the courthouse. They were released on bail as long as they would leave the state pending trial. On one occasion Worcester was arrested again after he re-entered Georgia from Tennessee. He was released after it became known that he was visiting his wife after the death of their youngest child.

David Greene, who became Secretary after the death of Jeremiah Evarts, asked William Wirt to represent Worcester and the others. Wirt advised the missionaries to defy Georgian jurisdiction, and Greene advised them not to voluntarily relinquish any property. They were to assess the value of their property so that they could sue for damages later if it was seized or damaged.

By September 15 nine of the eleven missionaries had either pledged allegiance to Georgia or had left the state. Worcester and Butler refused to obey and after fifteen minutes of deliberation were found guilty. They were sentenced to four years in prison, and the next day both were taken to Milledgeville Penitentiary. Within a month attorneys for the missionaries had petitioned the Supreme Court for a writ of error. There would be another opportunity for the Court to intervene on behalf of the rights of the Cherokee Nation, and the Cherokee were convinced that they would prevail. After Governor Gilmer was served noticed he too expressed concern that the Court would not find in favor of Georgia. Even the ABCFM worried that it would be successful, because if the Supreme Court found in its favor, the ruling could induce Georgia to secede and trigger a civil war.

1832

'Worcester v. Georgia'

Never before had the fate of the Cherokee played a more important role in American politics than in 1832. President Andrew Jackson was nominated by the new Democratic Party to run for re-election with Martin Van Buren as his running mate. The opposition was divided between Representative Henry Clay and former Attorney General William Wirt, but Jackson did not take his re-election for granted. South Carolina was incensed over the Tariff passed that year and by threatening to nullify it threatened the dissolution of the Union. Although Jackson harshly rebuked South Carolina over the nullification issue, he did so only after the election. The southerners were still anxious over the failed Nat Turner slave uprising and were apt to link any usurpation of their rights over the Indians as a threat to their rights over the Negro slaves. Clearly Jackson favored removal of all Indians from the eastern half of the United States, but he would have preferred that the issue be resolved without weakening the strength of the federal government. If he interfered with Georgia's occupation of the Cherokee Nation, Jackson risked losing the votes of all of the southern states, and also risked triggering the secession of South Carolina, Georgia, and perhaps Mississippi and Alabama.

During 1832 the United States succeeded in signing removal treaties with the Creeks, Seminoles, and Chickasaw. Only the Cherokee still held out in the southeastern part of the country. Meanwhile Black Hawk led a party of Sauks back across the Mississippi River in an attempt to take back lands ceded the year before. Within a few months Black Hawk had been defeated, and the Sauk and Fox Indians were forced once again to accept new lands west of the river. In the midst of all this activity Congress authorized the President to appoint a Commissioner of Indian Affairs, to serve under the Secretary of War. Ironically, in his first report to Congress, Commissioner Elbert Herring argued that the Indians should be brought into the white social system, especially in regard to ownership of private property.

Although the Cherokee had not signed a general removal treaty with the United States, individual Cherokees had been enrolled to move to Arkansas. Disbursing Agent William McClintock reported in January that he was having difficulty preparing for the first removal group because he was unable to procure the necessary equipment. Superintendent Benjamin F. Curry likewise found that his enrolling agents were ineffectual and thus had to be replaced. Curry also was concerned about the unusual case of individual Cherokees who held reservations. The Treaty of 1819 allowed some Indians to obtain titles to lands near the Cherokee Nation in return for becoming United States citizens. Undoubtedly most of the reservation holders did not understand the intent of the treaty and roamed freely within the territory of the Cherokee and considered themselves Cherokee citizens. Curry considered removing them as unlawful intruders in Cherokee territory!

Curry's first group of emigrants assembled at Florence, Alabama, on April 18. The party included about one hundred eighty Cherokees, an equal number of Negro slaves, and about fifty white men married to Cherokee women. The party boarded the steamboat *Tom Yeatman* on April 23, 1832, and navigated the Tennessee, Ohio, Mississippi, and Arkansas rivers before reaching their new home in early May. It turns out that there were some misunderstandings between Curry and his western counterpart, Agent George Vashon. Vashon did not understand that he was responsible for paying the new arrivals, nor was he aware that the slaves would be coming and would require provisioning. They had been listed as property and not persons, evidently. Naturally all parties involved were angry. In response to this fiasco the War Department issued new regulations that required all removal expeditions to be authorized and organized at a higher administrative level.

After Curry returned to the east he wished to organize another group of emigrants. Meanwhile, United States Agent Elisha Chester was in the Cherokee Nation trying to win approval of a general removal treaty. He argued against any further expeditions, saying that such small removals weakened his ability to obtain a general consensus for removal by siphoning off known removal advocates. Acting Secretary of War John Robb agreed with Chester and asked Curry to hold off at least until after the presidential elections. The new Disbursing Agent J.L. Dancy found that there was little interest anyway.

While Curry was busy organizing his first group of emigrants, Elias Boudinot and his cousin John Ridge were travelling in the east to raise public concern for the plight of the Cherokee and to raise money to support the continued publication of the *Cherokee Phoenix*. They reported excellent results in Philadelphia, as well as in Massachusetts. It did not really matter if every New Englander thought that the Cherokee were being treated unjustly by Georgia. What mattered was the opinion of one man: United States Supreme Court Chief Justice John Marshall.

In 1831 ABCFM missionaries Samuel A. Worcester and Elizur Butler had been imprisoned at Milledgeville Penitentiary for refusing to swear allegiance to Georgia. The missionaries appealed their cases all the way to the Supreme Court, but were doubtful of their chances since Marshall had refused jurisdiction over *The Cherokee Nation v. the State of Georgia* a few months earlier. They anticipated having to ask the governor of Georgia for clemency after their defeat. Georgia, on the other hand, confidently hired over five hundred surveyors to mark off ninety-two districts within Cherokee territory.

On March 3, 1832, John Marshall announced the decision of the Supreme Court in the case of *Worcester v. Georgia* and stunned the country. The Cherokee were a distinct nation independent of the individual states. The new laws of Georgia interfered with relations already established between the United States and the Cherokee Nation. Samuel Worcester was forcibly seized while performing humanitarian duties authorized by the President of the United States. The law by which Georgia condemned Worcester to four years of hard labor was repugnant to the Constitution, treaties, and laws of the United States and ought to be reversed and annulled.

The Cherokee were jubilant, but there was universal indignation in Georgia. Senator Troup suggested that the decision implied that the federal government might in the future claim jurisdiction over the Negro slaves and even push for abolition. Jackson has been credited as saying, "Marshall has made his decision, now let him enforce it," but he actually remained silent immediately after the announcement. United States Agent Chester forwarded a copy of the Supreme Court decision to the governor of Georgia and petitioned for the release of Worcester and Butler.

A month later Worcester and Butler remained in jail, and Georgian surveyors continued their work in Cherokee territory. The missionaries wrote to President Jackson asking him to intercede for their release since Georgia had not yet responded to the Supreme Court decision. Even they knew, however, that any federal action on their behalf could very well trigger the secession of Georgia and perhaps a civil war. As the summer dragged on and no relief came, it became clear that neither the Cherokee nor the missionaries could rely on the United States government for justice. Even if Jackson lost the election, Wirt had no real chance of winning and Clay had come to favor removal too. The Cherokee's old allies in Congress reluctantly began to advise them to agree to removal.

In late November while the missionaries remained in the penitentiary they informed the newly elected governor of Georgia, Wilson Lumpkin, that they would petition the Supreme Court to compel President Jackson to uphold the law. Lumpkin was under extreme pressure to detain the missionaries, especially if they pursued legal recourse. Nullification and secession pressures had never been stronger. Jackson was reelected early in December and immediately had to deal with the South Carolina nullification crisis. In this atmosphere the Prudential Committee of the ABCFM met on Christmas Day and (with David Greene dissenting) recommended that Worcester and Butler not pursue and further legal recourse. Even some Georgians began to favor the release of the missionaries since the law by which they were being held had been repealed. On December 29 Georgia offered to release the missionaries if they agreed to leave the state.

The plight of Worcester and Butler was not the only issue facing the missionaries in 1832. Georgia placed pressure on the schools, saying that they would no longer be allowed to enroll Negro students. The prevalence of disease forced the temporary closure of the school at Brainerd. Secretary David Greene could hardly justify sending more personnel or financing improvements in the face of all the chaos. Nonetheless, Sophia Sawyer, a teacher at New Echota, informed Greene at the end of the year that the schools were in good shape over all.

The political unity of the Cherokee was not in such good shape. Although all of the Cherokee seemed to be jubilant over Marshall's decision in the *Worcester v. Georgia* case, opinions began to differ after it became clear that Jackson would do nothing to enforce it. Congressman Daniel Newnan met with a delegation of Cherokee in April, arousing concerns that he might be trying to secure a removal treaty from unscrupulous Cherokee. Secretary of War Lewis Cass met with John Ridge and William Shorey Coodey also and apparently convinced them that removal was in the best interest of the Cherokee. With this in mind,

Agent Elisha Chester was sent to the Cherokee Nation to lobby for a removal treaty prior to the Council meeting in July.

The Cherokee National Council met at Red Clay, Tennessee, on July 19 and immediately a day of fasting was announced to protest Georgia's failure to comply with the Supreme Court's ruling. Elisha Chester's removal treaty proposals were presented to the Council and were favored by Elias Boudinot, John Ridge, William Rogers, William Coodey, William Hicks, Andrew Ross, John Walker Jr., and James Starr. The majority of the Council, however, was opposed to removal and expressed outrage over Newnan's behavior. Principal Chief John Ross expressed concern that Boudinot had favored the publication of pro-treaty articles in the *Cherokee Phoenix* and a law was passed forbidding the publication of such opinions. A few days later Boudinot resigned as editor of the *Phoenix* and was replaced by Elijah Hicks. Hicks did not have the editorial experience that Boudinot did, but he was the brother-in-law of Chief John Ross.

At the autumn Council meeting in October John Ridge, President of the National Committee, proposed sending a delegation to Washington to negotiate a removal treaty with Andrew Jackson. Once again, removal was rejected, and a delegation was appointed to go to Washington to lobby *against* removal: John Ross, Joseph Vann, John Baldridge, and Richard Taylor. Expressing concern that Georgia might prevent future elections, the Council declared that the current elected officers would hold their positions *ad infinitum*. Principal Chief John Ross and the anti-removal faction were guaranteed continued control of the Cherokee government (as well as the national press).

1833

Removal Openly Discussed at the Cherokee Council

At the beginning of 1833 South Carolina was poised to defy President Andrew Jackson's enforcement of the Tariff of 1832 and had even raised a militia for that purpose. Henry Clay, who had recently lost to Jackson in the presidential election, proposed a new compromise tariff and Force Bill. The proposals were eventually enacted into law and the crisis was averted. Jackson was inaugurated for a second term as President on March 4, and Martin Van Buren was sworn in as Vice-President. Disagreement over Jackson's decision to withdraw federal funds from the National Bank led to a cabinet reshuffling and the appointment of Roger B. Taney as Secretary of the Treasury. The day after Christmas Henry Clay expressed outrage over Jackson's policy and introduced a resolution calling for censure of the President for assuming powers beyond those allowed by the Constitution.

Meanwhile the stand-off between Georgia and the Cherokee continued. As the Cherokee lands were divided up and distributed by lottery to white settlers, encroachment led to more and more violent encounters. While Principal Chief John Ross was in Washington lobbying for the Cherokee cause, his home was taken over by a lottery winner and he was forced to move to Tennessee, near Red Clay. On the other hand, Georgia Governor Lumpkin gave instructions that the property of William Hicks was not to be disturbed since he had a record of supporting the laws of the state. Federal Agent Colonel Hugh Montgomery was ordered to remove intruders from the gold-mining districts for the third year in a row. By the end of the year, even the Springplace Mission Station had been taken over and converted into a new courthouse. Tennessee threatened to get into the action in November when the legislature extended its rule into the part of Cherokee territory within its boundaries.

John Ross and the Cherokee diplomatic delegation (Richard Taylor, John F. Baldridge, and Joseph Vann) arrived in Washington in January and met with President Jackson and Secretary of War Lewis Cass. Once again Cass refused to grant the annuity to the Cherokee except as payments to individuals. Ross also proposed that the United States buy the title to Cherokee lands lying within the State of Georgia. Naturally that proposal fell on deaf ears. Ross refused an offer of three million dollars for the removal of the Cherokee Nation. Apparently Ross had more faith that the United States would protect them against intruders from Georgia than was justified.

The Cherokee Council met in May at Red Clay, a month after the delegation returned from Washington empty-handed. John Ridge gave a speech criticizing Ross for refusing the best terms for removal. Following the first public discussion of removal in the history of the Council, twenty-five members introduced a proposal favoring negotiations for removal. The resolution did not pass, but the split in opinion among the Cherokee leaders had become public. This public dissent encouraged Benjamin F. Curry to renew efforts to enroll Cherokee for removal. Interestingly, such influential Cherokee as John Walker Jr. voiced support for removal but would not personally enlist. The Cherokee Council met again in October without any major events. John Ross was chosen once again to lead another delegation to lobby in Washington.

The missionaries were in an uncomfortable position of having to withdraw from their involvement in Cherokee politics. The Board of the ABCFM ordered Samuel A. Worcester and Elizur Butler to withdraw their legal challenge to Georgia's refusal to abide by the Supreme Court decision of 1832. Worcester and Butler wrote a letter to Governor Lumpkin indicating their decision, and within a few days they had been released from prison. The missionaries had come to believe that removal was in the best interest of the Cherokee. They feared that Ross' attitude was likely to lead to further encroachment and eventual extermination of the race. ABCFM Secretary David Greene commended Worcester and Butler for their exemplary behavior while in prison and yet they were now distrusted by Cherokees and Georgians alike. Greene encouraged Worcester to continue to work as much as possible on his translation of the New Testament and told both of the missionaries to prepare for eventual transfer to Arkansas.

Meanwhile in Arkansas the Creeks and the Cherokee had held a joint council with representatives of the United States (Montfort Stokes, Henry L. Ellsworth, and John F. Schermerhorn). The tribes signed two separate treaties at Fort Gibson on February 14, which defined the boundaries between the two nations. The Cherokee treaty also corrected a few inaccuracies of the Washington Treaty of 1828. The next week David Greene expressed his gratitude to Agent George Vashon for the kindness his office had shown toward the missionaries. A couple of months later, however, the Board petitioned Secretary of War Cass for indemnification for abandonment of their mission station caused by the new treaty's mandated removal of Osage Indians. Furthermore, the ABCFM wanted compensation for all losses caused by future removals.

1834

John Ross Struggles against Removal

Elias Boudinot and the Ridges Organize the Treaty Party

In 1834 while the Jackson administration struggled with economic issues, relations with Mexico were strained by Stephen Austin's work toward independence for Texas.

The Mexican government was also upset about the influx of Indian refugees fleeing oppression in the United States. Removal of the Indians from the eastern United States was nearly complete, although the Cherokee remained in place and the Seminoles were lingering in Florida despite having agreed to leave in 1832. Congress organized the new Department of Indian Affairs, thus eliminating a lot of the confusion over the roles of agents and commissioners and so forth. The Trade and Intercourse Act, also passed on June 30, codified the Indian trade policy.

The Cherokee found themselves in more desperate straits as Georgian citizens continued to displace them from their homes. Poverty and disease were rampant, and some mothers even resorted to infanticide. The leaders were divided over the merits of removal versus struggling to retain the ancestral homeland. The rights of Cherokee in their own nation were compromised by Georgia's policy of favoring those who supported removal. The *Cherokee Phoenix* reported that a Cherokee enrolling agent who murdered another Cherokee opposed to removal was protected from prosecution by Georgia law. Likewise the homes of Indians favoring removal were exempted from the lottery system.

The missionaries certainly were not exempted from the lottery system. When Elizur Butler's place at Haweis was granted to Jacob Putnam in January, he obtained an injunction. When Butler was evicted later that month, he complained to Secretary War Lewis Cass but to no avail. ABCFM Secretary David Greene told Samuel A. Worcester that if he got evicted he shouldn't bother to pursue legal remedies. Indeed when Worcester received his notice in February he moved on to Brainerd without protest. By March New Echota had been seized and only one ABCFM mission was left in Georgia. The Cherokee no longer held the missionaries in high esteem, even the ones who went to jail on their behalf. Greene told Butler and Worcester to move to Arkansas to join the missions there, and he encouraged Principal Chief John Ross to accept removal as inevitable. Editor Elijah Hicks ceased publication of the *Phoenix* in June, citing personal health issues and a lack of funds, so by the end of the year Greene had made arrangements to have the press moved to Arkansas. Not that everything was wonderful in Arkansas. James Orr reported from Dwight that there was disagreement among the missionaries there, and disease and death were prevalent as well.

Meanwhile John Ross led an official delegation of the Cherokee National Council to Washington, but he was the only member of the group who held out any hope of staving off removal. He offered to cede part of the Cherokee lands in Georgia in return for protected possession of the rest. The Cherokee would eventually become citizens of the various states in which they resided. Of course President Andrew Jackson rejected this proposal outright. When it became clear that the administration would not bend, Ross addressed a memorial to Congress rejecting removal. The judicial branch of the federal government had supported the Cherokee in the past and maybe the legislative branch would be helpful now.

Chief John Ross' efforts were being undermined by a rival delegation led by his brother Andrew. Andrew Ross was apparently willing to agree to removal for a very modest price. Chief John Ross protested that the delegation had no authority and held a petition with thirteen thousand signatures of Cherokees opposed to removal. In the end Andrew Ross could obtain only three other names besides his own and his treaty proposal was ultimately rejected. John Ross, however, was forced to consider the possibility at least of a partial removal.

The summer meeting of the Cherokee National Council convened at Red Clay in August. Andrew Ross spoke out in favor of removal, but the members of the Council were overwhelmingly against it. On the third day Thomas Foreman proclaimed that individuals supporting removal were enemies of the Cherokee. With near unanimous consent, the Council then proceeded to impeach the Ridges and David Vann. Their trials would occur at the fall meeting of the Council. The intensity of the bad feelings led to the assassination of John Walker Jr. on his way home from the Council meeting.

In response to the murder of Walker, President Jackson ordered

Agent Benjamin Curry and Colonel Hugh Montgomery to provide full protection to Major and John Ridge and their supporters. He put John Ross on notice that further violence against those favoring removal would be blamed squarely on him. John Ross met with the leaders of the pro-removal faction in September in hopes of reconciliation. The meeting did not go well and the divisions were, if anything, deeper.

At the autumn meeting of the Cherokee National Council in October Chief Ross decided not to proceed with the impeachment trials of Major Ridge, John Ridge, and David Vann. On the other hand he did not drop the charges to clear their names either, so the three resigned in protest. Meanwhile the Council appointed John Ross to lead a delegation to negotiate once again with the Jackson administration.

A meeting was held on November 27 at the home of John Ridge for the purpose of formally organizing a pro-removal political party. Elias Boudinot presided over the meeting and welcomed representatives of the Jackson administration. The party decided to send a delegation to Washington to negotiate fair terms for removal across the Mississippi River. The federal representative urged financial assistance for the fledgling organization. Furthermore Agent Curry was instructed to grant Boudinot the advantage of maximum security. Governor Lumpkin of Georgia agreed to withdraw Boudinot's property from the lottery. The stage was set for official American recognition of the pro-removal party as representatives of the Cherokee Nation.

1835

The Treaty of New Echota

In 1835 President Jackson decided not to seek a third term, and the Democrats nominated Vice President Martin Van Buren to succeed him. The Anti-Masonic Party chose William Henry Harrison, and the Whigs divided their support among Daniel Webster, Hugh Lawson White, and Harrison. As the campaign got started Jackson was given an opportunity to choose a successor to his nemesis, the late Chief Justice John Marshall. He selected Roger B. Taney (who had been denied the post of Secretary of the Treasury the year before) to the bench. On the international front, a crisis was looming with Mexico, as the American settlers in Texas began to rebel against Mexican rule. Jackson offered to purchase the territory, but Mexico was not interested in any deal.

The Jackson administration continued to push for removal of all Indians east of the Mississippi and began using force in the southeast. David Vann and John Ridge, who had served as negotiators on behalf of the Creeks, attended the Creek Council in June in order to obtain their fees. They found the Creeks to be angry over the way they had been treated since the signing of their removal treaty, and they were in no mood to pay the negotiators' fees. Within a few weeks the United States forcibly removed over two thousand Creeks who dared to rebel against the treaty. In Florida Osceola led the Seminoles in an attempt to resist removal. Osceola's rebellion triggered the second Seminole War, and by the end of the year the United States had been embarrassed by significant losses. Jackson felt compelled to justify his removal policy in his annual address to Congress in December.

Conditions for the Cherokee had also become critical by 1835. A census taken that year counted 16,542 Cherokee (plus 1,592 slaves and two hundred one whites married to Cherokees) distributed among Georgia (8,946), North Carolina (3,644), Tennessee (2,528), and Alabama (1,424). By that time over fifteen thousand white intruders from Georgia had settled within the boundaries of the Cherokee Nation and had confiscated the homes from the natives and missionaries. The Cherokee were impoverished, and diseases such as small pox were rampant. Although a vast majority opposed removal, the leadership of the nation was divided on the issue, and the level of debate had degraded to the point of violence and assassination.

Although many of the missionaries had opposed the removal efforts of the United States and Georgia, the ABCFM board officially recommended that the tribe accept it as inevitable. Many of the Cherokee were already resenting the fact that Christians were the ones displacing them from their homeland, and they also resented the fact that the missionaries were making profits from the intruders by milling their grain and lumber. The missionaries were themselves divided over the issue of slavery, and one even went so far to assert that God was punishing the Cherokee for having allowed the practice. The ABCFM wanted to make sure that their properties were properly appraised so that their losses could be appealed to the government. By the end of the year the last of the missionaries had been evicted from Georgia and most had moved to Arkansas. United States Superintendent Major F.W. Armstrong negotiated a treaty with the Osage Indians that winter, settling some of the territorial disputes between the two tribes in the area. The missionaries and some prominent Cherokee such as William S. Coodey began arriving in larger numbers. Samuel A. Worcester arrived at Dwight Mission in the spring and quickly set up a new press at the Forks of the Illinois at a place he called Park Hill.

Two rival diplomatic delegations arrived in Washington in February to address the removal issue. John Ross led the National Party delegation (officially appointed by the Cherokee National Council), and his mission was to negotiate an alternative to removal. John Ridge led the Treaty Party delegation and was eager to make the best deal for removal. The Treaty Party had been organized under the supervision of the Jackson administration and naturally Secretary of War Lewis Cass swiftly agreed to negotiate with Ridge. Cass authorized an offer of $3,250,000 in exchange for Cherokee removal, but Ridge talked him up to $4,500,000. The Reverend John F. Schermerhorn presented the draft to the Treaty Party leaders at the home of Elias Boudinot, and although he was able to get about a dozen signatures, the treaty stipulated that it must be approved by the nation in full council. Taking John Ridge's advice, President Jackson wrote a letter of friendship to the Cherokee people, in support of the new treaty. The old general recognized the contributions of the Cherokee in the past during the Creek War and outlined the many ways by which the tribe had suffered. He pointed out that the best way for the people to revive their old ways and avoid mischief at the hands of the white people was to remove to new lands across the Mississippi.

John Ross was forced to use a different tactic to derail the Ridge negotiations. For the first time he negotiated terms for full removal, but demanded twenty million dollars knowing that his request would not be met. Jackson dismissed the offer outright, so Ross decided to take his case to the Senate. Assuming that the Senate would find his offer reasonable, Ross mistakenly proposed that the Senate should decide upon a fair figure. To his dismay, the Senate suggested a five million dollar settlement. Stunned, Ross asserted that the Cherokee National Council must approve of any offer. At this point the Chief must have envisioned the futility of his efforts. He penned a letter to the Mexican government asking for permission to relocate the entire tribe there with the intention of becoming citizens. It is unclear whether Mexico considered the possibility of Cherokee immigration or not. If a response was ever sent it was never received and very likely would have been confiscated (mail to the Cherokee leaders was censored).

Immediately after the Senate's resolution, John Ridge began a conspiratorial campaign against Principal Chief John Ross. He wrote the Cherokee leaders saying that the Secretary of War, the President, and the Senate had rejected all of Ross' proposals. He would try to lie about his actions, but in truth the Chief had negotiated for removal and was a cheat. Prior to the spring meeting of the Council, Ridge wrote Georgia Governor Wilson Lumpkin asking for his help in destroying Ross' political organization. Accordingly, the Georgia Guard arrested White Path, Elijah Hicks, James Martin, and some others. Despite these efforts, ninety percent of the Cherokee people still supported Chief John Ross. John Ross did not suspect the treachery of John Ridge, and he suppressed efforts to condemn him (and others) to death for treason. The Council unanimously rejected the treaty proposal.

After the Council meeting The Reverend Schermerhorn desperately suggested that the United States use bribery and coercion to obtain full consent for the rejected treaty. These methods had worked well in the past. Senator Edward Everett reported that Secretary Cass had rejected such a notion but the efforts continued, and Lumpkin's "help" supplemented the negotiations.

The next step was to organize a rival Council meeting under the leadership of John Ridge. Schermerhorn attended the meeting at Running Waters in July with the intention of presenting a proposal for the individual distribution of annuities and to resurrect the removal treaty offer. Over twenty-five hundred Ross supporters attended the meeting to disrupt it. The Cherokee had developed a nickname for Schermerhorn that was the Tsa-La-Gi word for "Devil's Horn." Even the treaty supporters couldn't resist laughing at it. Benjamin Curry was allowed to speak and even John Ross was given his chance. Ross explained that his group had been prepared to discuss the annuity issue but had not brought enough provisions to give them time to talk about removal. Ross had succeeded in packing the meeting and the Council voted to reject the annuity distribution proposal. John Ross was approved as Chief over John Ridge by a vote of 2,225 to 114. The removal treaty was not discussed.

Schermerhorn, not yet defeated, made arrangements for a meeting between Chief John Ross and John Ridge, to occur before the fall Council meeting. Although Ross agreed to attend the meeting, he did not show up at the appointed date and sent a note indicating that he had been stricken with diarrhea. He suggested that they should meet later, perhaps after the Green Corn Festival (Ridge was organizing a big event).

Meanwhile John Ridge and the Georgia Guard stepped up the pressure against the Chief. Stand Watie claimed that the printing press rightfully belonged to his brother-in-law Elias Boudinot. He asserted that Ross had illegally gained control of it and that he was planning to use it for subversive purposes. The Guard seized the press and moved it to Watie's house at Springplace. At the suggestion of John Ridge, Governor Lumpkin "influenced" Judge William Underwood and Judge Hooper to drop The Cherokee Nation as clients. Chief Ross consulted a new attorney, Colonel Richard Rockwell, for help in gaining the release of his compatriots and the return of the press. His efforts were not effective.

The Cherokee National Council met at Red Clay in October and was attended by Treaty Party members as well as Ross supporters. John Howard Payne, a noted poet who had taken an interest in writing about Cherokee history and culture, had recently befriended John Ross. He attended the meeting as the Chief's special guest. Schermerhorn attended the meeting as well and was allowed to present his treaty proposal in detail. The United States was willing the grant $3,250,000 in return for the Cherokee's eastern lands. One hundred fifty thousand dollars would be granted for various losses including claims stemming from the Creek War. The United States reiterated Cherokee claims to thirteen million acres of western territory granted by treaty in 1828 and 1833 and added to these lands eight hundred thousand additional acres. The Council rejected the proposal, and even John Ridge and his cronies voted against it. Schermerhorn raised the offer to five million dollars, but even then the Council voted no.

Schermerhorn countered with a proposal to hold yet another Council meeting to discuss removal, this one to be held at New Echota in December. Encouraged by John Ridge's rejection of the treaty proposal, Ross decided that it was time to hold the meeting that had been postponed by his "illness" that summer. The two parties agreed to send a joint delegation to Washington, each sending five members. They agreed that neither side would accept less than five million dollars for removal, but they agreed to very little else. The delegation would leave for Washington before the proposed meeting at New Echota.

What can account for the sudden conversion of the Treaty party? It was all for show. John Ridge and the others knew that the treaty proposal would never pass in the full Council and by voting for it they would risk assassination. Ridge secretly wrote Governor Lumpkin to this effect and reassured him that the treaty would be ratified at New Echota. Shortly thereafter, the Georgia Guard crossed into Tennessee and arrested John Ross and his houseguest, John Howard Payne. The two were forced to travel under harsh conditions twenty-five miles to the prison at Camp Benton, Georgia. Other Cherokee had already been imprisoned at this jail, and it was said to reek of the smell of the rotting body of an executed Cherokee. Although the two were released without charges within a couple of weeks, Ross still did not suspect the involvement of John Ridge. Upon his release, Ross quickly organized his delegation and left for Washington.

Schermerhorn also tried to intimidate the Ross supporters into attending his Council meeting at New Echota. His men confiscated corn needed for food and committed other acts of coercion, but when the Council meeting opened on December 22, only five hundred Cherokee men, women, and children were present. No more than eighty were legal voters. Officers were selected on the first day, and on the second day Schermerhorn formally presented his treaty proposal. On Christmas Eve Benjamin Curry gave a detailed explanation of each article of the treaty. Major Ridge and Elias Boudinot both gave stirring speeches in favor of the proposal.

The Council adjourned for observance of Christmas and met a few days later after the participants had had time to recover from their revelries. A group of twenty leaders was chosen to sign the treaty and to travel to Washington for its official presentation. The group met at the home of Elias Boudinot on December 29 and after much discussion John Gunter was the first Cherokee brave enough to sign the document. Andrew Ross, John Ridge, Major Ridge, Stand Watie, and the others followed. Ironically, Major Ridge, executor of Doublehead, was heard saying that he had just signed his own death warrant. Agent Rev-

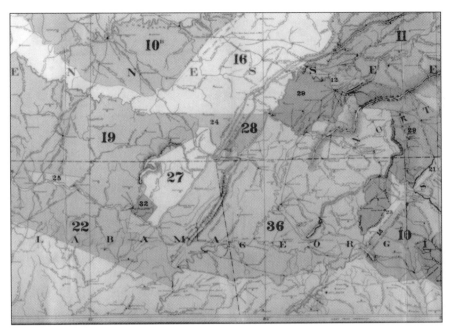

Map 13

erend John F. Schermerhorn signed the document on behalf of the United States.

The next day the rump Council voted unanimously to approve the treaty. This small group had approved on behalf of the other seventeen thousand Cherokee to cede all of the remaining eastern lands in return for five million dollars and rights to the land already held in Arkansas (now Oklahoma) and for a smaller tract (now part of Kansas). (See Map 13 #36.) The United States would pay for improvements and also for the travelling expenses. The Cherokee would be subsidized for a full year following the removal, which would take place within two years of the ratification of the treaty. Debts owed to individuals, such as pensions for service in the Creek War, would come out of the five million dollar settlement. The United States was granted the right to build roads and military posts within the western territories as needed. The United States would satisfy Osage claims and effect a peaceful understanding between the two tribes. The United States would put the annuities into a permanent national fund, to be disbursed according to will of the people expressed through their designated officers. The land allocated to the Cherokee would never be included within the boundaries of another state or territory without the consent of the Cherokee. The Cherokee Nation could establish its own government and apply its laws to its own citizens, so long as they were consistent with the Constitution of the United States. The United States promised perpetual friendship and guaranteed to protect the Cherokee from domestic strife and foreign enemies. In recognition of the extent of progress that the tribe had made toward civilization, the Cherokee would be entitled to a delegate in the United States House of Representatives. Furthermore, in recognition of the fact that certain individuals (the treaty signers) had made extraordinary progress toward citizenship, they would be allowed remain in the east and hold reservations of their properties.

Although twenty Cherokee leaders had signed the treaty, not one of them had been an officer of the Cherokee National Council. The treaty would not become law until after it was formally ratified by the United States Senate. In the meantime Schermerhorn reassured the missionaries that their rights and property would be respected. His dirty work was done.

Chapter Thirteen

1836–1840

Removal and Reunification

When Principal Chief John Ross learned about the illegal Treaty of New Echota he immediately protested to the Jackson administration. Despite his arguments that the treaty was not ratified by the Cherokee National Council and was not supported by ninety-five percent of the tribe, the United States Senate ratified it on May 23, 1836. Over the next two years Ross continued his efforts to stop the implementation of the treaty or at least to change its terms, but to no avail.

Although many of the Treaty Party members were able to organize their own removal with their personal goods, the majority of the Cherokee made no preparations to move at all. Most would rather starve than to accept government terms for removal and would just as soon murder those who would. After Chief Ross had exhausted all diplomatic efforts to avert the removal, General Winfield Scott (see Figure 14, page 289) issued a proclamation from his headquarters at New Echota on May 10, 1838, that the Cherokee would be given no more than a month to prepare for their removal. Although the General specifically ordered his troops to act with as little violence as possible, the cruelty of his soldiers when arresting these fiteen thousand people has been well documented.

After the tribe had been herded into three main detention camps, the government transported a few groups of Cherokee to Indian Territory by river, but these trips were not well organized. Chief Ross, who

Figure 14 — General Winfield Scott

had established a relationship with General Scott while still in Washington, argued that the Cherokee should be allowed to organize themselves for the journey. Ross was appointed superintendent for that reason and he personally took over the arrangements. He negotiated per capita reimbursements for the tribesmen. He was granted a delay because of a drought, but by October the thirteen remaining groups had started on the overland route west. Thousands of ill-fed and poorly prepared men, women, and children were forced to leave their homeland over the harsh winter months. Perhaps more than a fourth of the tribe died along this Trail of Tears.

The death and misery along the trail continued as the emigrants arrived in their new land without homes and with insufficient provisions. Famine and disease continued to take their tolls. Despite such misery, however, Chief John Ross, whose own wife had died during the removal, was determined to see his nation reunited under constitutional government. The Old Settlers—Cherokees who had lived in Arkansas for years before moving to Indian Territory—were not as sophisticated as the easterners in that they did not have a written constitution and had been resistant to formal education. There were not nearly as many Old Settlers as new emigrants, but their government was supported by the United States Agents, and the new arrivals were divided into those who supported the Treaty of New Echota and those who did not.

Chief Ross consequently invited the Old Settlers to join in Council with the new emigrants to form a new government. Although the westerners were reluctant at first, Sequoyah, the inventor of the Tsa-La-Gi syllabary, convinced his colleagues to join with Ross. Interest in merging the eastern and western groups especially increased after the assassination of the three main proponents of the Treaty of New Echota: Major Ridge, John Ridge, and Elias Boudinot. These executions effectively ended any chance that the Treaty Party would have a significant role in the new government. An Act of Union was signed on July 12, 1839, and a new Constitution was drafted on September 6, 1839. With the official approval of the Council of the Cherokee (western) on June 26, 1840, the new organization officially went into effect. The Council of the united tribe met in October at the new capital, Tahlequah. John Ross, who was elected Principal Chief, spoke before the Council and announced plans for the reconstruction of the Nation. Despite unimaginable hardship, the Cherokee Nation had endured and was looking forward to social progress under representational government.

1836

The Cherokee Protest the Treaty of New Echota

In 1836, during the last full year of Andrew Jackson's presidency, his handpicked heir, Vice President Martin Van Buren, was elected President. It was a quiet year for the United States. Arkansas was admitted as a slave state, and Wisconsin was organized as a territory forbidding slavery. Jackson's biggest foreign problem was the independence movement in Texas. Mexican General Santa Ana began the siege of the Alamo in an unsuccessful attempt to prevent the Texans from declaring independence. General Samuel Houston defeated Santa Ana at the Battle of San Jacinto and immediately petitioned Washington for recognition. Jackson was reluctant to recognize the new republic, fearing that such action would provoke a war with Mexico. The Cherokee had a relationship with Sam Houston long before the Texan War of Independence. Houston had lived among the Cherokee after his resignation as governor of Tennessee. He remained friendly to the tribe and in early 1836 met with Big Bowl and Mush in order to secure their friendship in return for the rights to stay on the lands already granted to them in Texas by the Mexican government (roughly modern Cherokee County, Texas). Despite President Houston's efforts, the Texas Senate rejected the treaty with the Cherokee in secret session.

In the east the Cherokee Nation was in a state of turmoil. The National Party (led by Principal Chief John Ross) and the Treaty Party (led by John Ridge) had agreed to send a combined delegation to Washington to negotiate a reasonable removal treaty. After Ross and his followers had left for Washington, Ridge's men stayed behind and illegally signed the twice-rejected Treaty of New Echota, ceding the homeland forever. Councils were held across the nation, and the treaty was rejected again and again. A letter of protest was drafted and given to General John Ellis Wool, Director of Removal, to be forwarded on to the President, Secretary of War, and the Senate. President Jackson reportedly was infuriated and insulted that Wool would have delivered such a letter. He forbade John Ross from any further communication with the United States, saying that no government among the eastern Cherokee would be recognized. Likewise the Cherokee would not be allowed to meet in Council to oppose the Treaty of New Echota.

President Jackson was not completely satisfied with the Treaty of New Echota as it had been drafted. He despised the article that would have allowed certain qualified Cherokees (the ones who signed the treaty) to become American citizens and to retain property in the east. Jackson felt that the entire Cherokee population should move, including their elite. On March 1 The Reverend John F. Schermerhorn, Major Ridge, Andrew Ross, John Ridge, Elias Boudinot, Stand Watie, and others signed a proclamation amending the treaty so as to disallow preemptions in return for six hundred thousand dollars to be distributed among those who qualified for them. The revised Treaty of New Echota passed by one vote in the Senate, after Tennessee Senator Hugh Lawson White unexpectedly changed his opinion. On May 23, 1836, President Jackson declared the treaty to be law and gave the Cherokee two years to move across the Mississippi River. Many in the United States Congress, among them former President John Quincy Adams, felt that the new treaty was a disgraceful blemish for the United States, but the Treaty of New Echota became law nonetheless.

Cherokees across their nation continued to meet in councils to voice opposition to the new treaty. The Cherokee in North Carolina complained that they had no representatives at the treaty negotiations at New Echota. The towns of western North Carolina (Qualla and others) selected William Holland Thomas to represent their interests. Thomas was a white man, but he had been adopted by the respected Chief Yonaguska. Thomas argued that the Cherokee of North Carolina wished to remain in their homes and become United States citizens, receiving their allotment of settlement money as had been outlined by Article XII of the treaty. This article applied to Cherokee not wishing to leave from North Carolina, Alabama, and Tennessee. Accordingly the War Department Office of Subsistence instructed the Superintendent of the Cherokee to prepare enrollment books listing those who wished to remove and those wanted to stay. General John Wool learned that the vast majority of the Cherokee in North Carolina were opposed to removal, but he was determined to effect their removal one way or another. He directed a policy of detaining the leaders of the Valley Towns in order to bait the other Cherokee men so that they could be forced to surrender their arms. Of course without weapons the Cherokee couldn't fight back, but they also couldn't hunt and feed themselves. Small pox and other diseases were already adding to the misery.

The Cherokee National Council met in the fall and decided to choose a delegation (again led by Principal Chief John Ross) to negotiate a new treaty, with full participation of the western (Arkansas) Cherokee. General Wool attended the Council and warned Ross and the others that the United States would meet with no more delegations, but the party traveled west and arrived in Arkansas early in December. While General Wool was at the Council he learned that ninety-five percent of the Cherokee opposed the Treaty of New Echota and that it had been signed illegally by a rump group of unauthorized leaders. Wool found his situation to be frustrating and distasteful and petitioned Acting Secretary of War Benjamin F. Butler to be transferred to another assignment.

With the preemption clause removed form the treaty, John Ridge and his allies had little reason to stick around where they were decidedly unpopular. He took care of some unfinished business he had as President of the National Committee and headed to Arkansas with his sister. The lot of the Cherokee was not exactly paradise in Arkansas, either. Poverty and disease were problems there as well. The missionaries complained of alcohol use and other bad behavior. The western population was anxious over the possible consequences of having seventeen thousand new neighbors show up over the next two years.

The missionaries in the east were having their problems too. The Cherokee were distracted with the removal process and many of them blamed all Christians for their plight. The ABCFM Board forbade the use of slave labor in both the eastern and western territories even though Arkansas had just been admitted as a slave state. Although the Board had reluctantly supported removal, it was appalled by the means that Treaty Party had used to attain it. The Treaty of New Echota granted the missionaries compensation for their losses caused by the removal and forced abandonment of their facilities. The Cherokee would be incensed if the Board accepted such funds, but the money certainly would not have been given to them.

1837

Treaty Party Followers Begin Their Exodus

In the last few weeks of President Andrew Jackson's administration the withdrawal of federal deposits from banking institutions and a collapse in cotton prices plummeted the economy into the Panic of 1837. On his last day in office, Jackson formally recognized the independence of the Republic of Texas. The former President was angry later when the Senate rejected annexation and statehood for the Lone Star Republic, but it was Martin Van Buren's problem now. Meanwhile the United States Army, under General Zachary Taylor, scored a major victory in the Seminole War at Okeechobee Swamp. Ironically, several Cherokee, including Jesse Bushyhead, received commendations by the United States for their assistance against the Seminoles. But the Cherokee had their own problems with the United States.

The United States Senate had ratified the controversial Treaty of New Echota and it was now the law of the land. Georgia and Alabama had already passed laws pertaining to the distribution of Cherokee lands. Tennessee had been a safe refuge for the Cherokee fleeing from Georgia, but authorities began arresting Cherokees crossing into the state and forcibly deporting them to Arkansas. By the end of the year Tennessee had enacted a law governing the disposal of the lands in the Ocoee District (to be vacated by the removal of the Cherokee). By contrast, North Carolina recognized that its Cherokee had not been represented at New Echota and actually passed a law designed to protect them from fraudulent business practices.

Meanwhile Principal Chief John Ross had returned from Arkansas with a delegation from the western Cherokee. They stopped in Brainerd briefly on their way to Washington to negotiate changes in the hated Treaty of New Echota. The delegation arrived by March, and Ross did secure a meeting with President Van Buren. The delegation made little progress and finally on March 24, Secretary of War Joel R. Poinsett wrote Chief Ross that having been legally ratified by the Senate, the Treaty of New Echota was in full effect.

Back in the Cherokee Nation the soldiers who were commissioned to remove the Cherokee became more and more repulsed by their assignments. The Tennessee Volunteers under Brigadier General R.G. Dunlap were reluctant to use force against the Cherokee when they saw that they were nearly universally opposed to removal.

General John E. Wool reported in February that almost the entire Cherokee population would rather starve to death rather than accept removal money. Despite his personal reservations, Wool issued a proclamation to the Cherokee urging them to prepare to move out or be forced. He advised them to accept their property valuations without argument.

The Cherokee Council met in Red Clay in June, with over three hundred attending religious services at its beginning. General Wool, who was becoming more and more sympathetic to the Cherokee, was finally relieved of his duties (as requested). The Council was allowed to meet again in August, this time with the permission of Colonel William Lindsey, Wool's replacement. General Nathaniel Smith (who had replaced the late Benjamin Currey as Agent) and United States Agent Colonel John Mason spoke at the Council. Lindsey specifically allowed the Council to meet so that Mason could lobby for acceptance of the Treaty of New Echota. Many of the Cherokee orators who might have spoken in favor of the treaty were gone, already having left for Arkansas. Mason influenced no one, of course, and managed to offend Chief Ross and the others. Ross gave his report to the Council about his negotiations. The Council once again chose him to lead a delegation to go to Washington that winter to meet with the Van Buren administration. White Path, Elijah Hicks, and Situwakee were appointed to accompany the Chief.

Not all Cherokee were opposed to removal; a few hundred had attended the meeting at New Echota. On New Year's Day 1837 a group of about six hundred wealthy Cherokee left the homeland with their slaves, oxen, and gear with the intentions of arriving in Arkansas in time for spring planting. Strategically placed payments to the leaders of this group allowed them to travel as aristocrats as they made their way over-land across Kentucky, Illinois, Missouri, and into Arkansas. The first set of emigrants to leave under the terms of the Treaty of New Echota was a party of four hundred sixty-six led by Major Ridge. Having said his fare-wells at Brainerd, Major Ridge led his flotilla from Ross' Landing early in March. The group navigated the Tennessee, Ohio, Mississippi, and finally the Arkansas rivers. Major Ridge disembarked two miles up from Fort Smith to reach Honey Creek, near the border with Missouri. The rest went on to Fort Coffee and then progressed on to Cherokee Terri-tory near Fort Gibson. Despite the difficulty of navigating the Arkansas River and problems with disease, fighting, and alcoholism, the party ar-rived by the end of March without the loss of life.

The second party of Cherokee to leave according to the treaty terms was a group of three hundred sixty-five Cherokees, led by James Starr. They left Calhoun's Landing on October 14 and headed overland to Nashville to pay respects to former President Jackson. From there they journeyed into Kentucky and across Illinois and Missouri into Ar-kansas. The party made it to their destination in late December, having lost fifteen lives along the way. Among the dead were eleven children.

The year 1837 was difficult for the missionaries as well. The Treaty of New Echota established that the missionaries should be compensated for the loss of property associated with the removal. The Cherokee were resentful that the funds to pay the missionaries would come out of the five million dollar general settlement. David Greene, Secretary of the Board of the ABCFM, recognized the anger of the Cherokee but in-sisted that all he wanted was to get enough money to build new missions among the Cherokee in Arkansas. The missionaries were disturbed, however, that the Agents were not evaluating their properties fairly. The Panic of 1837 had affected the ABCFM, and it was in serious financial trouble. Greene expressed concern as the year closed that he was not certain of the future of the missions or the attitude of the Cherokee to-ward them. John Ridge had invited some of the missionaries to join his group but others, including Elizur Butler, were snubbed.

1838

The Trail of Tears Begins

In 1838 war with Mexico was averted when the Senate rejected statehood for the Texas, but violent incidents had sparked an undeclared border war with Canada. No domestic issue was more significant, however, than the forced removal of the Cherokee from their homeland. Of the thirteen thousand Cherokee evicted in 1838 and early 1839, an estimated four thousand died on the Trail of Tears. (See Map 14.)

Principal Chief John Ross resisted removal until the last possible moment. He led a final delegation to Washington, arriving in January. President Martin Van Buren was cool toward the Ross delegation at first but finally opened up negotiations since Ross' help would be useful in effecting the removal. Ross hoped Van Buren would grant a delay in the removal so that he could obtain better terms than offered by the Treaty of New Echota. The President considered granting the delay, but Georgia Governor George Gilmer, already angered by the way the Cherokee population was ignoring the removal orders, threatened to provoke a states' rights crisis. Undaunted, Ross presented the United States Senate with a petition signed by 15,665 Cherokee rejecting removal and the Treaty of New Echota. On March 27, Commissioner of Indian Affairs C.A. Harris wrote Chief Ross informing him that the Senate had re-

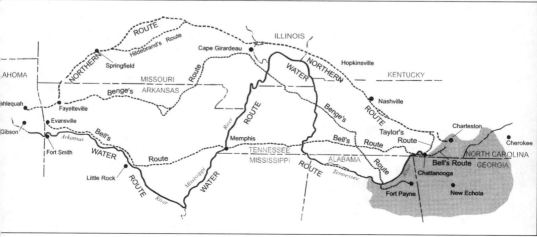

Map 14

jected his memorial and that it was clear that the legislature would not interfere with the implementation the Treaty of New Echota.

The removal policy of the Van Buren administration was not universally popular. Representative James Graham of Haywood County, North Carolina, spoke to the House of Representatives saying that the Cherokee were a peaceful and industrious people. Indeed the Senate's rejection of the delay sparked protests in Ohio and Philadelphia. Later in the year, in the midterm elections Van Buren's Democratic Party lost control of both houses of Congress. This came a few months too late.

Chief Ross stayed in Washington a little longer to negotiate for back annuities, the release of prisoners from jails in Georgia (so that they could be moved west), and for the exemption of the ill and infirm. John Ross also met with General Winfield Scott, who had just been assigned to lead a force of seven thousand soldiers to round up the Cherokee and move them west. The two had an amicable conversation, and the respectful relationship developed between the two would become useful later.

On May 10, 1838, General Scott issued a proclamation to the Cherokee from his new headquarters at New Echota. He rebuked them for having wasted the past two years not preparing for their journeys but promised them that his men would treat them in a most merciful way. He exhorted the Cherokee to cooperate so as to avoid forcing the soldiers to spill blood in the process, but within the month each and every Cherokee inhabitant must be in the process of moving. By the deadline fewer than two thousand Cherokee had voluntarily left. True to his word, General Scott instructed his soldiers to prosecute the round-up with as little violence as possible. Although the Cherokee were mostly disarmed already through the efforts of General John E. Wool, Scott promised that all of the confiscated weapons would be redistributed after they reached the west.

General Scott divided the nation into western, central, and eastern zones and established detention camps at Hiwassee (Calhoun, Tennessee), Ross' Landing (Chattanooga), and Gunter's Landing (Guntersville, Alabama). Despite orders to avoid unnecessary violence, the cruel actions of the soldiers are well documented. The missionaries witnessed the families being forced out of their homes at gunpoint without the benefit of packing supplies. They also reported death and suffering at the camps from measles, dysentery, and small pox.

General Scott assigned General Abraham Eustis the task of evicting the Cherokee from western North Carolina. General Eustis missed about three hundred Cherokees at Oconaluftee who claimed to be exempt as United States citizens with personal reservations. There were also many escaped Cherokee who had found refuge in the mountains. General Scott had already re-assigned Eustis to the Canadian frontier by the time he learned about the holdouts in the mountains outside of tribal territory. Over the summer and fall Scott sent small bands of soldiers to comb the mountains for the refugees and succeeded in capturing about one hundred forty of them.

It was during this period that the famous Tsali incident took place. A family of Cherokee, under some sort of provocation, killed all but one of the soldiers who were escorting them to a detention camp. The surviving soldier lived to tell his story so General Scott had no choice but to send in a large number of soldiers to seek revenge. He gave orders for the Tsali gang to be found and executed, but the Oconoluftee were to be left alone. Colonel William S. Foster successfully tracked down his quarry with the help of the Euchella gang of refugees. Tsali and all of his male adult relatives were executed. The Euchellas were allowed to stay in North Carolina.

On June 6, 1838, a first detachment of eight hundred Cherokee disembarked from Ross' Landing in 130-foot double-decked keelboats. They navigated the Tennessee River to the Ohio, Mississippi, and finally Arkansas rivers. Two more groups set out within the next few days. The third group walked from Ross' Landing to Waterloo, Alabama, to board since the river level was so low. Conditions were bad and many of the refugees were unruly. Acting without authorization in the absence of John Ross, Second Chief George Lowrey and his associates asked General Scott to delay any further passages until the drought and disease had subsided. The request was granted, but the rest of the Cherokee would have to go the overland route.

Chief Ross returned from Washington in July to find his people fenced into camps like livestock. He lobbied General Scott to grant better conditions and to prevent the sale of liquor to the refugees. The Council met and addressed a memorial to General Scott requesting that the Cherokee be allowed to organize their own removal if the United States would reimburse them for their expenses. Scott acceded to the request and named Chief Ross Superintendent. The Council submitted an estimate of $65,880 for wagons, horses, provisions, and so forth. The General rejected the estimate as too expensive and luxurious but accepted a smaller one. At the request of Chief Ross, the per capita expense was increased a few pennies to allow the refugees to take soap with them.

Chief Ross began preparing for his own departure and applied for compensation for his personal losses. Meanwhile he carefully preserved the written documents of the Cherokee Nation, including the official records of the Nation since its reconstruction and treaties from the earliest days of the United States. The Council met at Aquohee (meaning "Captured") on August 1, 1838. The Council approved the appointment of Ross as Superintendent of the Cherokee for Removal and Subsistence and authorized him to borrow money as needed to pay for their travel needs. Richard Taylor, President of the National Committee, and Going Snake, Speaker of the Council, signed a resolution asserting the eternal independence of the Cherokee Nation. The resolution rejected the Treaty of New Echota and vowed to preserve the constitutional law of the nation. The Council also approved his plan to divide the nation into thirteen groups of approximately one thousand each.

Ten groups were organized at Aquohee to travel a northern route through Tennessee, Kentucky, and Illinois, crossing the Mississippi River into Missouri and then moving through northwestern Arkansas into Indian Territory. An eleventh group organized at Aquohee was reserved for supporters of the Treaty Party. This contingent of about seven hundred people chose a southern route across Tennessee to Arkansas. Another group led by Richard Taylor and including The Reverend Daniel Butrick was organized to leave from Ross' Landing, taking the northern route. The thirteenth group left from Fort Payne (Willstown), Alabama, taking a route a little south of the main group.

Chief Ross notified General Scott that the groups were ready to go on August 28, but he was granted a brief delay because of the drought conditions. The rains came in late September so the first contingent of 1,103 individuals was ready to leave on October 1. This group, led by Hair Conrad, held a brief meeting at Rattlesnake Springs, Tennessee, and unanimously agreed to respect their constitution upon arrival in the west.

The misery that ensued is inestimable. Jesse Bushyhead, who was the leader of one of the groups, wrote Chief Ross on October 21 that among others, his wagon master had died. He reported also that the legendary White Path was dying. The missionaries Elizur Butler and Daniel Butrick both reported seeing hundreds die en route.

Three weeks before the last group left, Captain Page, Superintending Agent of the Cherokee Nation for Removal, paid John Ross $776,393.98 ($66.24 per capita) for expenses related to the removal. Later Ross would successfully argue for more money since all of the trips lasted longer than the estimated eighty days.

As the Cherokee approached their new land, the survivors would face the uncertainties of homelessness, unemployment, and civil unrest. How would the Old Settlers get along with the new emigrants? Would the Constitution be respected? How would the Ross supporters get along with the Treaty Party and their leaders? What role would Christianity and the missionaries play in the new home?

1839

Political Murders, An Act of Union, and a New Constitution

In 1839 the border dispute between Canada and the United States escalated into the Aroostook War. Meanwhile, the United States had avoided war with Mexico over Texas, but the Texans had avowed to remove all Indians from their territory. The Mexicans forged an alliance with the local Cherokee to challenge the Texans, but after a surprise attack on their villages on the Angelina River, the Cherokee were crushed. The two most powerful chiefs, Bowl and Hard Mush, were dead, and the tribe was scattered between northern Mexico and Indian Territory, in the new Cherokee Nation.

By January 1839 the only Cherokee left in the east were reservation holders in North Carolina and escaped refugees. Almost the entire nation was en route across the country enduring miserable conditions. The illness and death was legendary, and it struck those of all classes. Even Quatie Ross, the wife of Principal Chief John Ross, died in Arkansas. The first group of emigrants, led by Elijah Hicks, arrived in Indian Territory on January 4 and the last group arrived on March 25.

Tribal affairs were to be monitored from Fort Gibson in Arkansas, with Matthew Arbuckle and Governor Montfort Stokes acting as United States Agents for the Cherokee. Upon his arrival, the mourning Chief John Ross immediately complained to Arbuckle that the meat rations were unhealthy and the grains were infested with weevils. Unable to procure decent provisions from the United States, he was forced to purchase goods from private traders. The starvation, disease, and death continued for the new emigrants and their missionary friends.

The missionaries had long been thought of as friends to the Cherokee, but their position was challenged for many reasons. Samuel A. Worcester had worked closely with Elias Boudinot in translating the Bible, and both now were tainted with the shame of the Treaty of New Echota. Other missionaries who were seen as biased against the Treaty part, such as Daniel Butrick, found themselves endangered by treaty signers seeking revenge against them. The missionaries were blamed by some Cherokee as being partially responsible for the removal since the leadership supported it toward the end, and after all they were white and Christian just like the Georgians and Jackson administration. It did not help that the American Board of Commissioners for Foreign Missions accepted a $28,413.25 reimbursement for its losses connected with the removal. Even though the money came out of the funds set aside for the Cherokee by the Treaty of New Echota, David Greene, the Secretary of the ABCFM, said that Chief John Ross had not objected to the payment prior to the removal.

Upon the arrival of the last group of eastern Cherokee, Chief John Ross pursued a policy of political reconciliation with the Old Settlers, the western Cherokee who had settled in Arkansas decades before, and more recently in Indian Territory. The Old Settlers were by and large less sophisticated than their eastern counterparts since many of them had emigrated in the first place to avoid the evils of white customs and education. This group was less organized politically—it did not have a written constitution. Chief John Jolly, the leader of the Old Settlers, had recently died and the new leadership was reluctant at first to cede any power whatsoever to the new emigrants. The Old Settlers had two advantages over the emigrants: They already had a working government with an established location, and they were the favorites of the United States Agents. Arbuckle in particular did not trust John Ross and twice believed rumors that his people were planning massacres of Fort Gibson. While it was clear that members of the Treaty Party were spreading these rumors, Ross seemingly ignored the threat from this small faction to concentrate on the more important business of joining hands with the Old Settlers.

Early in June Chief Ross organized a Council meeting at Takotto-kah (Double Springs), to which representatives of the Old Settlers were invited. The cordial mood of the event was soured somewhat when A.M. Vann, President of National Council (West) asked the eastern Chief to clarify his specific proposals for him to consider. John Ross and George Lowrey responded by saying that they wanted to unite the eastern and western Cherokee on equal footing. The Cherokee National Council (East) authorized Ross, Lowrey, and Edward Gunter to meet with western counterparts for the purpose of devising a new government. Vann responded by asserting that the Cherokee were already united under the laws of the western Cherokee. The officers of the Council of the eastern Cherokee (Principal Chief John Ross, Second Chief George Lowrey, President of the National Committee Richard Taylor, and Speaker of the National Council Going Snake) expressed regret at the attitude of President Vann and asserted that the new emigrants would continue under their own laws, as was their right. The Council called for a joint council to be held in July for the purpose of forming a joint government with the Old Settlers. The Council adjourned on June 21, and on that day Chief Ross penned a letter to Agent Arbuckle asking him to make no payments or do any business with any Cherokee except for the eastern Council until the joint council should prove successful. Maybe a little financial pressure would bring the Old Settlers around to his way of thinking.

While the Council at Takattokah did not address the issue punishing the signers of the Treaty of New Echota, certainly it was on everybody's mind. John Ross had been widowed along the Trail of Tears and virtually every family had lost some relatives, in addition to their homes and property. According to the established laws of the Cherokee Nation, anyone selling tribal land without authorization of the Council could be punished by death. Major Ridge himself was one of the executioners of Doublehead, who had been guilty of selling prime hunting grounds. The Council was committed to working out a cooperative relationship with the Old Settlers and the Treaty Party issue was ignored.

Behind the scenes the Treaty Party issue was not ignored. On the morning of June 22, 1839, the day after the Council had adjourned, Major Ridge, John Ridge, and Elias Boudinot were murdered simultaneously. A group of assassins surrounded the home of John Ridge before dawn and then entered and dragged him outside to be stabbed to death. A few hours later, his father, Major Ridge, was shot and killed while travelling along the border with Arkansas. Later in the day Elias Boudinot was tricked into coming down from the roof of a new house where he was working in order to get medicine for a sick child. Once he was down, he was stabbed and bludgeoned to death.

While many members of the Treaty Party fled to Fort Gibson to safety, Stand Watie (the brother of Elias Boudinot) vowed to get revenge and called for the assassination of John Ross. Ross refused to be intimidated into leaving his house, but he did call on Arbuckle to provide assistance. The request was unnecessary since hundreds of his faithful supporters had already formed an armed guard around his home. Even though the murders occurred within the Cherokee Nation and were technically outside the jurisdiction of the United States, Arbuckle claimed that Major Ridge was killed in Arkansas, and a federal investigation ensued. Arbuckle advised Ross that the Ridge family wanted justice, not revenge, and accused Ross of harboring murderers. The Principal Chief refused to go to Fort Gibson to be interrogated and when asked about the murders at his home at Park Hill, Ross denied all knowledge of the murders.

The Council of the western Cherokee met at Fort Gibson on June 28 and expressed regret over the recent political murders, pleading for an end to the violence. The Council was angry over the letter Ross sent to Arbuckle but nonetheless agreed in principle to attend another joint meeting with the new emigrants and even suggested some rules of engagement. Ross' letter fell on deaf ears anyway as Arbuckle and Stokes told him that the laws of the Old Settlers should remain in effect until changed peacefully. The agents urged Ross to accept the westerners' proposals for the joint council. Ross responded to them that the eastern Cherokee Nation would not come to a joint council as supplicants; they had no say in the laws that governed the Old Settlers, and by the same token they would not want to impose their laws on the westerners.

The joint meeting sponsored by the eastern Cherokee met at Camp Illinois on July 1, 1839, and was attended by over two thousand Cherokee, almost all of whom were from the east. The Old Settlers stayed away in protest of the murders of the Ridges and Boudinot and because of the intimidating presence of Chief John Ross' armed guard. Among the western leaders who did attend was Sequoyah (George Gist). He was a strong proponent of unification and even drafted a letter to other western leaders urging them to join them in council. With unification sidelined as a major topic, the Council passed a resolution declaring the Treaty of New Echota null and void. All of the treaty signatories would be required to appear before the Council to apologize and would be banned from holding public office for five years. The murderers of the Ridges and Boudinot were granted amnesty.

While the Ross group was making overtures toward the Old Settlers for reunification, his actions drove the Treaty Party toward secession. The Treaty Party held its own Council at Tahlonteeskee on July 22. Among those in attendance were John Brown and John Rogers, two Old Settler chiefs who had disregarded Sequoyah's invitation to join Ross' group. On the other hand John Looney, another western chief, agreed to attend Ross' joint convention and work toward unification. The leaders worked in earnest and on July 12, 1839, the Act of Union Between the Eastern and Western Cherokees was drafted and signed at Camp Illinois by George Lowrey, President of the Eastern Cherokees; John Ross, Principal Chief; and Going Snake, Speaker of the Council. Sequoyah represented the Old Settlers. The Council of the Western Cherokee approved the Act of Union on August 23, with Acting Principal Chief John Looney and a large number of other Old Settlers signing the document.

A convention was held to form a new constitution, and it was dominated by the easterners. William Shorey Coodey (the nephew of John Ross), who had written the Act of Union, drafted the Constitution as well. George Lowrey, President of the National Convention, followed by Principal Chief John Ross, Going Snake, and thirteen other eastern Cherokee, signed the new Constitution of the Cherokee Nation at Tahlequah on September 6. Sequoyah, John Looney, and fifteen other Old Settlers signed the document of behalf of the western Cherokee. Tahlequah became the official capital of the united Cherokee Nation. The Convention elected John Ross Principal Chief and David Vann Second Chief. A delegation was chosen to represent the united Cherokee Nation in Washington.

By mid-October John Ross and William S. Coodey had left Tahlequah to head to Washington. The rest of the appointed delegation stayed behind to deal with Agent Arbuckle and his investigation of the Treaty Party murders. Although Arbuckle had seized Janus Foreman as a suspected murderer of Major Ridge, John Rollins Ridge was far from satisfied with the efforts of the United States Agent. Meanwhile John Ross sought the nullification of the Treaty of New Echota and asked that all money due to the Cherokee Nation be given to Lewis Ross, Treasurer. The War Department generally snubbed Ross, as the murder investigation was underway and he was suspected of complicity. He was also suspected of having supported or even fomented Creek and Seminole uprisings in the years before their removal.

William Holland Thomas had been in Washington for almost the entire year lobbying on behalf of the North Carolina Cherokee. The War Department finally agreed to grant per-capita claims of the Cherokee but not claims related to removal or subsistence. The victory was moot as Secretary Joel R. Poinsett refused to release the funds anyway. In late December Poinsett announced his decision that the Board of Commissioners set up by the Treaty of New Echota would have the final word on all such Cherokee claims.

1840

New Beginnings at Tahlequah

This was a year of endings and beginnings. The Trail of Tears was part of history, and the Cherokee Nation once again rose out of the ashes like the legendary phoenix. The eastern and western Cherokee had reconciled their differences in 1839, and the process of formally uniting their governments was underway. While Principal Chief John Ross was in Washington on a diplomatic mission a Council of almost two thousand Cherokees met and rescinded the earlier resolution declaring that all signers of the Treaty of New Echota were outlaws. The Treaty Party ignored the olive branch and declared itself independent from the rest of the Cherokee at its February council meeting at Fort Gibson. Agent Matthew Arbuckle threatened to unite the Cherokee under chiefs he would appoint himself, but nothing came of his words that year. Perhaps the wind was taken out of his sails after Tennessee Congressman John

Bell released the "Suppressed Report." In this document, which had been kept out of public view, the House Committee on Indian Affairs sharply criticized President Martin Van Buren and the War Department for interfering with the internal affairs of the Cherokee. The Committee faulted the administration for not recognizing John Ross as its legitimate leader during the debate over the Treaty of New Echota.

Meanwhile the hardship continued for the Cherokee people and the missionaries. Criticism of the Van Buren administration would not bring back those who died during the removal and would not take them all back to their homeland. Drinking and violence was rife and no one seemed to be immune from it. Daniel Butrick reported that he and his wife had been attacked by a cousin of John Ridge for having opposed congregational membership for Treaty signers. Some of the missionaries were under suspicion for having favored removal as well. Despite the hardships, Butrick was able to organize the Association of Ministers in the Cherokee Nation and Vicinity. The Christians were not going to give up on the tribe.

The Council of the Old Settlers met on June 26, 1840, at Fort Gibson and adopted the Constitution of September 6, 1839. The unification of the Cherokee was thus formally completed. In October the first united Council of the Cherokee Nation was held at Tahlequah. Principal Chief John Ross reported on the state of the Cherokee Nation and encouraged education to be a cornerstone of the rebuilding process. He discussed the frustrations of his diplomatic efforts in Washington and listed the Nation's grievances against the United States. John Ross and Lewis Ross were chosen as delegates to return to Washington. They did not know at that time that Van Buren would be in his final days as President and that they would have to look forward to dealing with another warrior famous for defeating an Indian nation—President William Henry Harrison.

When Hernando de Soto first encountered the Cherokee in 1540, the tribe was a self-sufficient people who took from nature what they needed. Men were respected for their attributes and accomplishments, not their material possessions. Over the next three hundred years the Europeans permanently affected the economy, culture, and government of the Cherokee. At the beginning of the fourth century after first contact, the Cherokee leaders were Christian capitalists serving under a formal constitutional government. The Cherokee had surrendered many of their old ways, but they had also adapted the ways of the white man in a way that no other native group had done. Instead of being recognized for their tremendous achievements, however, the racial bigotry and greed of their neighbors condemned them to expulsion from their own homeland. Despite the holocaust of the Trail of Tears the Cherokee immediately re-established the rule of law and set forth on a new pathway for peace and progress.

Bibliography

Pat Alderman, *The Overmountain Men* (The Overmountain Press, Johnson City, 1970, reprinted 1986).

Pat Alderman, *Nancy Ward / Dragging Canoe* (The Overmountain Press, Johnson City, Tennessee, 1978, Second Edition, 1990).

Fred Anderson, *Crucible of War* (Alfred A. Knopf, New York, 2000).

William L. Anderson and James A. Lewis, *A Guide to Cherokee Documents in Foreign Archives* (The Scarecrow Press, Metuchen, New Jersey, 1983).

William L. Anderson, editor, *Cherokee Removal Before and After* (The University of Georgia Press, Athens and London, 1991).

Colin G. Calloway, *The American Revolution in Indian Country* (Cambridge University Press, Cambridge, 1995).

Brent Yanusdi Cox, *Heart of the Eagle* (Chenanee Publishers, Milan, Tennessee, 1999).

Clifton Daniel, editor, *Chronicle of America* (Chronicle Publications, Mount Kisco, New York, 1989).

Walter T. Durham, *Before Tennessee: The Southwest Territory 1790–1796* (The Overmountain Press, Johnson City, Tennessee, 1990).

Walter Edgar, *South Carolina: a History* (University of South Carolina Press, Columbia, South Carolina, 1998).

John Ehle, *Trail of Tears: The Rise and Fall of the Cherokee Nation* (Doubleday, New York, 1988).

Stanley J. Folmsbee, Robert E. Corlew, Enoch L. Mitchell, *Tennessee: A Short History* (The University of Tennessee Press, Knoxville, 1969).

Grant Foreman, *The Five Civilized Tribes* (University of Oklahoma Press, Norman, Oklahoma, 1934).

William H. Goetzmann and Glyndwr Williams, *The Atlas of North American Exploration* (The University of Oklahoma Press, Norman, 1992).

Cherokee Chronicles

Donald R. Hickey, *The War of 1812: A Forgotten Conflict* (University of Illinois Press, Urbana and Chicago, 1990).

Stanley W. Hoig, *The Cherokees and Their Chiefs In the Wake of Empire* (The University of Arkansas Press, Fayetteville, 1998).

Duane H. King, editor, *The Cherokee Indian Nation: A Troubled History* (The University of Tennessee Press, Knoxville, 1979).

Paul Kutsche, *A Guide to Cherokee Documents in the Northeastern United States* (*Native American Bibliography Series, No. 7*, The Scarecrow Press, Inc. Metuchen, N.J., & London, 1986).

Thomas E. Mails, *The Cherokee People* (Marlowe and Company, New York, 1996).

William G. McLaughlin, *Cherokees and Missionaries, 1789–1839* (University of Oklahoma Press, Norman and London, 1994).

Richard Middleton, *Colonial America: A History, 1585–1776* (Blackwell Publishers, Oxford, 1996, 2nd Edition).

Jose Montero de Pedro, Marques de Casa Mena, *The Spanish in New Orleans and Louisiana, Translated from Spanish by Richard E. Chandler* (Pelican Publishing Company, Gretna, Louisiana, 2000).

James Mooney, *Myths of the Cherokee* (Dover Publications, New York, 1900, republished in 1995).

John Oliphant, *Peace and War on the Anglo-Cherokee Frontier, 1756–63* (Louisiana State University Press, Baton Rouge, 2001).

Frank L. Owsley, Jr., *Struggle for Gulf Borderlands: The Creek War and the Battle of New Orleans, 1812–1815* (The University of Alabama Press, Tuscaloosa and London, 1981 and 2000).

R. R. Palmer and Joel Colton, *A History of the Modern World, Fourth Edition* (Alfred A. Knopf, New York, 1971).

Theda Perdue, *Slavery and the Evolution of Cherokee Society, 1540–1866* (The University of Tennessee Press, Knoxville, 1979)

William S. Powell, *North Carolina Through Four Centuries* (The University of North Carolina Press, Chapel Hill, 1989).

Francis Paul Prucha, *Documents of United States Indian Policy, Third Edition* (University of Nebraska Press, Lincoln and London, 2000).

J. M. G. Ramsey, *Annals of Tennessee* (Walker and Jones, Charleston, 1853, Reprinted 1967).

Vicki Rozema, *Footsteps of the Cherokee* (John F. Blair, Publisher, Winston-Salem, North Carolina, 1995, Second Printing, 1998).

Arthur M. Schlesinger, Jr., General Editor, The Almanac of American History (Bramhall House, New York, 1983).

Emmet Starr, *History of the Cherokee Indians And Their Legends and Folk Lore* (The Warden Company, Oklahoma City, 1922, Kraus Reprint Company, Millwood, New York, 1991).

Rennard Strickland, *Fire and the Spirits: Cherokee Law from Clan to Court* (University of Oklahoma Press, Norman, 1975).

Russell Thornton, *The Cherokees: A Population History* (University of Nebraska Press, Lincoln, 1990).

Anthony F. C. Wallace, *Jefferson and the Indians: The Tragic Fate of the First Americans* (The Belknap Press of Harvard University Press, Cambridge, Massachusetts and London, England, 1999).

Samuel Cole Williams, *History of the Lost State of Franklin* (Revised edition, 1933, Reprinted by The Overmountain Press, Johnson City, Tennessee, 1993).

Grace Steele Woodward, *The Cherokees* (University of Oklahoma Press, Norman, 1963).

Index

Illustrations

Figure 1. Cherokee in London, 1730. Used by permission, Smithsonian Institution, National Anthropological Archives.

Figure 2. Cherokee in London, 1762. Used by permission, Smithsonian Institution National Anthropological Archives.

Figure 3. Major Ridge. Courtesy of the Library of Congress.

Figure 4. Tecumseh. Courtesy of the Library of Congress.

Figure 5. Major General Andrew Jackson. Courtesy of the Library of Congress.

Figure 6. John Ross. Courtesy of the Library of Congress.

Figure 7. John Ridge. Courtesy of the Library of Congress.

Figure 8. Elias Boudinot. Used by permission, Sam Watts-Kidd.

Figure 9. Sequoyah. Used by permission, Smithsonian Institution, National Anthropological Archives.

Figure 10. McIntosh. Used by permission, Smithsonian Institution, National Anthropological Archives.

Figure 11. Cherokee Phoenix. Courtesy of the Library of Congress.

Figure 12. William Wirt. Courtesy of the Library of Congress.

Figure 13. John Marshall. Courtesy of the Library of Congress.

Figure 14. Gen. Winfield Scott. Courtesy of the Library of Congress.

Map 1. Map: Regional Development of the Cherokee Tradition. Used by permission, University of Tennessee Press. Previously published in "The Origins and Development of Cherokee Culture" from The Cherokee Nation by Roy S. Dickens Jr., edited by Duane H. King, 1979.

Map 2. Map of the Former Territorial Limits of the Cherokee "Nation of" Indians (Royce, 1884). Used by permission, Hargrett Rare Book and Manuscript Library, University of Georgia Libraries.

Map 3. Map of the Former Territorial Limits of the Cherokee "Nation of" Indians (Royce, 1884). Used by permission, Hargrett Rare Book and Manuscript Library, University of Georgia Libraries.

Map 4. Map: British American Plantations (Bowen, 1754). Used by permission, Hargrett Rare Book and Manuscript Library, University of Georgia Libraries.

Map 5. Map of the Former Territorial Limits of the Cherokee "Nation of" Indians (Royce, 1884). Used by permission, Hargrett Rare Book and Manuscript Library, University of Georgia Libraries.

Map 6. Map of the Former Territorial Limits of the Cherokee "Nation of" Indians (Royce, 1884). Used by permission, Hargrett Rare Book and Manuscript Library, University of Georgia Libraries.

Map 7. Map: United States of North America with British and Spanish Territories (Faden, 1783). Used by permission, Hargrett Rare Book and Manuscript Library, University of Georgia Libraries.

Map 8. Map of the Former Territorial Limits of the Cherokee "Nation of" Indians (Royce, 1884). Used by permission, Hargrett Rare Book and Manuscript Library, University of Georgia Libraries.

Map 9. Map of the Southern Parts of the United States of America (Bradley, 1797). Used by permission, Hargrett Rare Book and Manuscript Library, University of Georgia Libraries.

Map 10. Map: The Southern Theater. Used by permission, University of Illinois Press. From The War of 1812: The Forgotten Conflict, by Donald R. Hickey, University of Illinois Press (1990).

Map 11. Map: The Battle of the Horse Shoe. Used by permission, Hargrett Rare Book and Manuscript Library, University of Georgia Libraries.

Map 12. Map of the Territory Belonging to the Cherokee and Creek Indians (Melish, 1816). Used by permission, Hargrett Rare Book and Manuscript Library, University of Georgia Libraries.

Map 13. Map of the Former Territorial Limits of the Cherokee "Nation of" Indians (Royce, 1884). Used by permission, Hargrett Rare Book and Manuscript Library, University of Georgia Libraries.

Map 14. Map of the Trail of Tears. Used by permission, Sam Watts-Kidd, Cherokee National Heritage Society.